Ambassadors in Chains

"I have read a number of books over the years that represent, in my mind, scholarship at its best. They have been clear, winsome, literate, learned, nuanced, and somehow relevant. I return to them often and consider them models worthy of emulation. Richard Steele has written such a book. I hesitate to call him 'old school,' but he is exactly that. He is learned. He writes with elegance. He exercises good judgment and manifests wisdom. And he loves his subject, loves it as only one who knows it well can, like a mother loves a child's face because she has gazed at it so often and with so much affection. I, too, came to love what he does because of the way he wrote this book. I found nothing but pleasure in reading it. I commend it to you with deep appreciation for both author and subject. You will not be disappointed."

—**Gerald L. Sittser**, professor emeritus of theology, Whitworth University

"Finally! Many of us have been anticipating this book for years, knowing that Richard Steele would do an incredible job of handling his source material with expert care and consideration. The subgenre of 'prisoners of conscience' is such an important one to explore in our context, one where people's opinions and endorsements are often 'on sale' to the highest bidder. Prisoners of conscience have actively shown throughout history with their very bodies that truth is worth suffering for. It is a precious affirmation of faith to be surrounded by a cloud of such witnesses. Steele faithfully and compellingly lifts up their voices for us to learn, be comforted, and ultimately challenged by their lives."

—**Daniel Castelo**, William Kellon Quick Professor of Theology and Methodist Studies, The Divinity School, Duke University

"Steele offers four intriguing, albeit inspiring profiles of discipleship in a martyr of blood, a confessor of truth, a statesman of esteem, and a preacher of justice. The result is a revelation of genuine Christian identity and integrity, against which we are all measured and judged. These are not just profiles of survival through sacrifice; they are symbols of life in abundance."

—**John Chryssavgis**, professor, Holy Cross School of Theology

"What enables some people to maintain their convictions under state threat and how do they do so in a faithful manner? With a storyteller's gift for narrative, Richard Steele helps readers explore these questions by expertly guiding them through histories of oft-complex theological debates, political machinations, and social upheavals. The result is a book engaging both for the stories it tells and the all-too relevant questions it raises about living a life of Christian conviction."

—**Sarah Ruble**, professor of religion, Gustavus Adolphus College

"Putting modern scholarly history to work for purposes of Christian theological anthropology, Richard Steele examines in four case studies an ecumenical cross-section of Christian conscience at work in the world. Christian conscience is understood as convictions of personal identity. Convictions so profound that to abandon them would constitute the moral disintegration of the person. To sustain them enables further conviction about the way this identity is to be enacted in challenging circumstances. Not only a solid contribution to the doctrine of humanity, but highly recommended reading for our challenging times!"

—**Paul R. Hinlicky**, Tise Professor Emeritus of Lutheran Studies, Roanoke College

Ambassadors in Chains

Four Christian Prisoners of Conscience

Richard B. Steele

CASCADE *Books* · Eugene, Oregon

AMBASSADORS IN CHAINS
Four Christian Prisoners of Conscience

Copyright © 2025 Richard B. Steele. All rights reserved. Except for brief quotations in critical publications or reviews, no part of this book may be reproduced in any manner without prior written permission from the publisher. Write: Permissions, Wipf and Stock Publishers, 199 W. 8th Ave., Suite 3, Eugene, OR 97401.

Cascade Books
An Imprint of Wipf and Stock Publishers
199 W. 8th Ave., Suite 3
Eugene, OR 97401

www.wipfandstock.com

PAPERBACK ISBN: 979-8-3852-1381-8
HARDCOVER ISBN: 979-8-3852-1382-5
EBOOK ISBN: 979-8-3852-1383-2

Cataloguing-in-Publication data:

Names: Steele, Richard B. [author].

Title: Ambassadors in chains : four Christian prisoners of conscience / by Richard B. Steele.

Description: Eugene, OR: Cascade Books, 2025 | Includes bibliographical references and index.

Identifiers: ISBN 979-8-3852-1381-8 (paperback) | ISBN 979-8-3852-1382-5 (hardcover) | ISBN 979-8-3852-1383-2 (ebook)

Subjects: LCSH: Prisoners—Religious life. | Martyrs. | Political prisoners. | Church work with prisoners. | Conscience—Religious aspects. | Persecution. | Perpetua, Saint, –203 | Maximus, Confessor, Saint, approximately 580–662 | More, Thomas, Saint, 1478–1535 | King, Martin Luther, Jr., 1929–1968

Classification: BV4340 S74 2025 (paperback) | BV4340 (ebook)

VERSION NUMBER 02/25/25

Quotations from *Why We Can't Wait* are reprinted by arrangement with The Heirs to the Estate of Martin Luther King Jr., c/o Writers House as agent for the proprietor New York. NY. Copyright © 1963, 1964 by Dr. Martin Luther King, Jr. Renewed © 1986 by Coretta Scott King.

Scripture quotations are from New Revised Standard Version Bible, copyright © 1989 National Council of the Churches of Christ in the United States of America. Used by permission. All rights reserved worldwide.

I dedicate this book
with gratitude to my faculty colleagues,
past and present, in the Seattle Pacific
University School of Theology

Contents

Acknowledgements | ix
Abbreviations | x

Introduction | 1
1. Vibia Perpetua | 10
2. Maximus the Confessor | 48
3. Thomas More | 93
4. Martin Luther King Jr. | 142
Conclusion | 181

Bibliography | 195
Subject Index | 203
Name Index | 207
Scripture Index | 213

Acknowledgments

THIS BOOK WAS A twinkle in my eye over twenty-five years ago, and it is a great relief to bring it to birth at long last. I won't bore the reader with the story of all the delays that impeded its completion. But I cannot fail to express my deep appreciation for my colleagues in the Seattle Pacific University School of Theology, who believed in this project—and who believed, even more astonishingly, in my ability to finish it—when I sometimes doubted both. I especially thank the deans with whom I served during my years at SPU: Les Steele, Doug Strong, Doug Koskela, Laura Sweat Holmes, Dave Nienhuis, and Brian Lugioyo. Their grace, patience, and encouragement always kept me going (or got me restarted).

I also thank SPU Librarians Steve Perisho and Johanna Staman for the courtesy and efficiency with which they supported my research, and my SPU faculty colleagues, Owen Ewald and Stamatis Vokos, for their help with the complexities of Classical and Renaissance Latin and Byzantine Greek. My deep gratitude also goes to Robin Parry, my editor at Wipf and Stock, and my dear friends, Gerald Sittser of Whitworth University and Sarah Johnson Ruble of Gustavus Adolphus College, who all possess the rare ability to identify the faults of a scholarly manuscript while reassuring the author of its promise. This is a better book for their efforts.

Finally, I want to pay tribute to the participants in the classes I taught on Christian prison literature at the Washington Corrections Center for Women in Gig Harbor, WA and the Cedar Creek Corrections Center in Littlerock, WA. Their determination to persevere with faith and courage in the straitened circumstances of prison life taught me much about the texts we were studying, but still more about the life we are all trying to live.

Abbreviations

DCT   Thomas More, *Dialogue of Comfort Against Tribulation*. Introduction by Gerard B. Wegemer. Translated by Mary Gottshalk. Princeton: Scepter, 1998.

LL   Thomas More, *Last Letters*. Edited by Alvaro de Silva. Grand Rapids: Eerdmans, 2000.

MCC   Pauline Allen and Neil Bronwen, eds., *Maximus the Confessor and His Companions*. Oxford Early Christian Texts. Oxford: Oxford University Press, 2002.

SC   Thomas More, *The Sadness of Christ and Final Prayers and Instructions*. Edited by Gerard B. Wegemer. Translated by Clarence Miller. Princeton: Scepter, 1993.

Introduction

THIS BOOK TELLS THE stories of four Christian prisoners of conscience—or "ambassadors in chains," as I shall be calling them. These were followers of Jesus who were imprisoned for holding religious convictions deemed subversive or treasonous by the government of their time, and who left a literary record of their experience of imprisonment and their continuing efforts to uphold and communicate their convictions in the face of the government's efforts to silence them or force them to recant. The four I have selected represent different nationalities, different historical and ecclesiastical situations, and different personal backgrounds. They are:

- Perpetua of Carthage (181–203), a young Roman noblewoman from North Africa who came from a pagan family but who had recently converted to Christianity and now refused in the name of Christ to offer sacrifice to the Roman gods.
- Maximus the Confessor (580–662), an elderly Byzantine Orthodox monk and theologian who opposed the state's efforts to introduce a heretical Christology in order win the allegiance of a large segment of its disaffected Christian population.
- Thomas More (1478–1535), an English Roman Catholic lawyer and statesman who denied the legitimacy of his king's divorce from his first wife, his marriage to a second, and his claim to be the "supreme head" of the English church.
- Martin Luther King Jr. (1929–68), a Black Baptist pastor who led the American Civil Rights Movement and who was repeatedly arrested

for organizing and participating in campaigns of mass nonviolent resistance against racist laws and customs.

Two of these figures, Perpetua and More, were ultimately executed for their refusal to capitulate to the state's demands and are recognized as martyrs of the Catholic Church. The other two also died for their faith, but not by state decree. Maximus endured long imprisonment, harsh interrogation, bodily mutilation, and exile. He died in prison from his wounds but was not directly put to death and is therefore called a "confessor" rather than a martyr. King was jailed on several occasions, but he was not treated as brutally during his lockups as our other three "ambassadors," and he was murdered by a lone gunman. Thus, although all four of these Christian prisoners of conscience ultimately gave their lives for their religious convictions, this book is not a study in martyrology. Rather, it is a study in how those who passionately held and fervently practiced religious convictions that contradicted the official ideology of the state were able to sustain those convictions despite the pressures brought to bear on them by the state (and often by the wider populous as well) during their incarceration(s).

We shall examine what I referred to above as the surviving "literary record" left by our four prisoners of conscience from their time of incarceration. For Perpetua, More, and King, much of this record comes in the form of diaries or letters, which they penned during their time in lockup. More's prison literature also includes two books and part of a third, several short meditations, and extensive marginal notations in his personal prayer book. King's also includes newspaper editorials that he wrote and sermons that he preached about his jail time. As for Maximus, very little of his own writing survives from his time in custody, but we have a great deal of material written by him prior to his arrest about his reasons for opposing the Byzantine government's new heresies, plus numerous documents by other writers about his lengthy imprisonment, including verbatim transcripts of two interrogations in which we hear his words and observe his conduct. This book, then, offers neither full-scale biographies of our four ambassadors nor comprehensive accounts of their respective theological visions. Excellent works of that sort are readily available for all four figures, and I draw upon these selectively in the chapters that follow. My task in this book is both more modest and more sharply focused. It is to analyze the surviving records of their experiences as prisoners of conscience and of the witness they bore to their religious convictions in defiance of state opposition. I include only such historical and biographical background information on these figures from before their incarceration—and in King's case, just afterward—as may help to explain why they later fell afoul of the authorities.

My investigation of the surviving literary record of these four prisoners of conscience means that this book deals with a subset of one genre of the vast and variegated body of what might collectively be called "Christian prison literature." Other figures who were incarcerated for their convictions and who left accounts of their prison experiences, include Michael Sattler (1490-1527), Avvakum Petrov (1620/21-82), John Bunyan (1628-88), Jeanne-Marie Bouvier de la Motte-Guyon (1648-1717), Dietrich Bonhoeffer (1906-45), and Nelson Mandela (1918-2013), to name only a few. But time and space considerations rendered their inclusion in this volume impossible. Moreover, there are many other genres of Christian prison literature that deserve systematic scholarly investigation. These include:

- Works *by* Christian prisoners who left writings of instruction and encouragement to their fellow Christians, but who said very little about their own experience *as* prisoners (e.g., Ignatius of Antioch and Polycarp of Smyrna).

- Works *about* Christian prisoners who left no writings of their own (e.g., the Scillitan Martyrs and the "disappeared" of Latin America, China, etc.).

- Works by authors who were not Christians at the time of their arrest, but who converted to Christianity during or after their incarceration (e.g., Chuck Colson).

- Works by Christian authors who were arrested for acts of conscientious objection to the state, but whose actions were not, at the time they were taken, explicitly religiously motivated (e.g., Fyodor Dostoyevsky and Alexandr Solzhenitsyn).

- Works by Christian authors who wrote extensively *during* their incarceration, but whose prison writings are not *about* (or at least not *directly* about) their reasons for or their experience of imprisonment (e.g., Anicius Boethius and John of the Cross).

- Works by prison chaplains or other religious professionals who offered spiritual care to inmates (e.g., Helen Prejean).

- Sermons by theologians who regularly visited local prisons (e.g., Karl Barth).
- Works by prison reformers who were motivated by their faith convictions (e.g., Elizabeth Gurney Fry and Bryan Stevenson).
- Works by critics of faith-based prisons (e.g., Tanya Erzen).

As far as I can determine, no comprehensive or comparative study of this sprawling body of literature has ever been made. It is work waiting to be done—but not here.

The title of this book is borrowed from a passage in one of St. Paul's prison epistles. He writes: "Pray in the Spirit at all times in every prayer and supplication. To that end keep alert and always persevere in supplication for all the saints. Pray also for me, so that when I speak, a message may be given to me to make known with boldness the mystery of the gospel, for which I am an ambassador in chains" (Eph 6:18–20a). There is a double irony in these verses. First, in calling himself an "ambassador" of the gospel (cf. 2 Cor 5:20), Paul is affirming the sovereign lordship of Jesus Christ and, while proudly asserting his Roman citizenship (Acts 21:39; 22:25–29), is also attesting to what he elsewhere calls his "citizenship in heaven" (Phil 3:20; cf. Eph 2:19). In effect, he is theologically "dethroning" Caesar. Second, in mentioning the "chains" he wears *as* an ambassador of the gospel, Paul is hinting that the Roman authorities have failed to honor the rules of international diplomacy whereby governments grant immunity from arrest and injury to visiting emissaries of foreign states. Of course, the Roman government assumed that, as a Roman citizen, Paul couldn't *have* any higher allegiance than to Rome and its state deities. But it was just that assumption that, from Paul's point of view, revealed the endemic error and ultimate futility of Rome's imperial ideology.

A similar assumption was made by the respective governments under whom our four ambassadors lived. By the early third century, Roman emperors (or at least their *genii*) *were* state deities. Accordingly, demonstrating one's allegiance to the empire meant offering sacrifice to a statue of a living person. Perpetua was martyred for refusing to do this. In the putatively "Christian" nations of seventh-century Byzantium, sixteenth-century England, and twentieth-century America, the situation was different—and in some respects more difficult for Christians to address. God was seen to be "above" the state, but the duties of citizens to God were assumed to be perfectly compatible, and indeed virtually identical, with their duties to the state. Maximus, More, and King argued otherwise, while nevertheless professing and displaying their civic loyalty. All four of our ambassadors sincerely loved the countries whose policies they opposed and recognized that their principled stands against the state were sometimes incomprehensible or flatly dangerous to their own families and friends. This gives their stories great pathos.

Crucial to my argument is the concept of "conviction," which I borrow from the work of James Wm. McClendon, Jr. and James M. Smith. They define it thus: "A conviction . . . means a persistent belief such that if X (a person or community) has a conviction, it will not easily be relinquished and it cannot be relinquished without making X a significantly different person (or community) than before."[1] Thus, a conviction is the kind of belief that shapes X's identity by delineating what X stands for and by regulating how X dwells in and acts upon the world. A person's convictions are of many sorts: religious, ethical, political, aesthetic, etc. But those we are studying here are *religious*, and specifically *Christian*, convictions, i.e., those which reflect our four ambassadors' faith in the Triune God. Of course, their *religious* convictions had immediate *political* implications, insofar as those convictions put them at odds with their respective governments. But the convictions that drove their public witness were religious—or were political only because they reflected their religious convictions.

I divide Christian convictions into two general types. Type A convictions delineate the believer's understanding of how she should conduct herself in the world as a faithful disciple of and witness to Jesus Christ. In contrast, Type B convictions delineate the believer's faith in God's providential governance of human affairs and her sense of God's presence and action in her own life. At times, a person's Type A convictions may contradict the official policies and social mores of the state in which she lives. When this happens, the state may react defensively and insist that she either relinquish her convictions or undergo punishment for clinging to them. Our four ambassadors all chose to endure punishment rather than betray their Type A convictions. Type B convictions provide the believer with her spiritual "center," with clarity of vision, with poise and confidence in the face of opposition, and with comfort in times of trial. Thus, their Type B convictions sustained our ambassadors' courage when their commitment to their Type A convictions landed them in

---

1. McClendon and Smith, *Convictions*, 5.

trouble. It was the firmness with which our ambassadors held their Type A convictions that explains their *willingness* to oppose their respective governments, and the firmness with which they held their Type B convictions that explains their *ability* to suffer for that opposition. Of course, both types of convictions define the ambassador's identity as a Christian, and the dividing line between these two types is sometimes fuzzy; indeed, some of their convictions might arguably belong to either category—or both. Nevertheless, the distinction is heuristically useful, for it allows us to differentiate those *for which* our ambassadors were incarcerated (Type A) from those *by means of which* they bore the tribulations of prison life (Type B). Each of the four main chapters of this book ends with a list of the religious convictions—of both types—that appear most prominently in the prison writings of the ambassador in question. A comprehensive table of the convictions I have extracted from the prison literature of our four ambassadors may be found in the Conclusion, on pp. 182–23 below. The Conclusion also offers an assessment of the theological significance of those convictions for the contemporary church.

Several clarifications about the distinction between these two types of Christian convictions are in order. First, putatively "Christian" societies typically don't fear Type B convictions as such. They may even regard those who profess them as paragons of piety and civic virtue. But when those who hold Type B convictions for which they are widely admired also hold Type A convictions that oppose the policies of the state, they become dangerous embarrassments to the authorities. Such were Maximus, More, and King. It was impossible for their respective governments to dismiss their opposition by simply impugning their character. Perpetua's situation was different. In her social world, Christianity was a *religio illicita*, and her conviction that the Triune God was the supreme good and sovereign power in the universe was both the cause of her arrest (Type A) and the source of her strength in facing martyrdom (Type B).

Second, the proportion of attention given to the two types of convictions in the expositions below varies from ambassador to ambassador. I assume that all four ambassadors held both types of convictions to be equally important, because equally central to their Christian identity and witness. The two types are distinguishable for purposes of analysis, but they are integrally related and existentially inseparable in the life of the believer—or at least they were for our four ambassadors. But the amount of space devoted to the two types in the prison writings of a given ambassador depends both on the causes of his or her conflict with the state and on the duration and severity of the prison conditions that he or she had to endure.

Third, all four of our ambassadors undoubtedly held *other* Christian convictions—of both types—besides those highlighted here. Maximus, More, and King elaborated these in their numerous other writings and put them into practice at other points in their lives. As for Perpetua, all that we know about her and the only piece of writing from her pen that has survived are contained in her brief martyrology. I do not wish to devalue such other religious convictions as our four prisoners of conscience may have held and displayed elsewhere in word or deed. I simply bracket them out of consideration here for the sake of brevity and focus.

Fourth, the willingness and ability of our four ambassadors to endure prison life was undoubtedly due to other factors besides their cherished convictions. Their age, their physical health, the specific conditions of the prison(s) in which were held, the severity of their punishments, the length of their sentences, and their access to their families, friends, and followers, all played a part—and will play a part in our story. But there would be no story at all apart from the religious convictions—of both types—that we are investigating.

Regarding my method of inquiry, I shall pose two distinct but closely related sets of questions to the prison writings of our four ambassadors. The first set pertains to their religious convictions *per se*. What precisely *were* the religious convictions—of both types—of each ambassador? Why did they lead to his or her arrest? How did they shape his or her prison experience?

In attempting to answer this first set of questions, I distinguish between "persons of conviction" and "dogmatic ideologues." A person of conviction is one who holds certain doctrines to be true and faithfully orders her life accordingly. She may seek to persuade others of the truth of those doctrines, but in doing so she displays respect and affection for those to whom she is witnessing, even if they inflexibly oppose her views; and she certainly abstains from using coercion. In contrast, a "dogmatist" is a person who harbors doubts, perhaps subconsciously, about the doctrines she professes and shores up her shaky faith by imposing it forcibly on others. The stories we investigate here vividly illustrate this distinction. As persons of conviction, our four ambassadors felt such deep confidence in the truth of the Christian gospel that, despite the urgent and courageous way they bore witness to it, they typically displayed humility, charity, courtesy, patience, and sometimes even playfulness toward their persecutors.

But the civil and ecclesiastical officials who dealt with them often come across as dogmatists, who felt a desperate need to protect the *status quo* and fiercely opposed dissenters. Persons of conviction will die for their beliefs; dogmatists may kill for theirs. Yet one who might be classified as a person of conviction in one set of circumstances might qualify as a dogmatist in others. For example, during his years as Chancellor of England, Thomas More furiously persecuted Protestants; later, after his fall from power, he held unswervingly to his convictions despite the immense pressure he was under to endorse the Henrician Reformation.

My second set of questions pertains to the types of writing and rhetorical strategies used by our ambassadors in communicating their convictions and describing their prison experiences. How did their felt need to formulate their convictions with precision and persuasive power shape the genre, style, content, and tone of a given piece of writing? To whom did they write, and why? Was it to persuade their captors of their innocence, or to ask their friends for support, or to console their own sorrows, fears, loneliness, and boredom, or to leave a record for posterity? How did the ever-present possibility that a work intended for a friendly audience might fall into the hands of the authorities shape its literary style and thematic content?[2] And how trustworthy are the records *about* our ambassadors' convictions and experiences that were kept by their enemies (such as the official court transcript of More's trial) or, conversely, by their devoted friends (such as the transcripts of Maximus' interrogations)?

With respect to this second set of questions, it is crucial to remember that an imprisoned author must always consider the impression his work might make on his readers, whether friends or foes, whether contemporaries or members of future generations. All prison literature is intensely *self-conscious* literature, even when it is not directly *self-revealing*. Its author is always, in some sense, "on trial," even when the work itself is not explicitly autobiographical. And as authors of *Christian* prison literature, our four ambassadors constantly faced the question of how to bear faithful witness to Christ instead of simply drawing attention to themselves. In inherently "dramatic" situations, they had to avoid gratuitous

---

2. From a penological perspective, much prison literature is contraband. Of the items surveyed in the following chapters, at least four—the prison diaries of Perpetua and Saturus, the manuscript of More's *Sadness of Christ*, and King's "Letter from Birmingham Jail"—were rescued from oblivion by their authors' friends, who displayed great ingenuity in duping—or great generosity in bribing—the prison guards.

theatrical self-display; in taking unpopular stands, they had to renounce the perverse pleasures of being merely "different" or "contrary." In articulating their principled resistance to the ideology of the state, they had to prevent their work from degenerating into sanctimonious bombast, spiteful diatribe, obsequious special pleading, or pious sloganeering. The aim of this book is to determine how well they succeeded.

CHAPTER 1

Vibia Perpetua

Introduction

The Passion of Saints *Perpetua and Felicitas* is one of the best-known martyrologies of the early church. Its fame is well deserved, resting on its remarkable combination of vivid description, historical reliability, theological depth, and human pathos. But although the literary genre to which it is usually, and rightly, assigned is that of martyrology, it also represents the earliest extant example of the kind of Christian prison literature we are investigating in this volume, and it includes the earliest extant writing of any kind by a Christian woman.

The *Passion* concerns the arrest, trial, imprisonment, and execution of six Christian martyrs in the city of Carthage, North Africa in the year AD 203. Their names were Vibia Perpetua, Felicitas, Revocatus, Saturninus, Secundulus, and Saturus. The first five were catechumens at the time of their house arrest, but managed to receive baptism before they were transferred to a military prison for trial. Saturus was their catechist. He apparently surrendered himself shortly after their arrest and may not have attended their baptisms, but he was certainly with them during their imprisonment, trial, and martyrdom. The text tells us that Perpetua was a noblewoman and that Felicitas and Revocatus were slaves (though not necessarily Perpetua's slaves), but it says nothing about the legal status or social standing of the other three.

During their time in lockup, the six prisoners had regular dealings with other members of Carthaginian church. One of these would become the editor of the *Passion*. He somehow gained possession of the prison diaries of Perpetua and Saturus and witnessed the deaths of the whole group. Believing the martyrs to have been imbued with the Holy Spirit and believing himself to be duty-bound to preserve their memory, he published the two diaries, along with a short introduction and a concluding narrative of their last day in prison and their contest in the arena. Thus, the *Passion* is a four-section document, with the editor's words "bookending" the diaries of the two martyrs. And the editor has done his work with great skill, having preserved the authentic voices of the martyrs, but also having incorporated them into a unified narrative.[1]

Before we investigate the *Passion*, we must face three plausible objections to our decision to take it as our first specimen of Christian prison literature. First, why start with *this* text, when it is certainly not the earliest datable literary work by a Christian who was under arrest for the faith at the time of writing? The apostle Paul wrote four letters from his prison cell in Rome in the late 50s or early 60s, and Ignatius of Antioch wrote seven letters to congregations in Asia Minor as he was being taken to Rome for execution sometime between 98 and 117. We need not doubt that imprisonment deeply affected Paul and Ignatius personally, but they say little about how it did so. Their primary aims were to elucidate Christian doctrines and practices and to address the needs and problems of those to whom they were writing. If they speak about themselves at all, they tend to refer to their impending martyrdom, rather than the circumstances of their imprisonment or its effects

---

1. I have consulted three editions of the Latin text of the *Passion*, each with an English translation: (1) that of Andrew S. Jacobs and L. Stephanie Cobb, in Cobb, *Passion*, 19–41; (2) that of Joseph Farrell and Craig Williams in Bremmer and Formisano, *Perpetua's Passions*, 14–32; and (3) that of Musurillo, *Acts*, 106–31. Cobb, *Passion*, 43–65, also includes the Greek text with an English translation. I have also consulted the English translation in Rader, "Martyrdom," 1–32. Unless otherwise specified, the translation of specific texts below is that of Jacobs and Cobb. A word about my method of citing passages from the *Passion* is in order here. The Latin text has twenty-one consecutively numbered paragraphs, each of which has several numbered sentences. The four main sections of the work—namely, the editor's introduction, Perpetua's diary, Saturus' diary, and the editor's conclusion—are not numbered in the Latin text. But it is often important for our purposes to note which section a particular passage belongs to, so in citations I will give three numbers: section, paragraph, and sentence. For example, "I.1.1" would refer to Section I (editor's introduction), Paragraph 1 (of the document as a whole), Sentence 1 (of Paragraph 1). A synopsis of the four sections and the contents of the twenty-one paragraphs is given on pp. 27–28 below.

on their own spiritual, intellectual, moral, or emotional state. Nor will the extant writings of such notable mid-second century martyrs as Polycarp and Justin serve our purposes, for they are scarcely autobiographical, except in passing, and they were apparently composed before their authors' imprisonment. Thus, although the extant writings of first- and second-century Christians who suffered imprisonment for their faith tell us much about their authors' convictions, they do not explain the effects of confinement on the authors themselves or on their relationships with others, nor do they feature extended reflections upon their experience in prison. Thus, they don't quite suit our purposes.

The second objection to taking the *Passion* as our starting point is that it may not deserve to be classified as a specimen of Christian prison literature at all, at least when taken in its entirety. Yes, it *contains* the kind of writing we are looking for, namely the prison diaries of Perpetua and Saturus. But the narrative bookends were written by the anonymous editor, and some scholars have even questioned the authenticity of the diary attributed to Saturus.[2] Moreover, Saturus' "diary" is little more than the record of a single vision he had about the afterlife that awaited Perpetua and himself; it says nothing about his experience of incarceration as such. So even *that* document, if taken by itself, would not match our selection criteria. Why not concentrate on Perpetua's diary alone and ignore the rest? A full reply to this objection must await our analysis of the *Passion*'s literary structure and rhetorical design. Here it suffices to indicate what our reply must show, namely that Perpetua's diary and Saturus' vision account are best understood in light of each other and in light of the editor's narrative additions. Thus, the *Passion* must be taken as a literary whole with three distinct "voices," each of which helps us to interpret the

2. For example, Dodds, *Pagan and Christian*, 49n2, doubts the authenticity of Saturus' diary, as well as its intrinsic worth: "If the author [= editor] of the *Passio* had decided . . . to omit the vision of Saturus, we should not, I think, have missed much of psychological or religious value." Dodds regards Saturus' vision as a "counterweight to Perpetua's unorthodoxy" with respect to the afterlife and presumes that the editor composed it himself. But if the editor wrote it *for* his narrative, why should he have "decided to omit" it *from* his narrative? My own view is that Saturus' "voice" is sufficiently different from that of the editor to argue for its authenticity. Saturus' vision highlights Perpetua's unusual spiritual authority as the *de facto* leader of the group of six martyrs (though it also establishes the limits of her authority), and I fail to see how its eschatology is any more "orthodox" than hers. Yes, Saturus' vision lacks the personal candor and literary vitality of Perpetua's diary, but it displays an interest in ecclesiastical protocol that we might expect of a church official. Accordingly, I regard Saturus' vision as genuine, and read the *Passion* as a three-author document whose literary unity is due to the editor's skill and theological acuity.

message of the other two. The artistic power and religious value of *this* martyrology is due precisely to the fact that embedded within it are the prison writings of two of the martyrs. These writings put a "human face" on the martyrs and keep the editor's account of their deaths from turning into mawkish didacticism or mock-heroic melodrama. The character of the witnesses is not eclipsed by the glory of their cause, nor is the content of their message obscured by the details of their deaths. Conversely, the content of their diaries is elucidated by the editor's narrative account and theological assessment of their words and deeds.

The third objection pertains to the catholicity of the document. Were its heroes orthodox Christians? As Musurillo has observed, the work's "phantasmagoric, and sometimes erotic, imagery may well represent the kind of mediumistic phenomena current in the Montanist church of Africa."[3] Certainly there is plenty in the *Passion* to suggest that its heroes and editor were associated with the "New Prophecy." But that does not necessarily imply that in 203, when the events described in the *Passion* occurred, they would have been regarded as schismatics. At that date the "proto-Montanist" party was still in communion with the "Catholic" party, and it would remain so for well over a decade.[4] Moreover, even after the breach occurred, the *Passion* was read in Catholic congregations on the martyrs' feast day. So, the document's catholicity is indisputable, even if it pointed in a direction that would eventuate in the rupture of the church.[5]

The point of view from which I shall analyze the *Passion of Saints Perpetua and Felicitas* can thus be summarized as follows: First, the text in its present form was prepared shortly after the events it recounts by an editor who knew the martyrs personally, was in contact with them during their imprisonment, and witnessed their deaths in the arena. Second, Perpetua's diary is certainly authentic, and Saturus' diary is probably

---

3. Musurillo, *Acts*, xxvi.

4. See Butler, *New Prophecy and "New Visions,"* 24–27; Markshies, "*Passio Sanctarum Perpetuae et Felicitas* and Montanism."

5. Later, however, sanitized versions of the text were produced that suppressed or downplayed the visionary, apocalyptic, and "feminist" elements of the original text. The shorter Latin *Acts of the Martyrdom of Perpetua and Felicitas* is available in Harris and Giffort, *Acts*, 70–73. See also Augustine, Sermons No. 280, 281, and 282 in *Works*, III.8, 72–82; Quodvultdeus, "On the Barbaric Age I," in Cobb, *Passion*, 229–31; and de Voragine, *Golden Legend*, 342–43. A rich and elegantly edited collection of all these shorter versions of the *Passion*, plus the sermons of Augustine and Quodvultdeus and numerous other sermons, occasional writings, and reproductions of relevant physical artifacts may be found in Cobb, *Passion*, 67–259.

so, even if they may have been retouched at points by the editor. Third, although three different authorial voices are present in the *Passion*, the document must be read as an integral literary whole. This coherence is secured by the editorial framework in which the diaries are set, and perhaps by the mild redactional surgery performed on them. But this literary coherence is all the more remarkable because the distinctive voices of the martyrs are faithfully preserved, not suppressed by any effort at artificial harmonization. Fourth, from a form-critical standpoint, the *Passion* is best understood as a Christian martyrology. But it is a highly unusual martyrology in also being the earliest specimen of the kind of Christian prison literature that we are investigating here. Conversely, it is a very unusual specimen of Christian prison literature in also being a martyrology—a situation that can only occur if someone else is able to preserve and publish the prisoner's written work. Fifth, from a theological standpoint, the *Passion* contains pneumatic and apocalyptic elements, which suggest that the editor and the martyrs were associated with the proto-Montanist movement within the Carthaginian church. The eventual schism between Catholics and Montanists, however, occurred at least a decade after the martyrdom of Perpetua and her friends, and well after the composition of the *Passion*. And even if the story's pneumatic and apocalyptic elements seemed "radical" to some members of the North African church at the time, there is no evidence that it was deemed heterodox. Finally, the text in its present form has been "received" by Catholics as the official account of the words and deeds of the Carthaginian martyrs of 203,[6] and therefore of the Carthaginian church that they represented. The anti-pneumatic, anti-apocalyptic, and anti-feminist trends that later arose in the Catholic Church may have shaped the way the text was interpreted and eventually led to the composition of "safer" versions of the story. But the original text was never suppressed and seems at times to have been regarded almost as sacred Scripture.[7] And

---

6. See Ronsse, "Rhetoric of Martyrs."

7. The editor's introduction may have contributed to this high estimate: "If ancient models of faith, bearing witness to God's grace and working to build people up, were disseminated in writing so that through reading them—as if by a reconsideration of matters—God might be honored and people comforted, why shouldn't new instances be disseminated which are suitable to both goals equally?" (I.1.1). If the deeds of recent saints are as edifying as those of the ancients, then the texts in which the deeds of recent saints are recorded may be expected to gain in prestige as times goes by. And in his *Treatise on the Soul and Its Origin* I.12[10], Augustine remarks that there is "no record in the canonical scripture" concerning Perpetua's brother, Dinocrates. The fact that he must state this suggests that some of his hearers may have regarded the text in which

the cult of the six martyrs, which depended heavily on the public reading of the document,[8] and which prominently featured the female members of the group, has proved enduringly popular.[9]

Historical and Religious Background

Thus, we shall take the *Passion of Saints Perpetua and Felicitas* as a reliable record of historical events that transpired in Carthage in 203 and accept Perpetua and Saturus as the true authors of the diaries attributed to them, which came into the editor's hands shortly before or shortly after their deaths. And we shall assume that the purpose of the *Passion* is to promote the same religious convictions to which the martyrs bore witness and to honor the way they did so. The editor tells us as much. He writes "so that ... God might be honored and people comforted" (I.1.1). And he has quite artfully composed his introduction and conclusion to provide literary integrity to the document as a whole. To assert that the *Passion* is a work of religious witness is not to deny either its basic historical accuracy or its evident literary artistry. That it is meant to be edifying does not imply that it is fictional.[10]

Indeed, it is precisely the historical plausibility and psychological verisimilitude of its contents that renders the narrative so edifying, and the religious aim of the work would be seriously compromised if readers had grounds for doubting them. The purpose of a religious narrative is to show how the convictions and virtues of the protagonists shape their actions and their responses to the hostility of their enemies. Such actions and responses express their deepest convictions. How a witness

---

the boy's story is told as quasi-canonical. Augustine, *Nicene and Post-Nicene Fathers*, 5:319–20.

8. Salisbury, *Blood of Martyrs*, 2–4, notes that the continuing devotion *to* a saint or martyr depends heavily on the availability of reliable written texts *about* her.

9. The popularity of the "cult" persists to this day, though it now takes new and sometimes regrettable forms. At this writing, two historical novels about Perpetua, two animated movies for children, and one volume of erotic poetry bearing her name—to say nothing of an enormous quantity of scholarly writings—are on offer.

10. For arguments questioning the authenticity of Perpetua's diary and the historical reliability of the *Passion* as a whole, see Halporn, "Literary History," 223–41, and Cobb, *Dying*, 94–113. But such arguments prevent us from making theological sense of an obviously theological text, i.e., one that bears witness to the providential activity of God in the lives of its protagonists. Moreover, the historical reconstruction of the events narrated in the work, which Salisbury provides in *Perpetua's Passion* and *Blood of Martyrs*, seems to me conclusive.

suffers, and how he understands his sufferings, is as much a testimony to his convictions as the actions that got him into trouble in the first place. And the power and persuasiveness of a "realistic historical narrative," whose purpose is to display those convictions, will depend largely on whether it "rings true," on whether it "fits" with what the readers may be presumed to know about the historical, social, political, and religious background of the events recorded.[11] Anything compromising the plausibility of a story that claims to record actual events would cast doubt on the validity of the convictions of its protagonists. Therefore, unless there is external evidence to suggest that the events recorded in such narratives did *not* take place more or less as reported, there is good reason to assume that they did. That doesn't mean that the primary purpose of the narrative is to offer character analysis or historical reportage as such. These are modern interests, and although they are quite legitimate in their own way, they are not the main concern of ancient religious narratives such as the *Passion*.[12] Their chief aim is to bear witness to the convictions for which the protagonists lived and died. They may achieve that by occasional embroidery and exaggeration, but too much of that sort of thing would strain the reader's credulity and diminish the story's power as religious witness. Thus, an author who uses realistic

---

11. I borrow the idea of "realistic historical narrative" from Auerbach, *Mimesis*, 3–23, and Frei, *Eclipse*, 1–16. Auerbach, 19, argues that Christian martyrologies are typically more "legendary" than realistically "historical." Legendary writing, he says, "runs far too smoothly. All cross-currents, all friction, all that is causal, secondary to the main events and themes, everything unresolved, truncated, and uncertain, which confuses the clear progress of the action and the simple orientation of the actors, has disappeared. The historical event which we witness, or learn from the testimony of those who witnessed it, runs much more variously, contradictorily, and confusedly." Martyrologies, in which a "stiff-necked and fanatical persecutor stands over against an equally stiff-necked and fanatical victim," illustrate the former kind of writing, whereas, for example, Pliny's letter to Trajan, which describes the legal complexities and moral conundrums of an actual situation, illustrates the latter. But stylistically, *The Passion of Saints Perpetua and Felicitas* is far closer to Pliny's letter than it is to many other early Christian martyrologies precisely because the editor inserts the prison diaries within a "historically realistic narrative" framework.

12. Taylor, *Sources of the Self*, describes the shift that has taken place over the centuries in the ways that people of the West engage in reasoning about morality. The ancients presumed that moral goodness depended upon achieving a vision of some transcendent moral Good (or goods) and upon conforming one's character and conduct thereto. Modern conceptions of morality, in contrast, emphasize the subjective experience of the agents, the intrinsic goodness of "ordinary life," and the value of "nature." Clearly the *Passion of Saints Perpetua and Felicitas* reflects the ancient approach, although it already points in the direction of the kind of "inwardness of radical reflexivity," which Taylor, 131, traces to Saint Augustine.

historical narrative to promote his religious convictions is prevented from overly fictionalizing events. Of course, the literary qualities of realistic historical narrative do not by themselves guarantee its historical accuracy. That can only be demonstrated by reference to other literary sources, archaeological evidence, etc. But when such tests are applied to the *Passion*, it stands up remarkably well.

What follows is a brief account of the historical and religious background of the *Passion*, highlighting only those aspects that we need to know to understand it *qua* prison literature. We begin by discussing the city of Carthage and its place in the Roman Empire of the early third century. Then we identify a few aspects of the character of the North African church relevant to our purpose. Finally, we look briefly at the Severan persecution of 202–3.

Roman Carthage[13]

According to legend, Carthage was founded about 800 BCE by sailors from the Phoenician city of Tyre, who were exploring the western Mediterranean in search of new markets and raw materials. The expedition was led by a Tyrian princess, Elissa, better known from Virgil's *Aeneid* and other Roman sources as Queen Dido. One evening, as they were scouting the North African shore for overnight moorage, they spotted a magnificent harbor, and upon putting in, immediately realized the strategic, commercial, and agricultural advantages of the spot. According to the legend, Dido negotiated skillfully (or perhaps unscrupulously) with the inhabitants and secured title to the place. The new trading colony made good use of its deep, protected harbor and its commanding location—an easy sail to Italy, Spain, and the islands of the Western Mediterranean—to establish one of the greatest commercial empires of antiquity. It maintained its cultural ties with Tyre but was entirely self-governing.

Between the seventh and fourth centuries BCE, the Carthaginians competed fiercely with the Greeks of Sicily and southern Italy for control of the Mediterranean trade routes. In the third century, when the Romans established hegemony over Magna Graecia, they inherited the conflict with Carthage. Efforts at diplomacy and cooperation failed, and between 264 and 146 BCE, Rome defeated Carthage in three great wars, the third

---

13. This and the following subsection are heavily indebted to Salisbury, *Perpetua's Passion*, 33–83.

of which ended in the complete destruction and depopulation of the city of Carthage. In about 40 BCE, however, the site was recolonized by Julius Caesar, and the new city was promptly made the capital of the Roman province of Proconsular Africa. Its population, which had peaked at about four hundred thousand during the Phoenician period, may have reached five hundred thousand during the Roman period, making it the second largest city in the western half of the empire after Rome, and roughly comparable in size to Alexandria and Antioch in the East. Culturally, Carthage was a rich mixture of Punic, Berber, and Greco-Roman elements. Perpetua, who was a member of the lower nobility from a nearby suburb,[14] and who received a first-rate education,[15] appears to have been fluent in Greek, Latin, and probably Punic (I.2.1; II.5.2; III.13.4). The city's architecture—including its great amphitheater, where Perpetua and her companions were martyred—was renowned for its grandeur and elegance. In short, by the early third century CE, it was the seat of power and the hub of culture, commerce, and education for Roman Africa, and the imperial and local governments would have been swift to crush any activities that might have disturbed its peace and prosperity. This would have included dissident "religious" activities—though as noted earlier, the Romans did not differentiate as sharply between "religious" and "political" activities as we do. Indeed, any "religious" activities that would have seemed to challenge the divine authority of the imperial government or the temporal stability and security of the region would have been punished at once as both impious and seditious.

Joyce Salisbury has pointed out two features of early-third-century North African society that are especially relevant to our study of the *Passion*. First, like Greco-Roman society in general, it was patriarchal, but there was also an impressive tradition of female strength. The example of Queen Dido has already been mentioned. Additionally, the popular literature of the Hellenistic and Roman imperial period was replete with female characters who successfully resisted the social strictures placed on women at that time. Of particular note is *The Golden Ass*, a novel by Lucius Apuleius, a native of the Numidian city of Madaurus (modern M'Daourouch, Algeria), about two hundred kilometers southwest of Carthage. This work, which was written in the mid-second century, and

---

14. The Greek text (I.2.1) of the *Passion* states that Perpetua and her companions came from Thuburbo Minus (modern Tebourba), about thirty kilometers west of Carthage. See Cobb, *Passion*, 46–47.

15. See Ameling, *"Femina Liberaliter Instituta."*

which Perpetua may have read,[16] features young characters, both male and female, who defy conventions and overcome misfortunes to achieve their ends. Female strength was also represented at the highest level of society and government during this period. Empress Julia Domna, the spouse of Septimius Severus (himself from North Africa), was a powerful and popular figure in her own right, a patroness of literature and the arts, and the recipient of a remarkable honor, namely the mintage of coins bearing her image and the title *mater castrorum* ("mother of the camp"), because she accompanied her husband on his military campaigns. Whether or not Perpetua consciously regarded any of these strong figures as role models cannot be determined. But the portrait of her that emerges in the *Passion* mirrors the independent-mindedness, resourcefulness, and courage they displayed. Second, Salisbury points out the strong Phoenician/Carthaginian tradition of human sacrifice (particularly of one's own children) and sacrificial suicide (particularly by women). This tradition culminated in the writings of Tertullian, Perpetua's contemporary and a fellow member of the Carthaginian church. Tertullian stoutly insisted that the expected outcome of the Christian life would be martyrdom.[17] Although Salisbury's arguments that the pagan Punic tradition of human sacrifice presages the later North African Christian stress on martyrdom are suggestive, they seem a bit overdrawn. Killing one's children or oneself in a frenzy of grief over the calamities that have befallen one's city or in hopes of persuading the gods to come to its aid is different from refusing to renounce one's convictions at the behest of the government under penalty of death.

The North African Church

One of the striking features of the *Passion* is the evidence it gives of the organizational complexity of the Carthaginian church, but also the intimate familiarity that its members seem to have enjoyed with one another. We read of Optatus the bishop (III.13.1), of Aspasius the presbyter (III.13.1), of Tertius and Pomponius the deacons (II.3.7; cf. II.10.1), of Saturus the catechist (II.4.4; III.11:1), and of a variety of catechumens, including five of the six martyrs (I.2.1), Perpetua's unnamed brother

---

16. Dronke, *Women Writers*, 285, cited in Salisbury, *Perpetua's Passion*, 46 and 187n56.

17. See his *Apology*, and his treatises, *To the Martyrs* and *Of Flight in Persecution*.

(I.2.2; IV.20.10), and Rusticus (IV.20.8). And a number of pagans, including Pudens the military adjutant (II.9.1; IV.21.1–5) and "many people from among [the crowd]" (IV.17.3), are converted to the faith by the example of the prisoners. We also read the names of ten members of the Carthaginian church who were martyrs. Six are the subjects of the *Passion*; the other four—Jocundus, Saturninus, Artaxius, and Quintus—had died earlier "in the same persecution" (III.11.9).

The narrative does not describe the specific duties of bishops, presbyters, deacons, and catechists in much detail, but what little it says matches what we know from other ancient sources. The bishop and presbyter, who appear in Saturus' vision, are responsible for maintaining church discipline, and presumably also for preaching and administering the sacraments. (Unfortunately, they are neither setting a very good example for their flock nor carrying out their duties very effectively—a point whose significance we shall elaborate below.) The deacons are charged with caring for the prisoners, a job that included bribing the jailors into giving them better accommodations. And Saturus the catechist is described by Perpetua as "the one to edify us" (II.4.5). (The term "catechist" is not explicitly used in the narrative, and the title of the office in the Carthaginian church may simply have been "edifier.") The care taken by the editor and the diarists to identify the officials of their church by name, together with the reference to the maladministration of Optatus and Aspasius, suggests that the church was large and mature enough to require the full array of ecclesiastical ranks, but still small enough for its members to know each other personally, to feel responsible for each other's physical and spiritual welfare, and to hold each other accountable in Christian discipleship—despite their evident differences in social status and ecclesiastical rank. This squares with Salisbury's conjecture that the number of Christians in Carthage at the time of the Severan Persecution was about two thousand.[18]

---

18. Salisbury, *Perpetua's Passion*, 61. But her figure presumes three things of which we are uncertain: (1) that the percentage of Christians in Carthage was roughly that of Christians in the empire as a whole; (2) that that percentage was no more than 0.05 percent; and (3) that the population of Carthage was about five hundred thousand. Salisbury's estimate is based partly on the demographic studies of Stark, *Rise*, especially chapter 6. But Stark's figures are for 100 CE, about a century before the events narrated in the *Passion*. A somewhat lower figure for the number of Carthaginian Christians in this period—between three and four hundred, organized into several house churches—is given in Tabbernee, "To Pardon or Not to Pardon?," 381.

Later we shall analyze the religious convictions to which the characters in the *Passion* bore witness, but here we should note two issues that were hotly contested in the Carthaginian church and that suffuse our narrative. These are the issues of *pneumatic phenomena* and *ecclesiastical authority*. By pneumatic phenomena, I refer to "ecstatic" experiences of God's power and presence. These responses might be immediate, unreflective, and intensely emotional, such as visions, prophecies, and the power to heal. Or they might be more sedated, measured, and enduring, involving the onset of a wide array of emotions and character traits, such as remorse for sin, gratitude for blessings, joy in forgiveness, and love of neighbors and enemies. Or they might be both. By ecclesiastical authority, I refer to the policy- and decision-making offices of the church and the formal procedures for setting policies and enacting decisions. Now when a sizable portion of a church's members experience profound and life-changing pneumatic phenomena, the question immediately arises about how the authenticity and validity of those experiences are to be assessed, and, if found authentic and valid, how they are to be sustained, nurtured, enriched, galvanized into constructive action, kept within acknowledged doctrinal, moral, and social boundaries, and communicated to those have not yet enjoyed them. Religious experience without religious authority may become lawless; religious authority without religious experience may become lifeless. Those who have undergone pneumatic experiences are likely to regard them as self-authenticating and in no need of testing or disciplining by church officials, whereas the appointed guardians of orthodoxy and canonical order may view the pneumatic party under their jurisdiction as reckless and immature.

The *Passion* reveals that in the Carthaginian church of the early second century, pneumatic phenomena were occurring with growing frequency and intensity. The "new prophecies and new visions" (I.1.5) which the martyrs of 203 had experienced, recorded, and entrusted to the editor for publication could be understood as a fresh fulfillment of Pentecost (Acts 2:17–18, paraphrasing Joel 2:28).[19] But the very fact that the editor felt that a "revival" of Pentecost was now needed indicates that some Carthaginian Christians were worried about the spiritual declension of their church. They believed that Pentecost was supposed to be an ongoing reality, not an isolated event in the distant past. As yet, no breach in the church had occurred, but squabbles were breaking out. In

---

19. See Robeck, *Prophecy in Carthage*, 1–94.

Saturus' vision, the martyrs visit the quarrelling bishop and the presbyter, who immediately fall on their faces before them and implore them to "reconcile us" (III.13.2), an action that the martyrs find both emotionally moving and socially embarrassing. For the position of the martyrs is decidedly equivocal: they are, on the one hand, newly baptized—and two of them are women. Accordingly, they should not be expected to exercise disciplinary authority over ordained ecclesiastical officials. On the other hand, they are visionaries and martyrs-to-be, and thus possess a degree of spiritual authority that equals or exceeds that of the clergy. It should be noted that even after the schism between Catholics and Montanists had taken place, the Montanists established their own array of ecclesiastical officers, while the Catholics, for their part, canonized "proto-Montanist" martyrs as saints and even preserved the later and avowedly schismatic writings of Tertullian. Thus, both groups recognized the need for promoting genuine religious experience and for maintaining legitimate religious authority. The dispute was over what kinds of religious experiences were genuine and what kinds of people could exercise legitimate authority in the church. This dispute was already underway in 203, and traces of it are detectable in the *Passion*. Indeed, one reason the narrative has such power is that its heroes were obliged to articulate their religious convictions not only before the secular authorities, who doubted their patriotism, but also before the officials of their own church, who doubted the authenticity and spiritual validity of their pneumatic experiences.

The Severan Persecution

The crime for which Perpetua and her friends were tried and executed was *being* Christians (II.6.4). According to de Ste Croix, "from at least 112 onwards (perhaps . . . from 64) the normal charge against Christians was simply 'being Christians': they were punished, that is to say, 'for the Name', the *nomen Christianum*."[20] It is important to distinguish this charge from three other things that made Christians hateful to the Roman people and authorities.[21] First, some Roman writers, such as Tacitus, believed that Christians were guilty of committing abominations (*flagitia*) during their services of worship. Those who were found guilty of them by

20. De Ste Croix, "Why Were the Early Christians Persecuted?," 9. For a general account of Roman antipathy toward Christianity, but with no specific reference to the Severan Persecution, see Wilken, *Christians*.

21. Sherwin-White, "Early Persecutions," 199–213.

a magistrate would have been punished. But the charge that Christians were guilty of *flagitia* apparently rested on mistaken understandings of their worship practices. Their "love feasts" were never proved to involve incest, nor were their Eucharistic feasts ever shown to involve cannibalism. To be hated on suspicion of abominable acts is not to be convicted of committing them, and none of the surviving trial transcripts charge Christians with that crime. Second, Christians sometimes displayed "obstinacy" (*contumacia*) when interrogated in court. But one cannot be guilty of infractions of courtroom etiquette unless one is already on trial for something else. When Perpetua appeared before Hilarianus the Procurator, she refused to "make the sacrifice for the health of the emperors" (II.6.3). But it was that refusal itself, grounded in her profession of the Name of Christ, for which she was punished, not her disrespectful attitude in court. (Curiously, it was not Perpetua, but her father, who took a beating during her trial, for disrupting the proceedings in his zealous attempt to persuade her to renounce her new faith.)

The third complaint—the supposed crime of abandoning the ancestral Roman deities and *converting* to Christianity—requires a bit more discussion. The reigning emperor in 203 CE was Septimius Severus. Of him the *Historia Augusta* states:

> After this, having first raised his soldiers' pay, he turned his steps toward Alexandria, and while on his way thither he conferred numerous rights upon the communities of Palestine. He forbade conversion to Judaism under heavy penalties and enacted a similar law in regard to the Christians. He then gave the Alexandrians the privilege of a local senate, for they were still without any public council, just as they had been under their own kings, and were obliged to be content with the single governor appointed by Caesar. Besides this, he changed many of their laws. In after years Severus himself continually avowed that he had found this journey very enjoyable, because he had taken part in the worship of the god Serapis, had learned something of antiquity, and had seen unfamiliar animals and strange places. For he visited Memphis, Memnon, the Pyramids, and the Labyrinth, and examined them all with great care.[22]

If accurate, this passage may help us to understand several features of the *Passion*, but probably *not* the legal charge for which Perpetua and her friends were arrested. For example, the passage indicates that

---

22. Aelius Spartianus, *Severus* 17.1–4, 408–11.

Severus was a devotee of Serapis, the Romanized version of the ancient Egyptian god Osiris, and if that fact were known to Perpetua, it may have found its way into her fourth vision, where she does battle in the arena with "an Egyptian ... horrible in appearance" (II.10.6). But we cannot be sure that Perpetua knew of Severus' devotion to Serapis, nor is it safe to "psychoanalyze" her visions.[23] Yet it is noteworthy that it is not the Egyptian, but the other figure in the vision, the gladiatorial trainer or referee (*lanista*), who possesses "imperial" or quasi-divine features and who ultimately pronounces Perpetua the victor.[24] Perhaps that is a cryptic indication of her understanding of where true authority lies. We also know from Dio Cassius that Severus "built a temple of huge size to Bacchus and Hercules,"[25] and from Eusebius that he "instigat[ed] a persecution of the churches."[26] So his antipathy to Christianity may have been connected with his zeal for Serapis and for the deities of the traditional Greco-Roman pantheon.[27] But whether Severus actually issued an edict that forbade conversion to Christianity, as the *Historia Augusta* claims, is disputed.[28] And even if he did, that may not have been the law that Hilarianus found Perpetua and her friends guilty of breaking, for the charge against them was that they *were* Christians, not

23. See, e.g., Rouselle, "Dreams," 193–206, who takes a Freudian approach; and Von Franz, *Passion of Perpetua*, and Rossi, "Everywoman of Late Antiquity," 53–86, who use a Jungian framework. The great problem with psychohistorical approaches to Perpetua is that they do not sufficiently explain the connection between the symbolism of her visions and her actual experiences and conduct as a Christian martyr. Yet she wrote her diary, and it was preserved and cherished by the church, precisely because that connection was patent.

24. He is described as "a man of marvelous stature," who wore "a purple outfit with two stripes through the middle of his chest" and "fancy shoes made out of gold and silver," and who was carrying "a rod ... and a green branch which had golden apples on it" (II.10:8).

25. Dio Cassius, *Roman History* 17.16, 273.

26. Eusebius, *History* 6.1, 179.

27. Davies, "Devotion," 73–76. A general assessment of "philosophy and religion" during the reign of Septimius may be found in Platnauer, *Septimius Severus*, 141–57. Platnauer, 154–55, affirms that "the emperor was opposed to Christianity as a religion and to Christians as a class," but notes that he had positive dealings with several Christian individuals.

28. Frend, *Martyrdom and Persecution*, 238–42 and 482n66, asserts that Severus prohibited conversions to both Judaism and Christianity in the wake of his pacification campaign in Palestine in 200–201. But Barnes, "Legislation," 40–41, argues that although Severus may have forbidden conversions to Judaism, the statement in the *Historia Augusta* that "put ... Christians and Jews on the same level [is] an indubitable fiction."

that they had recently *converted* to Christianity. If he did indeed learn that five Christian catechumens had been baptized while under surveillance, he might have deemed that evidence of *contumacia*. But he did not arrest them *for* that offense.[29]

This brings us to another point: the role of Hilarianus in the persecution of the Carthaginian martyrs. Frend contends that "the Severan persecution was the first co-ordinated worldwide move against Christians." But he promptly qualifies this remark by admitting that it "affected only the relatively small class of Christian converts" (Frend accepts the historicity of the edict), and that it "was confined to the major centers," such as Carthage, Alexandria, Rome, Corinth, and Antioch).[30] And even if the persecution of 202–3 set a precedent for the much more extensive pogroms launched by Decius in 250 and Diocletian in 303, as Frend contends, it appears that direct legal action against Christians (or Christian converts only?) depended largely on the initiative of local governors, perhaps prompted by zealous local mobs. For the governors of other areas were not forced by the imperial administration to persecute local Christians. Perhaps Hilarianus, who had recently "received capital authority (*ius gladii*)" (II.6.3) in the province, knew of Severus's hostility to Christianity. And if there *was* a new edict prohibiting *conversion* to Christianity, he may have known of that, too, even if the law that he cited against Perpetua and her friends was the older one against its *practice*. But the decision to act against the Christians and the manner in which he acted were apparently largely his own—perhaps a function of his own devotion to traditional Roman religious practices and cultural values, and perhaps also a function of some desire to curry favor with Severus.[31] On the whole, then, it seems the Carthaginian persecution described in the *Passion* was an instance of a widespread wave of fierce hostility against Christians, fomented or encouraged by the emperor's own religious views, perhaps abetted by a new imperial edict, but still left to local governors to put into effect. And the older

---

29. The *Passion* states that the five prisoners were held *cum prosecutoribus* (II.3.1) for several days before being placed *in carcerum* (II.3.5). But what exactly does that mean? Jacobs and Cobb, in Cobb, *Passion*, 23, read "with the prosecutors." Musurillo, *Acts*, 109, translates it as "under arrest." Rader, "*Martyrdom*," 20, has "with the police authorities." Salisbury, *Perpetua's Passion*, 82, describes the situation as "some sort of house arrest." However we take the phrase, it is astonishing that the authorities didn't prevent the prisoners from receiving baptism.

30. Frend, *Martyrdom and Persecution*, 240.

31. See Rives, "Piety of a Persecutor," 1–25.

law, not the new edict, could still be used in legal proceedings, as it had been for a century or more. Hilarianus asked Perpetua, "Are you a Christian?" To which she replied, "I am a Christian" (*Christiana sum*) (II.6.4). For that she was sent to the arena.

Structure, Rhetorical Design, and Literary Devices

In his classic work, *Christ and Culture*, H. Richard Niebuhr delineates a spectrum of ways in which Christians through the centuries have understood their respective responsibilities to God and the state. Those on the extreme "right" of the spectrum believe that loyalty to the state and loyalty to God are perfectly compatible, and that the performance of one's civic duties is a Christian responsibility. On the extreme "left" stand those who believe that loyalty to God inevitably puts one at odds with the state. Between these poles are three mediating positions, all of which acknowledge that "Christ" and "culture" both lay legitimate claims on a Christian's life and suggest various ways for the Christian to negotiate these claims when they compete.[32] The *Passion* certainly belongs on the far left of this spectrum, in what Niebuhr calls the "Christ against culture" type.[33] Niebuhr cites Tertullian as a paradigmatic exemplar of this type, and whether or not Tertullian was the editor of the *Passion*, the rhetorical design of the text certainly makes a very Tertullianic point: the faithful proclamation of the Christian gospel is dangerous to one's temporal interests but crucial for one's eternal blessedness. In this section, we examine how the rhetorical design and literary structure of the *Passion* establish this point.

Narrative Structure

We have seen that the *Passion* is a three-author document, consisting of four sections: the editor's introduction and conclusion, with the prison

---

32. Niebuhr, *Christ and Culture*. The 2001 edition includes a new preface by James M. Gustafson, xxi–xxxv, which rightly warns us against construing Niebuhr's typology as an ironclad taxonomy into which a given theologian's "position" on the relationship between Christ and culture can simply be "located" without further ado. Even the description of his typology as a "spectrum," on which there is a "left" and a "right," is reminiscent of political categories that don't match it very well. So, the way I have formulated this paragraph should be taken advisedly.

33. Niebuhr, *Christ and Culture*, xliii–xlv and 45–82.

diaries of Perpetua and Saturus sandwiched in between. But it will help our analysis of the text as a specimen of prison literature to provide a synopsis of the action, using the numbered paragraphs as guidelines. This will show which parts of the story, and how much of the story, each of the three authors contributed.

I. Introduction
   1. The Holy Spirit at work in the persecuted church.
   2. The martyrs introduced.
II. The Prison Diary of Perpetua
   3. The arrest of the martyrs; Perpetua's first conversation with her father; prison conditions improve.
   4. Perpetua's first vision: the ladder to heaven.
   5. Perpetua's second conversation with her father.
   6. The hearing before Hilarianus; Perpetua's father's protest.
   7. Perpetua's second vision: Dinocrates in torment and Perpetua's prayer on his behalf.
   8. Perpetua's third vision: Dinocrates refreshed.
   9. The prisoners honored by Pudens the prison officer.
   10. Perpetua's fourth vision: her combat with the Egyptian.
III. The Vision of Saturus
   11. The martyrs arrive in heaven.
   12. The martyrs meet the Lord.
   13. The martyrs and the heavenly angels settle a dispute in the Carthaginian church.
IV. Conclusion
   14. Secundulus dies in prison.
   15. Felicitas gives birth prematurely.
   16. Perpetua rebukes a military tribune.
   17. The prisoners' last meal; Saturus rebukes the mob.
   18. The prisoners enter the arena.
   19. Saturninus, Revocatus, and Saturus fight with the beasts.

20. Perpetua and Felicitas fight with the beasts.
21. Saturus gives a bloodied ring to Pudens; Perpetua helps a gladiator slit her throat; concluding words of praise to the martyrs.

The seam points between the four sections are clearly indicated. The editor concludes his introduction (Section I) with the words, "This entire account of her own martyrdom from this point she has narrated, just as she left behind written in her own hand and from her own experience" (I.2.3). Perpetua ends her diary (Section II) with the remark, "This is what I did up until the day before the show. But what happened at the show itself, if someone wants to, let him write it" (II.10.15). Saturus' diary (Section III) begins with a brief note by the editor: "Now also blessed Saturus made public this vision of his own, which he himself wrote down" (III.11.1); it concludes with Saturus' remark: "Then rejoicing I woke up" (III.13.8). The editor begins his conclusion by remarking, "These were the very remarkable visions of these most blessed martyrs, Saturus and Perpetua, which they themselves recorded" (IV.14.1), and then begins his account of their last days.

From this outline we can glean several things. First, the editor's introduction comprises about 10 percent of the text, Perpetua's diary about 40 percent, Saturus' diary about 15 percent, and the editor's conclusion about 35 percent. Thus, the length of the introduction and conclusion taken together is about 10 percent less than that of the two diaries taken together. The bookends are no shorter, but also no longer, than necessary for explaining the historical context of the diaries, the purpose of their composition, and the fate of their authors.

Second, about half of Perpetua's diary and all of Saturus' are devoted to accounts of their visions. Most of these accounts are quite detailed. The remainder of Perpetua's diary consists in her account of her experiences in prison, her tangled relationship with her family, especially her father, and her trial before Hilarianus. Thus, well over a third of the *Passion* is composed of material that was "shown" to the two martyrs while the other two thirds are narratives of events.

Third, the editor and the martyrs agree that it was the Holy Spirit who "showed" the martyrs their visions. The editor makes this point explicit in his introduction. He announces that God has given "an overflowing of grace . . . for the last interval of the world" (I.1.3) in the form of "new prophecies and new visions" to the church. He quotes Acts 2:17–18 to affirm that these manifestations of spiritual power are both "for God's glory" and according to God's promise (I.1.5). Two of the seam verses quoted above (III.11.1 and IV.14.1) make the same point. The martyrs themselves are somewhat more circumspect about claiming direct divine inspiration, but it is not hard to read between the lines. Perpetua introduces three of her visions with the words, *ostensum est mihi hoc* ["this was shown to me"] (II.4.2; II.7.3; II.8.1) and the fourth with *video in horomate hoc* ["I see in this vision"] (II.10.1). She thus affirms that she was the recipient of divine favor and declares that she only asked for this favor after her brother the catechumen had prompted her to do so and had assured her that she was worthy of it (II.4.1). Thus, the visions are presented as products of divine inspiration: they are to be read theologically, with the narrative bookends providing the necessary historical context.

Fourth, the sequencing of authorial voices in the *Passion* (editor → Perpetua → Saturus → editor) and the careful proportioning of the lengths of the four sections of the text indicate that the work is to be taken as an integrated whole, with each voice providing a distinctive but essential component of the work's overall message. The martyrdoms cannot be rightly understood unless the prophetic authority of the martyrs is established; but the prophetic authority of the martyrs depends on their having been granted visions by the Holy Spirit during their imprisonment; and the authenticity of the records of the visions is guaranteed by the fact that the martyrs wrote them out by hand and passed them on to a fellow church member for publication. The editor puts this point forcefully: "Now since the Holy Spirit has allowed and by allowing has wished for the account of that show to be recorded, even though we are not worthy to add anything to so great a wonder as must be described, nevertheless we shall execute it as if it were the command of most holy Perpetua—or, really, her bequest—adding one instance of her steadfastness and the loftiness of her mind" (IV.16.1).

Contrasts, Parallels, and Transformations

But there is another way in which the literary unity of the *Passion* is secured, namely, a stylistic device whereby themes and images introduced at one point in the narrative are echoed at a later point, and often in a different section and therefore by a different authorial voice. These reduplicating images often occur in pairs, though sometimes in triads and still larger groupings. And they come in three forms. In some cases, the two (or three, or more) coordinated themes or images stand in sharp *contrast* to each other, often with one representing the demonic power of Rome and the other representing the spiritual authority of the martyrs. In other cases, the themes or images are closely *parallel* to each other—and usually both (or all) are "positive." In still other cases, the first item of the pair represents an early stage of a physical or spiritual *transformation* which a character in the narrative is undergoing, while the second item represents the culmination of that process. Let us first tabulate these pairs and groups of coordinated images and themes according to their form, and then examine the rhetorical force of each form in turn.

Contrasts

1. Perpetua identified as a member of *gens Vibius* (I.2.1) vs. Perpetua addressed as a member of the church, her new family: as "Lady sister" [*Domina soror*] by her brother the catechumen (II.4.1), as "Child" [*teknon*] by Saturus, her catechist (II.4.9), as "Daughter" [*filia*] by the gladiatorial trainer (II.10.13), and as "Christ's lawful wife" [*matrona Christi*] and "God's sweetheart" [*Dei delicata*] by the editor (IV.18.2).

2. The white hair of the divine shepherd in Perpetua's first vision signifying venerability (II.4.8) vs. the white hair of Perpetua's father signifying feeble old age (II.5.2, II.6.3).

3. The identification of various Roman officers and soldiers: proconsul (II.6.3), procurator (II.6.3–6), Caesar (II.7.9), military adjutant (II.9.1; IV.16.4), military tribune (IV.16.2), and various soldiers, prison guards, and gladiators (passim) vs. the identification of various church officials: deacons (II.3.7; II.6.7; II.10.1), catechist (II.4.5), bishop (III.13.1), presbyter (III.13.1), and various catechumens and martyrs (passim).

4. The identification of various elements of Roman religion, such as the sacrifice to the gods for the emperor (II.6.3), the belief in magical spells (IV.16.2), and the costuming of the prisoners as deities (IV.18.4) vs. the identification of various elements of the Christian religion, such as belief in the Holy Trinity (I.1.1–6; IV.21.11),[34] the

---

34. The term "Trinity" is used here for convenience but does not appear in our text. Its first known use in Christian Greek (*trias*) was by Theophilus of Antioch, *To Autylocus* 2.15 (ca. 180). Its first known use in Christian Latin (*trinitas*) was by Tertullian,

celebration of baptism (II.3.5), the celebration of a post-baptismal ritual or Eucharist (II.4.9–10), prayers (II.7.1; II.7.10), the kiss of peace [*pacem* or *sollemnia pacis*] (III.12.6; IV.21.7), the celebration of the love feast [*agapem*] (IV.17.1), and psalm-singing (IV.18.7).

5. The chiding of some Carthaginian Christians for approaching their bishop "as if they're coming home from the racetrack and arguing about the factions" (III.13.6) vs. the praising Carthaginian martyrs for "march[ing] from the prison into the amphitheater as though into heaven, joyful, with handsome faces" (IV.18.1).

6. Mention of "other criminals" (IV.15.2) vs. the six prisoners of conscience (passim).

7. The mocking chant of the Carthaginian mob after the bloodbath in the arena: "Saving bath, saving bath!" [*Salvum lotum, salvum lotum*] (IV.21.2) vs. the pious chants of the heavenly host: "Amen!" (II.4.9), "They are here, they are here!" (*Ecce sunt, ecce sunt*) (III.11.7), "Holy, holy, holy!" [*Hagios, hagios, hagios!*] (III.12.2), and "Let us stand" [*Stemus!*] (III.12.6).

Parallels

1. "Ancient models of faith" for building people up spiritually (I.1.1) ‖ "the one to edify us" (II.4.5) ‖ "these examples for building up the church" (IV.21.11).[35]

2. Perpetua as mother and martyr (I.2.1–3; II.3.6–8; II.6.7–8) ‖ Felicitas as mother and martyr (IV.15.1–7; IV.20.2).

3. Perpetua tells her father: "I cannot call myself anything but what I am, a Christian" (II.3.2). ‖ Perpetua tells Hilarianus: "I am a Christian" (II.6.4).

4. Perpetua argues with her father (II.3.1–4; II.5.1–6; II.6.2–5; II.9.2–3). ‖ Perpetua's sees a vision of herself battling with the Egyptian (II.10.1–14). ‖ Perpetua is attacked by a ferocious heifer (IV.20.1–5). ‖ Perpetua is slain by the gladiator (IV.21.9–10).

Against Praxeas 2–4 (ca. 213) and *On Modesty* 21 (ca. 217?). See Kelly, *Early Christian Doctrines*, 109–15; Quasten, *Patrology*, 1:237–41; 2:284–86, 312–15.

35. The first and third references to edification are in sections penned by the editor. For the literary and theological significance of this, see Boeft, "Editor's Prime Objective."

5. The "darkness" (*tenebras*) of the prison (II.3.5–6). ‖ The "shadowy place" (*de loco tenebroso*) of Dinocrates' place of torment (II.7.4).³⁶

6. Perpetua nurses her child (II.3.8). ‖ The divine Shepherd milks sheep and feeds Perpetua the curds (II.4.8–9).³⁷ ‖ Felicitas' breasts drip with milk (IV.20.2).

7. Perpetua's brother the catechumen affirms that because she is "already in great esteem" [*magna dignatione*] she may "request a vision" (II.4.1). ‖ Perpetua realizes that she is "worthy" [*statim dignam*] to intercede for her other brother, Dinocrates (II.7.2).

8. Perpetua states: "And this was shown to me" (II.4.2; II.7.3; II.8.1). ‖ Perpetua states: "I see in this vision" (II.10.1). ‖ The editor states: "Saturus made public this vision of his own" (III.11.1).

9. After each of Perpetua's visions, she "understands" or "knows" its significance: *intelleximus* (II.4.10), ‖ *intellexi* (II.8.4), ‖ *intellexi* (II.10.13), and ‖ *cognovi* (II.7.9).

10. In her first vision, Perpetua sees Saturus climbing a deadly ladder to heaven and "holding on" for Perpetua, who follows (II.4.5–6;

---

36. The text does not explain whether Dinocrates had been condemned to this "dark place" because he had died unbaptized or, as Augustine thought, had committed some unrepented post-baptismal sin. See Musurillo, *Acts*, 115n11. The reference in Perpetua's second vision to the *grande diastema* (II.7.6; literally "great gap," but translated as "great distance" by Jacobs and Cobb in Cobb, *Passion*, 29) may echo the *chasma mega* ("great gulf") of Jesus' parable of Lazarus and Dives (Luke 16:26). In the Old Latin version of the Bible, Luke's *chasma mega* is rendered *chaos magnum*, while the ancient Greek version of the *Passion* reads *mega diastēma*. Whatever this may say about the textual history of the *Passion*, the parallels between Jesus' parable and Perpetua's second vision are not exact. In the parable, the *chasma mega* separating Lazarus from Dives is uncrossable. In Perpetua's vision, the *grande diastema* is uncrossable, but Perpetua is not explicitly said to be in heaven, nor is Dinocrates, though in torment, said to be in hell. Moreover, in Perpetua's third vision, Dinocrates is beside the same pool of water as before, but now he can drink from it, so wherever he was, conditions have greatly improved (as they never do for Dives).

37. This is part of a vision, and is, in the strictest sense of the word, "wonderful." The shepherd, presumably representing Christ, is "milking sheep" (*oues mulgentum*) (II.4.8). He gives some of the "curds which he had milked" (*caseo quod mulgabat*) (II.4.9) to Perpetua, which she eats, with those around her exclaiming "Amen!" When she wakes from her vision, she is "still chewing something sweet (*dulce*)" (II.4.10). Exactly what sort of dairy product is meant here—raw milk, curds, whey, or sweet cheese—is unclear. Also unclear is whether the image in the vision has any direct reference to the sacramental practices of the ancient church. Tertullian indicates that the newly baptized are given a drink of milk and honey (*The Chaplet* 3.3), and Hippolytus says that a cup of milk and honey is taken during the Eucharist which immediately follows the baptism of initiates on Easter morning (*Apostolic Tradition* 21.28, 113). Tertullian's treatise was written in 209 and Hippolytus' around 215, per Quasten, *Patrology*, Vol. 2, 309 and 209, respectively.

IV.21.8). ‖ In his vision, Saturus sees Perpetua and himself climbing a "gentle slope" to heaven together (III.11.3–4).

11. In her first vision, Perpetua states: "Saturus climbed up first" (II.4.5). ‖ In the conclusion, the editor refers to that scene in Perpetua's vision when mentioning that Saturus was also the first of the six friends to die in the arena (IV.21.8).

12. Perpetua steps on the head of the dragon (II.4.7). ‖ Perpetua repeatedly kicks the Egyptian during their combat and steps on his head (II.10.10–11). ‖ Perpetua sings a psalm and "was already treading on the head of the Egyptian" (IV.18.7).

13. Perpetua's vision of heaven as "immense expanse of a garden" (II.4.8). ‖ Saturus' vision of heaven as "a great expanse . . . like a green garden, with rose bushes and all kinds of flowers" (III.11.5).

14. Perpetua awakes from her first vision "still chewing something sweet" (II.4.10). ‖ Saturus' vision ends with him and many others "nourished by an indescribable odor which sated us" (III.13.8).

15. God's power (*potestate*) determines the future (II.5.6). ‖ God's splendor and great power (*claritas et immensa potestas*) last forever (IV.21.11).

16. Perpetua's baby is entrusted to the care of her parents (II.6.2).[38] ‖ Felicitas' daughter is entrusted to "a certain sister" (presumably a Carthaginian Christian woman) (IV.15.7).

17. Gynecological "miracles": Perpetua's lactation ends suddenly during her baby's absence (II.6.8). ‖ Felicitas gives birth prematurely in response to her prayers and those of her fellow prisoners (IV.15.2, 5).

18. Perpetua's prayer for Dinocrates' healing is granted (II.7.10–8.4). ‖ Perpetua's wish is granted (III.12.7). ‖ The martyrs' prayer that Felicitas will give birth prematurely is granted (IV.15.4–5). ‖ Saturus' prayer to be mauled by a leopard, not a bear, is granted (IV.19.4; 21.1–2).

19. Dinocrates goes "from the water to play, having fun like children do" (*accessit de aqua ludere more infantium gaudens*) (II.8.4). ‖ The

---

38. Perpetua's baby was apparently taken from her at her arrest (II.3.6) but was soon brought back and allowed to stay with her for a time (II.3.8–9). At some point, he was entrusted to Perpetua's parents, for during her interrogation by Hilarianus, her father brings him back again, hoping that her maternal anxiety will induce her to recant her faith (II.6.2). In the interval, the child had somehow been weaned (II.6.8). Presumably, he remained in his grandparents' care after his mother's death.

heavenly "elders" tell the martyrs to "Go and play" (*Ite et ludite*) (III.12.6).

20. Perpetua is stripped and anointed in preparation for combat with the Egyptian (II.10.7). ‖ Perpetua and Felicitas are stripped and garbed for combat in the arena (IV.20.2).

21. After defeating the Egyptian, Perpetua "began to go with glory to the Gate of the Living" (II.10.13). ‖ "The throng's harshness was subdued, and [Perpetua and Felicitas] were called back to the Gate of the Living" (IV.20.7).[39]

22. Felicitas goes "from blood to blood, from midwife to net-fighter, ready to wash after birth in a second baptism" (IV.18:3). ‖ Saturus, "after he was thrown out to a leopard, shed so much blood from a single bite that the throng shouted back to him as he returned, in witness to his second baptism, 'Saving bath, saving bath!'" (IV.21:2-3).

Transformations

1. Perpetua worries about her infant, who has been taken from her (II.3.6). → Perpetua's baby is restored to her; she nurses him but confides her continuing anxieties to her mother (II.3.8). → Perpetua's worries over her child are relieved when she gets permission for him to stay with her (II.3.9). → The baby is weaned, her lactation ends, and she is no longer "tormented neither by concern for my baby nor by pain in my breasts" (II.6.8).[40]

2. Perpetua writes in her diary, "Suddenly the prison became my palace, and there was nowhere else I wanted to be" (II.3.9). → Perpetua says to Saturus in his vision, "Thank God that, as happy as I was in the flesh, I am happier here and now" (III.12.7).

3. Dinocrates, with an open cancer lesion of the face, is in anguish by a pool whose water he cannot reach (II.7.7–8). → Dinocrates, with facial lesion scarred over, is able to reach the pool of water and is refreshed (II.8.2–4).

---

39. This instance might just as well be included in the list of Contrasts above. Roman amphitheaters had two gates, the *Porta Sanavivaria* ("the Gate of the Living," lit. The Gate of Life and Health"), where victorious gladiators made their exit, and the *Porta Libitinensis* ("The Funeral Gate"), where the corpses of the defeated were dragged for burial. See Musurillo, *Acts*, 119n12. The entire story turns on the irony that what for the Romans was a public execution of dangerous criminals was for the Christians a glorious victory over the demonic power of the empire.

40. See Parallel 17 and n38 above.

4. A spectacle in the arena is staged to celebrate the birthday of Geta Caesar (II.7.9). → The martyrs celebrate their "day of victory" (IV.18.1).[41]

5. Pudens the military adjutant shows honor to the prisoners (II.9.1). → Pudens becomes a believer (IV.16.4). → Saturus give Pudens a bloodied ring as a memento (IV.21.4–5).

6. The prisoners eat their "last meal" (*cenam ultimam*) or "free meal" (*cenam liberam*) (IV.17.1). → But they do so as if celebrating a "love-feast" (*agapem cenarent*) (IV.17.1).

7. When Saturus is bitten by the leopard, the crowds mockingly compare his imminent exsanguination to a visit to a public bath house (IV.21.2). → The editor overturns their mockery by defining Saturus' martyrdom as a spiritual cleansing (IV.21.2).

The seven *contrast* groups listed above illustrate the sharply counter-cultural stance of the *Passion*. Various aspects of Roman society are set in stark opposition to corresponding aspects of the Christian community, which the prisoners have now joined—at their peril. For example, numerous Roman officials are mentioned, often by name, but within the narrative the performance of their duties always involves the direct use of coercive force or the administration of what is repeatedly shown to be a deeply violent society. Caesar Geta's birthday is celebrated with "murderous games" in the arena.[42] Hilarianus the Procurator receives the *ius gladii* ("capital authority," lit., "the right of the sword"); later, while officiating at the prisoners' trial, Hilarianus has Perpetua's father beaten for disorderly conduct in court and condemns (*damnat*) the accused to the beasts. Prison guards extort bribes. A military tribune punishes the prisoners severely. Mobs mock the condemned and satisfy their blood-lust at the arena. Gladiators struggle to control the beasts in the arena, and when the beasts don't cooperate, the gladiators dispatch the prisoners with their swords. Pudens the military adjutant is the exception that proves the rule: he shows the Christians "great honor," realizing that they possess "great power" (*magnum virtutem*) (II.9.1), and eventually converts to their faith (see Transformation 5).

41. Early Christians regarded the date of a martyr's death as his or her "birthday." See, e.g., *Martrydom of Polycarp* 18 in Lightfoot and Harmer, *Apostolic Fathers*, 196, 209, and Augustine, *Works III:8*, Sermons 280, 281, and 282, which are all titled, "On the Birthday of the Martyrs Perpetua and Felicitas," 72, 78, and 81, respectively.

42. On the socio-political functions of violent spectacles in Roman society, see Hopkins, "Murderous Games," 1–30.

Standing over against this picture of Roman brutality and authoritarianism is the picture of the Christian community, whose officials and members—most of them also identified by name—are consistently shown engaging in acts of benevolence, nurture, and mutual support. Deacons Tertius and Pomponius care for the prisoners. Saturus, who had "edified" the catechumens before their arrest, gives his bloodied ring as a memento to the newly converted Pudens. Perpetua's son is cared for by her mother, who was apparently a Christian (as II.5.6 seems to imply). Felicitas' daughter is adopted by a Christian woman, who "reared [her] as a daughter for herself" (IV.15.7). In the arena, Perpetua preserves her "modesty" (*pudor*) when her body is exposed to the prurient gaze of the mob, and then offers a hand to the injured Felicitas, helps her to her feet, and stands by her (IV.20.4–6). Rusticus the catechumen stands by Perpetua as she is ushered from the arena (IV.20.8). And once again, the exception proves the rule: when Bishop Optatus and Presbyter Aspasius fail to perform their official duties, they are respectfully called to account by martyrs and angels. But instead of being disgraced, they are encouraged to properly exercise their office by "correcting" their flock for approaching them with unbecoming familiarity, as if they themselves were squabbling spectators at the arena (III.13.6). So, in Pudens, we have a "good" Roman becoming a Christian, while in the undisciplined Carthaginian church, we have a number of "bad" Christians behaving like a Roman mob.

Other sharp contrasts between Roman civilization and Christianity are illustrated in our text. Particularly noteworthy are those in which Roman religion and family life are set against the practices of the church (Contrasts 3, 4, and 7). Reference is made to the Roman practice of having citizens perform sacrifices to the gods for the health of the emperor (II.6.3), but here this act of civic piety is a test of patriotism. A military tribune treats the prisoners with unnecessary cruelty because he believes a superstitious rumor that they might use magic spells to escape. While being marched to the arena, the condemned are temporarily dressed as priests of Roman deities, but Perpetua insists that they be allowed to die without nullifying the glory of their martyrdom by going along with this cynical and degrading farce. The mob in the arena mocks Saturus' "baptism by blood" with the conventional greeting exchanged by Romans after leaving the public bathhouses, *salvum lotum* (IV.21.2). Meanwhile, the Christians manage to celebrate a baptism and a love feast during their imprisonment; quasi-Eucharistic imagery occurs in the visions; the kiss of peace is exchanged; the Trinity is honored; angels sing all the proper liturgical chants (Contrast 7). Conventional social norms dissolve among the Christians. Perpetua is a member of the local nobility, but the obedience she would be expected to give to her *paterfamilias* is nullified by her new allegiance to Christ. Felicitas the slave girl is eight months pregnant, and according to Roman law, cannot be executed until she gives birth (IV.15.2). But her prayer to deliver early is answered and she joins her comrades in the arena, where Perpetua the noblewoman serves *her*.[43] Two quarrelling clerics throw themselves at the feet of those who are newly baptized and soon to be martyred and cry out, "Reconcile us, since you went away and you left us in this way" (III.13.2), suggesting that the unity of the church, as well as its public witness, depends on the rank and file no less than the clergy. Are the Christian beliefs and practices featured in the narrative meant as parodies of their Roman equivalents? Not quite. Rather, the latter appear to parody themselves, while the former are described with dignity and reverence.[44]

Let us turn now to the groups of *parallel* images or themes. Like the contrast groups, and like the transitions that we will examine momentarily, the parallels establish a network of repetitions, foreshadowings, inter-textual cross-references, and literary "echoes," which bind different sections of the narrative into a tightly woven literary whole. But whereas the contrast groups differentiate Christianity from the dominant Roman society, the parallels emphasize the unity of belief and experience among the Christians. A careful inspection of the citations listed above for any pair or group of these parallel passages will show how often one or more items of that pair or group occurs in one section of the narrative, while the other item or items occurs in a different section. This binds the various sections together without muting the distinctive voices and thematic interests of the different authors. This paralleling of spiritual experiences among different Christians is a literary cue that "the same Spirit" (cf. 1 Cor 12) is at work in all of them, despite their various gifts, needs, offices, and social roles.

---

43. Felicitas' role in the story is stressed by Amat, *Passion de Perpétue et de Félicité*; Bremmer, "Felicitas."

44. Davies, *Writers in Prison*, has rightly drawn attention to the fact that prison literature often parodies the dominant society. But although some of the authors whom Davies studies—such as Boethius, Bunyan, Dostoyevsky, and Solzhenitsyn—are Christians, he has not given much attention to the possibility that the social and political criticisms that their prison writings contain are meant to serve positive theological and missiological purposes and are rarely intended solely as parody or mockery.

A conspicuous feature of the parallels is the way they underscore the spiritual power and eschatological joy that the Christians experience in their new faith, despite the conflicts and sufferings that the transfer of their primary allegiance from Rome to Christ entails. Indeed, the experience of such power and joy is an essential element of the new identity that a baptized Christian receives upon joining the church. Thus, while two young mothers, Perpetua and Felicitas, would naturally have many things in common, what the text underscores are the similar ways in which their experiences of maternity and childcare and their relationships with their co-religionists and the members of the wider community are shaped by their common faith, despite their difference in social rank (Parallels 2, 6, and 20). We are told nothing about their husbands—because neither of them is defined any longer by her marriage. We are told that both suffered the physical discomforts associated with childbirth and early maternity—but also that the inflammation in Perpetua's lactating breasts soon subsided "as God wished" (*Deus voluit*) (II.6.8) and that Felicitas' premature delivery was an answer to prayer (IV.15.4). We are told, finally, that both surrendered their infants to face martyrdom—and to face it together.[45] Similarly, there are striking parallels between the visionary experiences of Perpetua and Saturus (Parallels 8, 10, 11, and 13), and equally striking parallels in the efficacy of the martyrs' prayers (Parallel 18).

But it would be mistaken to suppose that the prospect of enjoying the delights of heaven, which is so prominent a feature of the *Passion*, was simply a form of psychic self-compensation for the martyrs' sufferings (*à la* Nietzsche and Freud) or to suppose that it was an "opiate" distributed by the authorities to dull the senses of the oppressed masses (*à la* Marx). On the contrary, one of the most touching features of the narrative is that Perpetua displays genuine mental anguish over the personal costs of her new allegiance to Christ. In her two avowals that she is a Christian (Parallel 3), she repudiates her rights and responsibilities as a female member of the Roman nobility. This repudiation is decisive and dramatic, as symbolized in her visions by her treading upon the heads of the dragon and the Egyptian (Parallel 12). But it involves mental anguish, physical pain, and mortal combat. Victory comes through, and beyond,

---

45. The relationship between motherhood and martyrdom has been carefully analyzed by Salisbury, *Blood of Martyrs*, 70–79. See also van Henten, "*Passio Perpetuae* and Jewish Martyrdom"; Weitbrecht, "Maternity and Sainthood in the Medieval Perpetua Legend."

earthly suffering. The spiritual power and eschatological joy that the martyrs experience through faith in Christ enable them to endure their humiliations and sufferings; but these agonies remain poignantly real. Christian faith is sharing personally in the sufferings of Christ (cf. 2 Cor 1:5), and the authenticity of the martyrs' commitment is demonstrated by the realism with which the human cost is described.

The third group of coordinated images and themes are cases in which a character in the story passes through multiple stages of a *transformation* or in which something meant for ill by the Romans is changed by the martyrs' faith into something edifying, encouraging, or life-giving. Consider Transformation 7: When Saturus is bitten by a leopard, the mob roars, "Saving bath, saving bath!" This was a common greeting in Roman bath houses. But the editor turns this piece of brutal mockery on its head: "Clearly indeed he was saved who bathed in this way" (IV.21.3). He knows, as the crowd does not, the saving efficacy of dying *with* Christ through baptism and dying *for* Christ in martyrdom.[46] Thus, what the Romans regard as a legal procedure for punishing crime, the Christians redefine—and personally experience—as a ritual of salvation. The crowd's scurrility becomes a "witness" (*testimonium*) to the very thing they imagine themselves to be lampooning, and the government's severest method of executing prisoners becomes a means of "saving" them. Similarly, in Transformation 4, the emperor's birthday, celebrated with a bloody spectacle in the arena, becomes the martyrs' "day of victory," and in Transformation 6, the traditional "last meal" eaten by condemned prisoners before their execution is turned into a Christian love feast. The most dramatic transformations, however, are the healing of Dinocrates (Transformation 3) and the conversion of Pudens (Transformation 5), both of which deserve closer attention.

Perpetua's brother Dinocrates had died at the age of seven from a disfiguring facial cancer. His death took place some years before the events narrated in the *Passion*, and well before Perpetua and several other members of his family had come under the influence of Christianity. Perpetua is surprised when his name suddenly pops into her head while she

---

46. I suspect that the editor's remark alludes to 1 Peter 3–4, in which the themes of witnessing to Christ, suffering for Christ, and undergoing baptism into Christ are elaborated. See especially 1 Peter 3:21: "Baptism . . . now saves you, not as a removal of dirt from the body but as an appeal to God for a clear conscience, through the resurrection of Jesus Christ." In bathhouse greetings, *salvum* meant "healthfully" or "soundly." But among Latin-speaking Christians, the word had soteriological and eschatological resonances which the pagan mob would never have suspected.

and her comrades are at prayer, and she takes this unbidden memory as a call to intercede for him. That night she sees a vision of Dinocrates in torment: he emerges from a "shadowy place... very hot and thirsty, with filthy appearance and ashen color" (II.7.4). This recalls the "darkness" of the Carthaginian prison in which she herself was lodged (II.3.5) (Parallel 5). There is a pool of water nearby, but the rim is too high for him to reach.[47] Perpetua awakes from this vision (her second) believing that her brother is in torment, but also believing that her prayers can improve his lot. She proceeds to pray for him "every day until we were transferred into the military prison" (II.7.9). And then, "on the day we were kept fettered" (II.8.1), she has another vision (her third) of Dinocrates. His sores have healed, leaving scars, and the rim of the pool is now within his reach. Perpetua writes: "And above the edge was a golden cup full of water. And Dinocrates approached and began to drink from it; this cup did not empty. Sated, he set out from the water to play, having fun like children do" (II.8.3–4).[48] Upon awaking from her third vision, she realizes that Dinocrates had been "transferred from punishment" (II.8.4). This pair of visions indicates the efficacy of the martyrs' prayers. Their holy influence extends even to the afterlife: as they progress toward their own salvation, they gain the "power" (*virtu*) to save others.

But something else is going on here. We learn that the life of the blessed consists not simply in health and refreshment, but also in play. In her interpretation of this scene, Salisbury notes that the ancient dream-interpreter, Artemidorus, claimed that "drinking from a bowl symbolized great safety, and a scar 'signifies the ending of every care.'"[49] Both of these

47. Compare the story of Tantalus, whom Odysseus met in the underworld (*Odyssey* XI.582–92). Tantalus' punishment for sins committed during his lifetime was to spend eternity standing up to his chin in a pool of water and gazing up at boughs of delicious fruits, only to have the water vanish whenever he stooped to take a drink and the fruits blown out of his reach by the wind whenever he tried to pluck them.

48. It is not entirely clear whether the boy was splashing *in* the water or simply playing *near* it. But either way, the phrase, *ludere more infantium gaudens*, suggests carefree enjoyment.

49. Salisbury, *Perpetua's Passion*, 106. That said, the methods of dream analysis, whether ancient or modern, can only be applied to visions with the greatest caution. The distinction between dreams and visions is impossible to draw with precision, nor is any such distinction drawn in the *Passion*. The use of both terms in the quotation from Acts 2:17–18, "the young men shall see visions (*visiones*) and the old men shall dream dreams (*somnia*)," in the editor's introduction (I.1.4) seems to be a case of synonymous parallelism. Perpetua's first and second visions come to her at night, presumably during sleep (II.4.2; II.7.3), but her third and fourth apparently came during the daytime (II.8.1; II.10.1). Yet both she and Saturus consistently refer to "waking" (*experrecta*

aspects of the scene clearly take on an added eschatological significance in a Christian context that would have been missing in Artemidorus. But Salisbury construes the reference to Dinocrates' play in domestic terms, as a memory from some happy earlier period in the family home. Perhaps so, but there seems to be more to it. In Saturus' vision, the martyrs, after being welcomed into God's throne room and given the kiss of peace, are told, "Go and play" (III.12.6). Heavenly "play" is thus pictured as the eternal reward for the martyrs' mortal combat in the arena, just as the Sabbath is the crown and completion of the week's labors for the faithful on earth. And in Saturus' vision, this heavenly play is explicitly pictured as participation in the angelic liturgy—the singing (in Greek!) of the *Sanctus* (cf. Isa 6:3; Rev 4:8) that goes on "without ceasing" in God's presence (III.12.2). Now, play is closely related to joy, but whereas joy is an emotion, play is an activity. True, it can be both a cause and a result of joy, but it is characterized by the vigorous involvement of the whole person. One at play is freed from the compulsion to produce anything or to perform labor for others: hence the close analogy between Sabbath rest and playful "leisure." But play is not idleness or indolence. Rather, it is creative activity that is carefree, innocent, festive, and "ecstatic"—again, like properly conducted liturgy.[50]

The other case of transformation that deserves careful analysis is that of Pudens. He appears three times in the *Passion*. On the first occasion, he honors the prisoners when he realizes that they possess some "great power" (*magnam virtutem*) (II.9.1). The Latin term *virtu*, like its English cognate, refers to moral goodness, but also suggests dynamic strength or causal efficacy. Rader renders the term as "persistence," which catches the idea that the prisoners have the moral strength to endure their sufferings but doesn't hint at their power to effect actual changes in other people or outward events.[51] The point is that both aspects of the prisoners' *virtu* may well have impressed Pudens and precipitated his conversion.

---

sum) from them (II.4.10; II.7.9; II.8.4; II.10.13; III.13.8). Whatever the psychodynamics of such experiences may be, the crucial point for our purposes is that the visions described here are believed to come from the Holy Spirit and are therefore to be interpreted *theologically*, along the lines of prophecy. We are to determine the "meaning" of the images in these visions not by consulting a manual on dream interpretation, but by analyzing their religious function in the visions themselves.

50. On the relationship between "leisure" and liturgy, see Pieper, *Leisure*, 65–74. On the "civilizing" and spiritually edifying aspects of play, though without much attention to liturgy, see Huizinga, *Homo Ludens*.

51. Rader, "*Martyrdom*," 23.

When Pudens is mentioned for the second time, by title, though not by name (IV.16.4), he has embraced their faith. Indeed, the very fact that his title is foregrounded in this second reference suggests that his conversion may jeopardize his role in the Roman military and social order. His third appearance is during the story's final scene, when the martyrs are being executed. He is standing at one of the gates into the arena, when Saturus, who is about to be sent in, tells him that, just as he had "anticipated and predicted," he would be killed "from the single bite of a leopard" (IV.21.2, referring to IV.19.4). This immediately happens, and as Saturus is dying, he advises Pudens, "Don't let these things disturb you but let them affirm you" (a play on words: *non conturbent, sed conferment*) (IV.21.4). Saturus then asks Pudens for his ring, touches it to his gushing wound, and returns it to him "as an inheritance, leaving it to him as pledge and a monument of blood" (IV.21.5). The transformation of Pudens from Roman soldier to Christian believer recalls Tertullian's famous remark, "The oftener we are mown down by you, the more in number we grow; the blood of Christians is seed."[52] In short, the moral example of the martyrs *is* causally efficacious in the realm of the Spirit: we are told that many other spectators of these dramatic events also "became believers" (IV.17.3).

In summary, despite the complex structure of the *Passion of Saints Perpetua and Felicias*, with its four distinct sections and three different authors, it displays remarkable literary unity. This is secured by the frequent citation of or allusion to sacred Scripture, by the narration of heavenly visions which elucidate the meaning of the story's "real-time" events, and by the frequent repetition of vivid images and key themes.

Theological Convictions

Let us now examine three theological convictions that appear prominently in the *Passion of Saints Perpetua and Felicitas*. As mentioned in the introduction, the fact that early-third-century imperial Rome regarded Christianity itself as an "illegal religion" meant that both Type A and Type B convictions were equally objectionable. Perpetua and her friends were imprisoned *for* holding firmly to all three convictions, and they endured incarceration and martyrdom *by* holding them so firmly. It

---

52. Tertullian, *Apology* 50. Quasten, *Patrology*, 2:255, dates the *Apology* to 197, about six years before the events in the *Passion*.

should also be stressed that all three of these convictions were held by the entire North African church, not simply by the "proto-Montanist" party to which Perpetua and her friends appear to have belonged.

1. The Triune God is the supreme good and the sovereign power in the universe

This conviction belongs equally to Type A and Type B, as it both caused Perpetua and her friends to challenge the totalizing power of Rome and suffuses their attitude toward their captors and the jeering crowds. In the introduction, the editor states that "God always makes good on his promises, as a testimony to those who do not believe and a blessing to those who do" (I.1.5). In his conclusion, the editor offers the following Trinitarian doxology: "These new virtues also testify to the one and only eternal Holy Spirit still in operation, [and] the all-powerful God the Father and his Son Jesus Christ our Lord, to whom is the splendor and great power forever and ever. Amen" (IV.21.11). And in one of her conversations with her frantic father, Perpetua states: "What will happen in that dock is what God wanted; know that we are not going to be determined by our own power, but by God's (*in nostra esse potestate constitutos futurus, sed in Dei*)" (II.5.6). This conviction carries three implications: First, when Christians face tribulation, they must draw strength from the knowledge that God's purposes are mysteriously being worked out through their sufferings. Second, when Christians realize that their earthly blessings are distracting them from their loyalty to God, they must unhesitatingly renounce them. Third, when earthly powers and principalities, such as the imperial government, demand an allegiance that is due only to God, Christians must resist at all costs.

2. God freely and continuously communicates his will and grace to his followers

The defense of this conviction is the stated objective of the *Passion*. Indeed, the entire narrative is virtually a midrash on Acts 2:17–18. The editor is addressing a church that is flirting with the notion that the apostolic age is over and that the "extraordinary graces" of the Spirit—visions, prophecies, healings, and glossolalia—are no longer available to it. Hence his remark: "So then we, who also in this way both acknowledge and honor new visions similarly promised, reckon the other powers of the Holy Spirit (*virtutes Spiritus Sancti*) as the tool of the Church to which it was sent, ready to administer all gifts among all, just as the Lord distributed to each one" (I.1.5). This would seem to classify Conviction No. 2 with other Type B convictions. Yet there are immediate overtones of Type A here, too, because a church that has lost the animating power of the Spirit is in danger of capitulating to the power of Rome. Thus, what the editor takes to be significant about Perpetua and her comrades is not merely that they were pneumatics and visionaries, but that precisely *because* they were pneumatics and visionaries, they were willing to defy the state and face the beasts.

Note that Perpetua does not think her visions require "interpretation"—as dreams did in ancient times, and still do.[53] Rather, she regards her visions themselves as revelations from the Holy Spirit that explain her prison experience, enable her to bear witness to her father and the procurator, and strengthen her for the ordeal in the arena. She ends each of her four vision accounts with a brief formula of what she "understood" or "knew" that vision to mean (Parallel 9). The conviction that underlies these formulae is that the Spirit communicates to believers what is going to happen to them and how God expects them to respond.

Note also that the prisoners seem to feel no tension between being the beneficiaries of the "extraordinary graces" of the Spirit and being faithful participants in the customs and rites of the church. They arrange to receive baptism while under government surveillance and carry out such "routine" Christian activities as meeting for prayer, exchanging the kiss of peace, celebrating a love feast, singing psalms, and bearing witness to jailers, soldiers, magistrates, family members, fellow prisoners, and the madding crowd (per Contrast 4). It would be too much to say that by doing so they somehow "normalized" their lives while in lockup. There must have been a note of fierce determination, perhaps even of defiance, in the way they performed these activities. But in practicing them openly they were not simply expressing contempt for Roman values and prison regulations. For these are just the things that Christians do, both to express their identity as Christians and to sustain their faith in time of trial.

---

53. See, e.g., Price, "Future of Dreams," 3–37.

3. The church is a community of witness in a world indifferent to God and hostile to God's church

This conviction, too, clearly belongs both to Types A and B and reflects the "Christ against culture" or "proto-Montanist" posture of the narrative. It coheres with Conviction 1, which requires the church to regard the state as evil, at least insofar as it ignores God's sovereignty and forces Christians to renounce their faith. It also links with Conviction 2, which affirms that the church's opposition to the state is empowered by the Holy Spirit. What Conviction 3 adds to Convictions 1 and 2 is the note of missiology. The proper ways for the church to bear witness to God in this fallen world are, first, by establishing a radical new form of community life, one flatly contrary to the empire's cultural norms, religious practices, and pervasive violence, and second, by willingly enduring persecution for that opposition. The Christian community witnesses by being a new kind of *family*, which redefines the gender roles and ignores the social and legal boundaries of ancient Mediterranean society. The *Passion* mentions the many endearing terms the Christians used to address each other (Contrast 1) and the many nurturing actions they performed for each other (securing improved conditions for the imprisoned, adopting the martyrs' orphans, supporting each other in the arena, praying and worshipping together, etc.).

But Christians who take a contrarian stand vis-à-vis their social world are tempted to over-identify the evils they deplore with those who practice those evils. It is a short step from hating worldliness to hating worldlings, and another short step from hating worldlings to hating the world they rule. Prophetic critique can easily turn into pharisaical faultfinding, and the latter into Manichaean nausea.[54] Several of the protagonists in the *Passion* do seem to have succumbed to this temptation. When the six prisoners were being marched to the arena, three of them—Revocatus, Saturninus, and Saturus—displayed a rather unsavory pleasure in warning their captors of the doom awaiting them: "When they arrived under Hilarianus's gaze, by gesture and nod they began to say to Hilarianus: 'As you do to us, God will to you,' they were saying. At this the throng, provoked, called for them to be tortured by whips through the rank of gladiators. At any rate they gave thanks that they were attaining something of the Lord's sufferings" (IV.18.8-9). Here, principled opposition to Roman brutality has degenerated into self-righteous gloating over

---

54. Cf. Niebuhr, *Christ and Culture*, 80-82.

the anticipated damnation of the pagans and into an almost masochistic delight in baiting their enemies into intensifying their punishment.

Disturbing as this scene is, it is only the most egregious illustration of the "counter-cultural" posture of all the protagonists of this story. But to understand this posture correctly, we must remember that what Perpetua and her friends stood *against* was a function of what they stood *for*. If they sacrificed hearth and home, it was not because they despised or devalued them, but because the social bonds and spiritual fulfillment of their new family transcended and relativized them. If they willingly endured death, it was not because they hated life, but because they had found a new depth and quality of life that death could not destroy. As Charles Taylor has written:

> The Christian martyr, in giving up health, freedom, or life, doesn't declare them to be of no value. On the contrary, the act would lose its sense if they were not of great worth. To say that greater love hath no man than this, that a man give up his life for his friends, implies that life is a great good. The sentence would lose its point in reference to someone who renounced life from a sense of detachment; it presupposes he's giving up something. Central to the Judaeo-Christian notion of martyrdom is that one gives up a good in order to follow God. What God is engaged in is the hallowing of life. God first called Israel to be a "holy nation" (Exodus 19:6). But the hallowing of life is not antithetical to its fullness. On the contrary. Hence the powerful sense of loss at the heart of martyrdom.[55]

Perpetua's conversations with her father exemplify this. Yes, she regards her father's blandishments as "the devil's arguments" (II.3.3) and finds his repeated efforts to dissuade her from her new faith deeply distressing. But for her father himself she feels love and pity, and she clearly treasures his love for her, irksomely as he expresses it (II.5.5–6; II.6.5). And every other mention of her family members—her mother, her brothers, her aunt, and above all her baby—suggests tender devotion and family intimacy.

Perpetua and her companions are certainly defiant when the authorities expect them to cooperate with the brutal spectacle of public humiliation, torture, and execution planned for them: they refuse to wear the garb of pagan deities in the arena (IV.18.4–6) and Perpetua rearranges her ripped tunic and fixes her disheveled hair after being

---

55. Taylor, *Sources of the Self*, 218–19.

tossed by the heifer (IV.20.1–5). (And given Perpetua's general feistiness, I suspect that what the editor there calls her "modesty" is a function, not of any stereotypically "feminine" bashfulness, but of her stout refusal to play along with the pornographic spectacle of the arena.) Yet the prisoners show no hostility to their families of origin or to their country as such. Indeed, one of the points of Perpetua's visions is precisely the insight they give her into the true nature of her situation and the courage they give her to hold fast to her new commitment. During her "waking" moments, she must face the loss of things she loves, and she experiences genuine anguish over this. Her visions, however, reinforce her religious conviction that the worth of her new faith surpasses that of her worldly loves and enables her to surrender them—with pain, no doubt, but also with fierce joy—for the sake of a greater good.[56] Indeed, it is precisely because she ascribes divine authority to these visions that she is able to heed their message, even when they contradict her temporal interests and personal inclinations. In short, what Perpetua opposes in the Roman family and state are their sacral pretensions, and her acts of defiance bear witness to her commitment to an authority that transcends them and whose authority they refuse to acknowledge.

---

56. Here I take exception to the otherwise insightful interpretation of the *Passion* offered by Alvyn Pettersen in "Perpetua—Prisoner of Conscience," 139–53. Petterson is surely right to understand that Perpetua and her comrades were acting according to their deepest religious convictions and in full knowledge of the dangers that doing so entailed. In this respect, his reading is significantly superior to psycho-historical accounts, which fail to see the connections between the martyrs' visions and their concrete actions. But the *tone* of Petterson's essay misses those aspects of the *Passion* that make it such an emotionally arresting and spiritually edifying read. For example, he writes: "It is not that for Perpetua the family is innately evil. Rather, it is that in a clash of interests within this ambivalent world, the lesser good, the interests of the family, must yield place to those of the greater good, God. For a family, being contingent, valued apart from the heavenly Father, upon which it is dependent, is 'vanity'" (152n62). Well, yes. But that statement seems so bloodless and abstract in comparison with the earthy realism and human vitality of Perpetua's diary. It is impossible to imagine her looking down at her nursing baby and calmly thinking, "There lies a contingent and lesser good, which I must not overvalue." But it is not hard to imagine her weeping as she hands him for the last time to her mother. She certainly has theological reasons for her actions, but she does not intellectualize her experiences.

CHAPTER 2

Maximus the Confessor

Introduction

LIKE VIBIA PERPETUA, MAXIMUS the Confessor was a citizen of the Roman Empire, a state that regarded religious conformity as the key to political stability, and religious non-conformity as treason. But immense changes had taken place in the empire between the deaths of Perpetua in 203 CE and Maximus in 662 CE, and many of these changes are reflected in their respective prison writings. Perpetua lived at a time when Christianity was an *illegal* religion in the Roman Empire. She was martyred simply for *being* a Christian, and the record of her imprisonment and death reflects the stark ideological differences between Greco-Roman paganism and early Christianity. In contrast, Maximus lived at a time when Christianity had been the *official* religion of the Roman Empire for well over two centuries, and he was arrested for being the *wrong kind* of Christian, or rather, for opposing a doctrinal innovation recently promulgated by the imperial church for the sake of political advantage. But his efforts to show the imperial government and the state church the subtle but fatal errors implicit in this innovation required a great deal of technical scriptural exposition and subtle doctrinal argumentation, and the records of Maximus' imprisonment and trials are filled with these. One is tempted to say that whereas Perpetua died for bearing the *Name* of Christ, Maximus died for defending the *doctrine* of Christ. But that would be grossly unfair to both. For theological convictions—embryonic in their formulation, to be sure, but pointing ahead to the "orthodox" doctrinal developments of the following centuries—suffuse the *Passion of Saints Perpetua and Felicitas*. Conversely, the records of Maximus' long dispute with the agents of Constans II bear witness to his conviction that to forsake orthodox doctrine is to deny Christ himself.

Historical and Religious Background[1]

When we speak of the "Roman Empire" in the time of Maximus, we must keep two geographical points in mind. First, we are referring to what was left of what had been the eastern half of the Roman Empire in the time of Perpetua. Almost two centuries after her death, in the year 395, the empire was formally divided into the Western and Eastern Empires to improve administrative efficiency and military effectiveness. But within a century, the Western Empire had fallen to an assortment of Germanic tribes. At the time of the division, the Eastern Empire was much richer, more populous, and generally better governed than the West. It escaped the worst ravages of the "barbarian" migrations and held on to the Balkans, Anatolia, Syria, Palestine, and Egypt. Furthermore, portions of the old Western Empire were conquered in the 530s by the emperor of the Eastern (or "Byzantine") Empire, Justinian I, (r. 527–65). These additions were later organized into the Exarchate of Ravenna (584–751), which controlled Sicily and parts of Italy, and the Exarchate of Africa (591–698), which covered most of the northern coast of Africa, the southeastern coast of Spain, and the islands of the western Mediterranean. Thus, the great western cities of Rome, Ravenna, and Carthage remained under Byzantine control throughout the period covered by this chapter.

But second, the Eastern Roman Empire steadily shrank during Maximus' lifetime. Upper Mesopotamia, the Holy Land, and Egypt were lost to the Persians in the 610s, regained in the mid-620s, but then lost permanently to the Arabs by the mid-640s. And the northern Balkans came under the control of the Avars from the 560s through the 610s. The panic felt by the Byzantine emperors of the seventh century over these losses plays a major part in our story.

And that panic was not due solely to border threats. It was also due to the religious disaffection of large segments of the population in its

---

1. This and the next section of the chapter are heavily dependent on Ekonomou, *Byzantine Rome and the Greek Popes*; Haldon, *Byzantium*; Norwich, *Byzantium*, 284–327.

easternmost provinces. This disaffection was the downstream result of the fierce Christological controversies of the fourth century between the "Nestorian," "monophysite," and "Chalcedonian" parties, respectively.

The Nestorians were adherents of the Christology that had been developed in the third and fourth centuries in the theological school of Syrian Antioch. It strongly emphasized the humanity of Jesus and the literal-historical reading of Christian Scripture. Antiochene Christology was promulgated with great enthusiasm, but without sufficient caution, by Nestorius (c. 386–c. 451), who was appointed patriarch of Constantinople in 428. Nestorius so emphasized the distinctness of Christ's divine and human natures that he seemed to compromise the integrity of Christ's person. He was condemned and deposed at the Third Ecumenical Council (Ephesus, 431), and again at the Fourth Ecumenical Council (Chalcedon, 451). Within a century, many of his outraged followers, who dwelt in eastern Syria and Upper Mesopotamia, had emigrated into Sassanid Persia and were lost to the Byzantine Empire altogether.[2]

On the other end of the christological spectrum were the monophysites, who reflected the religious sensibilities and hermeneutical methods of the theological school of Alexandria. The monophysite heresiarch was Eutyches (c. 378–458), who was the archimandrite of a large monastery in Constantinople when Nestorius became the patriarch of that city. To refute Nestorius, Eutyches emphasized the unity of the person of the incarnate Christ in a way that suggested that Jesus' humanity was virtually obliterated by its union with divinity. Monophysitism (lit. "one-nature-ism") was condemned at Chalcedon, but Eutyches' views were refined and corrected by another opponent of Nestorius, Cyril, patriarch of Alexandria (c. 376–444), and it was Cyrilline Christology that gained the favor of large majorities in western Syria, Palestine, and Egypt—provinces essential to the economic prosperity and military security of the Byzantine Empire. Unlike the Nestorians, the monophysites could not easily emigrate from Roman territory in protest, but their opposition to Chalcedon led them to reject the authority of the imperial church and eroded their loyalty to the imperial government. Under the leadership of Severus of Antioch (c. 465–538) and Jacob Baradaeus (c. 500–578),

---

2. To this day, the Assyrian Church of the East claims Nestorius as its spiritual father. But it insists that it does not hold the heretical teachings for which he was condemned, and indeed, that Nestorius himself did not hold those teachings, at least in the extreme form often attributed to him.

they established an extensive and well-organized counter-church in the eastern provinces of the Byzantine Empire.[3]

The Chalcedonian party included the papacy of Rome and the patriarchate of Constantinople, which were in doctrinal agreement throughout the fifth, sixth, and most of the seventh centuries. Its Christology was intended to mediate between the positions of the Antiochene and Alexandrian parties, to incorporate the key insights of both, and to correct the exaggerations and false conclusions to which they were inclined in their equal but opposite ways. This Christology, known as dyophysitism ("two-nature-ism"),[4] was classically delineated in the *Tome* (449) of Pope Leo I (r. 440–61) and formally adopted two years later at the Council of Chalcedon. The "Definition" of Chalcedon taught that the divine and human natures of Christ were preserved in the union "without confusion and without change," but that their conjunction was "without division and without separation." The distinctive "properties" or characteristics of each nature remained intact, but they were harmoniously integrated in the "theanthropic" person of Jesus. Because this position was promulgated by a duly convened ecumenical council, it was taken to be irrevocable. Henceforth, it would be the official Christology of the imperial church.

But therein lay a problem. The empire could not afford to lose the support of its eastern provinces, whose citizens heavily favored monophysitism. The religious unity of the empire was felt to be crucial to its political stability, and its political stability was felt to be crucial in meeting the military threat posed by the Avars and Persians. The monophysites were implacably opposed to the dyophysite Christology, but the

---

3. Or counter-churches. The Syrian "Jacobites" (followers of Jacob Baradaeus) and the Egyptian Copts, though both monophysite, were not always on friendly terms. Nicetus, a senior military figure under Heraclius the Elder, exarch of Africa, managed to bring the two networks of churches into union in 616 as part of the Byzantine strategy to retake the East from the Persians.

The Oriental Orthodox Churches of today prefer to be called "miaphysites," rather than "monophysites," insisting that the prefix *mia* ("one") denotes their commitment to the integral personhood of the incarnate Christ, whereas the prefix *mono* ("only one") implies the Eutychian notion—which they disclaim—that Jesus' human nature was erased by its union with the divine nature.

4. This term must be used with caution, for it can refer either to the Nestorian or the Chalcedonian Christology. The major difference between the two is the greater care taken by the latter to emphasize the integral unity of Christ's person, and this is the sense it will bear in this chapter. The related term, "dyothelitism" ("two-wills-ism"), will be used here to identify the "Neo-Chalcedonian" Christology of Maximus the Confessor, who taught that Christ has two *wills*, just as he has two *natures*, but remains a single integral *person*.

imperial church was unalterably committed to it. From the emperor's perspective, monophysites either had to be forced to accept the Chalcedonian Definition or offered a carefully crafted "interpretation" of it that they could find palatable. Both strategies were repeatedly tried, and both ultimately failed.

One early attempt to resolve the impasse was made by Emperor Zeno (r. 474–91) in 482 with the publication of the *Henotikon* (*Act of Union*). This decree was co-authored by Acacius, patriarch of Constantinople (r. 471–89) and Peter Mongo, patriarch of Alexandria (r. 477–90), and featured a harsh denunciation of Nestorius, high praise of Cyril, and no reference to Leo. Pleasing as this approach might have been to the monophysites, it backfired by alienating the papacy and eventuated in the so-called Acacian Schism, a breach in communion between Rome and Constantinople, which lasted from 484 until 519. Emperor Justin I (r. 518–27) healed the rift, but the dispute between the Chalcedonians and the monophysites was left unchanged.

Another attempt was made by Justin's co-emperor, Justinian I, who promoted a doctrine known as theopaschitism (lit. "God-suffered-ism"), according to which "one of the Trinity suffered in the flesh." Although this formula emphasizes the union of the two natures in the person of Christ in a manner that was intended to pacify the monophysites, the fact that the Fifth Ecumenical Council (Constantinople II, 553), which was convened and controlled by Justinian, did not revoke the Definition of Chalcedon, negated the imperial effort at conciliation. Subsequent efforts by Justin II (r. 565–78), Tiberius II Constantine (r. 574–82), and Maurice (r. 582–602), sometimes by appeasement and sometimes by repression, also failed. By the beginning of the seventh century, not only were the monophysites and the Chalcedonians as far apart theologically as they had been since 451, but the former had, in disgust and disillusionment, established their counter-church.

Yet ecclesiastical unity throughout the empire remained the objective of the government, and the felt need for it was exacerbated in the early decades of the seventh century. In 602, a junior army officer named Phocas murdered Maurice and usurped his throne, thus incurring the wrath of Maurice's erstwhile friend and ally, the Persian king, Chosroes II. Persian armies captured Syria in 613, Palestine in 614, and Egypt in 618. The monophysite Christians of those provinces may not have actively welcomed Persian rule, but they seem not to have forcefully opposed it.[5] To make matters worse, the Avars and Slavs began attacking the empire's Balkan provinces. Phocas' inability to deal effectively with the military crisis led to a revolt by Heraclius, who sailed with a large military force from his base in Northern Africa. Heraclius deposed and executed Phocas in 610, assumed his throne, and inherited all his problems. In the face of the growing threat by a coalition of Persians, Avars, and Slavs, Heraclius (r. 610–41) managed to reform the Byzantine economy and military machine and take the offensive. Between 622 and 629 he pacified the Balkans, invaded Persia, repeatedly defeated the armies of Chosroes, reclaimed the lost Eastern provinces, and retrieved the True Cross, which had been captured by the Persians in 614. In 626, while Heraclius was on maneuvers, a coalition of Slavs, Avars, and Persians besieged the imperial city, but, under the leadership of Sergius I, the patriarch of Constantinople (r. 610–38), they were repulsed. By 628, the Byzantine Empire was once again politically and militarily secure. But Heraclius still faced the problem of religious disunity in the East, and within a few years he found himself facing a new threat in that region: the unconquerable armies of Islam.

Both problems—the continuing quest for religious unity in the East and the need to stem the Arab onslaught, which dominated the closing years of Heraclius' reign, also dominated most of the reign of his successor, Constans II (r. 641–68). To establish rapprochement with the monophysites, he proposed a subtle doctrinal adjustment—two of them, in fact—to the interpretation, though not to the text, of the Definition of Chalcedon. These proposals are known, respectively, as monenergism, which asserted that Christ possessed only one *energeia* ("energy," "operation," or "mode of activity"), and monotheletism, which asserted that Christ possessed only one *thelēma* ("will"). Both proposals ultimately proved unacceptable to the monophysites and therefore failed as a political measure. But as Constans' great opponent, Maximus the Confessor, was to show, they implicitly contradicted dyophysite Christology, and therefore had to be repudiated if the Byzantine Empire—with or without its holdings in the Eastern Mediterranean—was to rest upon the "orthodox" Christian faith.

---

5. According to Haldon, *Byzantium*, 300, the Persian conquest "encouraged the self-confidence of the monophysite clergy and people; and upon the completion of the reconquest [under Heraclius], it became evident that throughout the Eastern provinces—Egypt, Syria, Palestine, and Armenia in particular—a potential or actual hostility to, and a resentment of, Constantinopolitan rule now constituted a real danger, both to the unity of the empire politically and ideologically, and to the authority of the emperor and of the Chalcedonian Church."

To tell that story properly, we must backtrack a bit and examine the life and times of Maximus the Confessor.

The Life and Times of Maximus the Confessor

Two ancient biographies of Maximus come down to us, and they contradict each other at many points. The Greek *Life* is effusively sympathetic—and staunchly Chalcedonian in its doctrinal position.[6] The Syriac *Life* is fiercely hostile—and just as staunchly monothelite.[7] Both accounts reflect the theological views of their authors, but on the whole the story told in the Greek *Life* squares better with what we know of Maximus from his surviving writings and other contemporary sources, and most modern accounts (including this one) follow it wherever it disagrees with the Syriac account.[8] Yet both *Lives* agree that Maximus was the central character in the religio-political conflicts of the mid-seventh century. Taken together they help us understand the reasons both for Maximus' sanctified intransigence and for Constans' relentless efforts to make him capitulate.

According to the Greek *Life*, Maximus was born in Constantinople about 580. His parents were wealthy patricians and devout Christians, who brought him up strictly and provided him with an excellent education at the university in the capital. There he distinguished himself as a brilliant student and demonstrated a particular aptitude toward "philosophy," which in that context meant not only metaphysical speculation and logical argument, but also the life of ascetic discipline and contemplative prayer.[9] His abilities were soon noticed, and when Heraclius came to power in 610, he appointed Maximus as chief secretary of imperial records, a very high post in the new government. But Maximus' period of imperial service ended in 613, when he entered monastic life. In 618, he acquired a disciple named Anastasius the Monk, who remained his

---

6. The Greek text and an English translation are found in Neil and Allen, *Life of Maximus*, 35–185.

7. The Syriac text and an English translation are found in Brock, "Early Syriac Life," 302–19.

8. Three modern reconstructions of Maximus' career on which I have relied heavily are Louth, Introduction to Maximus, *Maximus*, 3–18; Sherwood, *Annotated Date-List*, 1–22; Thunberg, *Man and the Cosmos*, 11–30.

9. Maximus' Greek biographer is careful to emphasize his "reason and prudence" (*logos kai phronēma*), but also his rejection of another, and very inferior, kind of philosophy, namely "the sophistic approach, and whatever it contained of deceit and errors," i.e., the approach typical of the universities. See Neil and Allen, *Life* §3, 42–43.

companion for the rest of his life.[10] In the next few years, Maximus and Anastasius moved several times to escape the invading Persian armies. Finally, in about 630, they entered the Eucratas Monastery in Carthage, whose founder and abbot was the Syrian monastic theologian Sophronius of Jerusalem.[11] They remained there until 646, although Maximus apparently travelled extensively during those years.

Heraclius' victory over the Persians had left him in political control of his eastern provinces, but reigning over them was not the same as ruling them. Governance depended upon religious unity, and Heraclius took the steps in that direction that unleashed the monenergist/monothelite controversy.[12] As early as 616, with the Persians still in control of Syria, Palestine, and Egypt, Heraclius and his agents began using the monenergist doctrine to coax the monophysites back into unity with the imperial church. After reestablishing control of the East, Heraclius stepped up his efforts. In 631 he appointed Cyrus, previously the Chalcedonian metropolitan of Phasis in Lazica (modern Poti, Georgia), both as patriarch of Alexandria and as prefect of Egypt. On June 3, 633, Cyrus issued a document known variously as the *Plērophoria (Assurance)*, the *Pact of Union*, and the *Nine Chapters*.[13] This document sought to conciliate the monophysites by referring to Christ in Cyrilline terms as "one Son, from two natures, that is from both Godhead and humanity, 'one incarnate nature of God the Word.'" Strict Chalcedonians balked at this, for the Definition of 451 asserted that Christ was "one person and subsistence *in* two natures," not "one incarnate person *from* two natures." They feared that the preposition "from" might be taken in a Eutychian sense to imply the obliteration of the human nature by the divine. But the Chalcedonians could not dispute either the authority of Cyril or the authenticity of the quotation, and in an age less given to creedal precisionism, this trope

---

10. Anastasius the Monk should not be confused with Anastasius the Apocrisiarius, a Roman papal diplomat who in later years became another of Maximus' close associates.

11. The name "Eucratas" indicates loyalty to the Council of Chalcedon. Both Sophronius and his friend, John Moschus, bore it as a surname. See Chadwick, "Moschus and Sophronius," 59, 59n1; Allen and Neil, *Maximus and His Companions*, 178–79n30. Sophronius founded the Eucratas Monastery around 626 and presumably gave it its name as a badge of its theological identity.

12. On this controversy, see Hovorun, *Will, Action, and Freedom*; Hussey, *Orthodox Church*, 10–27; Pelikan, *Christian Tradition*, 2:62–75; Wolfson, *Philosophy of the Church Fathers*, 1:473–93; Verghese, "Monothelite Controversy," 196–211.

13. For the Greek text and English translation of the *Pact*, see Allen, *Sophronius*, 168–73.

might have softened hearts. But Cyrus was not done. He added a quotation—or rather a misquotation—from another impeccable patristic authority, Pseudo-Dionysius the Areopagite (c. 500). Dionysius had spoken of "a certain new theandric [i.e., compositely divine and human] activity" in Christ, a phrase that can be taken in a perfectly orthodox sense to mean that the characteristic "energy" or "activity" of each nature is preserved in the hypostatic union, without the divine and human natures being in moral or psychic conflict with each other.[14] But some years earlier, the monophysite theologian Severus of Antioch had interpreted Dionysius' idea of "one theandric activity" to imply "the rejection of every duality" in Christ's person.[15] And Cyrus actually changed Dionysus' wording in a Severan direction, referring not to "a *new* theandric activity," but to "*one* theandric activity." Perhaps this was meant as a sop to the monophysites, although he gave it an explicitly Chalcedonian spin, insisting that the natures remained "without change and without confusion after their natural and hypostatic union," thereby undoing any rhetorical advantage he might have gained with his hostile flock. But the reference to *one* theandric activity was immediately recognized by Sophronius, who was visiting Alexandria on the eve of the promulgation of the *Pact*, as a dangerous innovation and an implicit rejection of Chalcedonian Christology. Despite Sophronius' objections, Cyrus retained the offending passage in the *Pact of Union*, and Sophronius promptly sailed to Constantinople, intending to ask Patriarch Sergius to arbitrate the dispute.

Sergius' intervention only made matters worse. In August 633 he issued the *Psēphos* (*Resolution*), which did not repudiate Cyrus' doctrine—the doctrine now known as monenergism—but merely forbade public wrangling over whether Christ had one or two *energeiai* and underscored the moral and psychological harmony of Christ's two natures.[16] Cyrus refused to be silenced and appealed to Pope Honorius. Honorius wrote to Sergius in 634, supporting his efforts to suppress debate on the number of Christ's energies. But in that letter, he invented a variant strain of the same error, the new heresy of monotheletism: "We confess one will (*hen thelēma*) of the Lord Jesus Christ, since manifestly our nature was assumed by the Godhead, there being no sin in it." Furthermore, Honorius

---

14. Dionysius, "Letter 4 to Gaius Therapeutēs," §1.

15. See his Letter to John the Hegumenos, which may be found in Allen and Hayward, *Severus*, 152–53.

16. The text of the *Psēphos* has not survived, but its content seems to have been incorporated into Sergius' *Ekthesis* of 638. See n19 below.

took the Lord's statements, "I did not come to do my will, but that of the Father who sent me" (John 6:38), and "Not as I will, but as you will, Father" (Matt 26:39), "not [as] expressions of a different will (*diaphorou thelēmatos*), but of the economy of the humanity which he assumed."[17] As it stood, this statement was not heretical, and in the subsequent disputes, Maximus defended Honorius's orthodoxy. But in trying to defend Christ's moral integrity and psychological intactness, Honorius had used an expression that seemed to imply that the incarnate Christ, though composed of two natures, was possessed of only one will. It was some years before Maximus recognized the unacceptable consequences of this move for Christology and theological anthropology.

But if monotheletism was not yet fully born, monenergism was not yet fully dead. Or at least Sophronius didn't think so. And when he was elected patriarch of Jerusalem in 634, he published a *Synodical Letter*, which attacked the one-energy doctrine. In doing so, he defied the gag orders of Sergius and Honorius, and both senior prelates promptly censured him for doing so. This phase of the quarrel might have continued, but in the year 638 several events occurred that changed the game significantly. In February, Jerusalem fell to the Arabs. Sophronius himself negotiated the city's surrender and died a year or two later. Thus, the strongest anti-monenergist voice of the age was silenced, and the power base of Chalcedonianism in the East was lost to the Byzantine church. A few months later, Sergius promulgated a document known as the *Ekthesis* (*Exposition*), which again forbade debate on the question of whether Christ had one or two energies, leaving the dogmatic issue unresolved. And it generated fresh controversy by expatiating on Honorius' ill-fated suggestion that the incarnate Christ had but one will. Sergius wrote:

> The expression "one activity," even if it was uttered by some of the Fathers, nevertheless alienates and confuses some who hear it, who suppose that it will lead to the destruction of the two natures which were hypostatically united in Christ our God. In a similar way the expression "the two activities" scandalizes many; on the grounds that it was uttered by none of the holy and select spiritual leaders of the church, and certainly to follow it is to uphold also two wills at variance with one another, such that while God the Word wished to fulfill the salvific suffering, his humanity resisted and opposed him with its own will, and as a

---

17. The Greek text and English translation of Honorius' First Letter to Sergius may be found in Allen, *Sophronius*, 194–205.

result two persons with conflicting wills are introduced, which is impious and foreign to Christian teaching.[18]

Late in 638, both Pope Honorius and Patriarch Sergius died. The almost simultaneous change of leadership in the two great sees proved significant for subsequent events. The next four popes, Severinus (r. May–August, 640), John IV (r. 640–42), Theodore I (r. 642–49), and Martin (r. 649–55) were convinced Chalcedonians, whereas the next three patriarchs of Constantinople, Pyrrhus I (r. 638–41, 654), Paul II (r. 641–53), and Peter (r. 654–66) followed the monothelite policy of the reigning emperors. This drove a wedge between the papacy and the imperial church. Many Chalcedonians, including Maximus and his closest disciples, eventually emigrated to Rome, although that did not automatically guarantee their safety from imperial pressure, as long as the reigning exarch of Ravenna was loyal to the emperor.

During this period of ecclesiastical turmoil, the Arab armies were rapidly expanding westward, scoring decisive victories over the Byzantines at Damascus (635), Yarmuk (636), Jerusalem (638), Alexandria (642), and Tripoli (643). The Byzantines retook Alexandria in 645, but lost it again, and permanently, in 646. Whatever loyalty the monophysite inhabitants of the East felt toward Constantinople had been severely compromised by nearly two centuries of imperial efforts to induce them to embrace Chalcedon, and their resistance to the Arabs was as tepid as their resistance to the Persians had been two decades earlier. During this time, a large proportion of the Melkite (i.e., theologically Chalcedonian and politically pro-Byzantine) Christians of the East fled to more secure areas—many to Carthage. Before his death in February 641, Heraclius seems to have realized the futility of his religious policy. Or at least he yearned to die in the peace of the (Roman!) church, and when he learned that Pope John had condemned the *Ekthesis*, he claimed that he himself had approved it only very unwillingly. But his successors failed to learn their lesson. After the brief reigns of Heraclius's sons, Constantine III and Heracleonas in 641, his grandson, Constans II Pogonatus assumed the throne and eagerly embraced monotheletism. His commitment to it must have been sincere, for whatever political advantages the doctrine might have offered at his accession were gone within a year or two. Or at least his hostility toward the leading Chalcedonians of the

---

18. See Allen, *Sophronius*, 213–15. Allen gives the full Greek text and an English translation, 208–17.

age, Maximus and Pope Martin, was fierce, although the records suggest that his ferocity was due not only to the sincerity of his beliefs but to his outrage over their opposition to his authority.

Between 630 and 646, while living at the Eucratas Monastery in Carthage, Maximus underwent a significant theological transformation. Some of his earliest musings on the will of Christ have a distinctly monothelite ring to them, though of course they were penned before Honorius first enunciated the doctrine that would later be deemed heretical. He was probably first alerted to the dangers of monenergism by his study of Sophronius' *Synodical Letter* of 634. It was not until about 640 that he publicly spoke out against the *Ekthesis*,[19] but from that point forward he was the leading opponent of the two imperial heresies—especially the one-will doctrine, the one-energy doctrine having by this time been abandoned by its original proponents. One of the key events in his campaign occurred in July 645, when he engaged in a public debate in Carthage with Pyrrhus, the former patriarch of Constantinople, who had been deposed for political reasons shortly after the accession of Constans II, and who understood that his reinstatement depended on his endorsement of the emperor's pet heresy. Presiding over the dispute was Gregory, exarch of North Africa (r. 641?–48), a fact that signals the political as well as the religious significance of the proceedings. The transcript of the *Disputation with Pyrrhus* survives and provides one of the clearest statements of Maximus' refutation of monotheletism.[20]

Note that the number of *natures* in Christ was not here in dispute: Maximus and Pyrrhus agreed that both the human and divine natures coinhered in the hypostatic union and remained fully "activated" and "energized." This shows that monotheletism was originally proposed by the Chalcedonians as a conciliatory measure, but it also shows why it could never satisfy the monophysites, for whom all talk of two natures *in* Christ implied a crypto-Nestorian fracturing of his integral personhood. It also shows that by this time monenergism was a dead letter, the *Psēphos* and *Ekthesis* having closed debate on the number of Christ's energies. The dispute now turned on whether Christ possessed two wills, that is, on whether the will of a person was to be ascribed to his *human nature* or to his *individual personhood*. If, as Maximus contended, the will of any sentient being (whether God, angel, or human being) was a function of

19. In *Opusculum 20*, per Sherwood, *Annotated Date-List*, 41–42.
20. Maximus, *Disputation with Pyrrhus*.

that being's nature, and if Christ possessed two natures (divine and human), then Christ must have possessed two wills. If, on the other hand, the will of a sentient being was a function of that being's personhood, and if the hypostatic union in Christ was complete, such that his personhood was perfectly integral, then Christ must have possessed but one will: this was Pyrrhus' position. But even here the disputants were not too far apart. As the quotation from the *Ekthesis* suggests, the monothelites were afraid that if Jesus were thought to possess two wills, he might also be thought to have gone through life in a state of constant moral conflict or psychic division. The dyothelites certainly had no intention of suggesting that Jesus experienced two simultaneous or alternating states of consciousness, like a person suffering from a dissociative identity disorder or severe moral indecisiveness. Both parties shared the concern to picture the Savior as a spiritually and morally "whole" person.

Given such agreement, the question of the *number* of his wills may seem speculative or hyper-technical, a matter over which Christians might safely be allowed to disagree without breach of communion. Indeed, is there any need to have an opinion on the matter at all, and are there any rational warrants for supposing that one could know? One of Maximus' greatest contributions to Christology and theological anthropology was to show that there *is* a need to decide the matter, that there *are* rational warrants for doing so, and that the answer *must* be that the incarnate Christ had two wills. First, there was exegetical evidence supporting the dyothelite reading of the Gospels. The story of Jesus' temptation by Satan in the desert, and especially the story of his prayers in the Garden of Gethsemane, where his fear of death was starkly juxtaposed against his filial obedience, both attest to the fact that the needs and intentions characteristic of his human nature had by no means been erased or suppressed by his deity. But Maximus' arguments go far beyond proof-texting. He writes:

> Christ exists as God and as man by nature. Then did He will as God and as man, or only as Christ? If it were Christ who willed and initiated actions, being both God and man, then it is clear that, being one and the same, He willed dually and not singly. For if Christ be nothing else apart from the natures from which and in which He exists, then obviously he wills and operates in a manner corresponding to each of His natures, in other words, as each nature is capable of operating. And if he has two natures,

then He surely must have two natural wills, the wills and essential operations being equal in number to the natures.[21]

The crucial point here is that the human *will* must be construed as an essential and constitutive feature of human *nature*, not of the *personhood* of a particular human being. Of course, human nature is only instantiated in persons, such that each person possesses her own will. And her actual possession of a human will is inseparable from her own instantiation of human nature. In most people, therefore, the question of whether the will is a feature of their human nature or of their individual personhood never arises, for they instantiate only one nature in their personhood. Human beings differ from each other as to their personhood, but not as to their nature; and one key marker of their personhood is what Maximus calls their distinctive "mode" (*tropos*) of willing—what they desire, how they act, how effectively they govern their passions, how thoroughly they subordinate their individual preferences to divine law or the social good, and so forth. What does not differ among them is *that* they are willing beings, for that is a function of their kind of being, their human nature. But the case of Jesus Christ is different. According to the Definition of Chalcedon, *his* personhood instantiates *two* natures in such a way that those natures are united without either of them being "confused" with the other or "changed" into the other; and yet those natures retain their distinctness without being "divided" from each other and without operating "separately" from each other.

If Jesus' will had been a feature of his unique manner of embodying both his natures in his integral personhood, as the monothelites contended, then his will would have been other than an ordinary human one. Accordingly, his humanity would have been defective, his identification with the human condition incomplete, and his salvific work on our behalf ineffectual. This soteriologically disastrous conclusion shows where monotheletism went awry.[22] The truth must be that Christ possessed two wills, as well as two natures, and that those wills, like the natures of which

---

21. Maximus, *Disputation with Pyrrhus*, 4. I have modernized several English archaisms in Farrell's translation.

22. Both the Niceno-Constantinopolitan Creed (381) and the Definition of Chalcedon (451) explicitly assert that the incarnation occurred "for us human beings and our salvation." No doubt the Christological debates of the fourth through the eighth century reflected regional rivalries, personal jealousies, and linguistic confusions, but the underlying driver was always the need to articulate the incarnation in a way that best accounted for Christ's saving work.

they were constitutive elements, interacted "without confusion, without change, without division, and without separation."

Maximus concedes that the hypostatic union affects Jesus' *mode* of willing, and that his sinlessness exempts him from the tortuous deliberations, moral uncertainties, and psychic conflicts that afflict fallen human beings.[23] He manifests a clarity of purpose, a fixity of resolve, and a freedom from the insurgent passions that is unique among human beings—but in a way that strikes pious readers of the Gospel narratives as *perfectly* human, not *super*-human or *in*-human. And as the scenes of his encounter with Satan in the desert and his agony in the garden indicate, he is not free from temptation: he feels the typical joys and sorrows of human existence, experiences the natural needs of body and soul, and treasures life in the face of death. Yet he does so in a way that is revelatory of God and salvific for human beings—and in *that* sense alone his experience of life and his actions in the world differs from yours and mine.

At the end of their public disputation, Pyrrhus declared himself convinced, and sometime in 646 he sailed to Rome to recant his monotheletism before Pope Theodore, suggesting that he had also, at least temporarily, given up his ambition of being restored to the patriarchal throne. Maximus, too, went to Rome in that year, intending to join forces with Theodore in the struggle against imperial heresy, although it is unclear whether he sailed with Pyrrhus or followed later. Not surprisingly, word of Pyrrhus' defection enraged Emperor Constans and the reigning monothelite patriarch of Constantinople, Paul II. Whether cowed by imperial disfavor, or driven once again by his old ambitions, or sincerely re-persuaded by the one-will doctrine, Pyrrhus switched sides again. He fled Rome for Ravenna in 647, took refuge with the monothelite exarch, Plato (r. 646–49), renounced his obedience to Pope Theodore, and once again embraced the imperial heresy. Theodore promptly excommunicated him.

Our story now sub-divides into five distinct though inter-related chains of events. The first involves the growing dissatisfaction with imperial policy by the civil and ecclesiastical authorities of the exarchate of Africa. In the wake of the disputation between Maximus and Pyrrhus, and shortly after their departure for Italy, several regional councils in

---

23. For a penetrating explanation of Maximus' contention that Christ possessed a natural human will (like all other humans), but not a "gnomic" or deliberative will (which is the mode of the natural will's activity under the conditions of fallenness—a condition that Christ did not share), see Louth's Introduction to Maximus, *Maximus*, 59–62.

North Africa condemned monotheletism. This allied the North African church with the papacy against the emperor and the ecumenical patriarch. Then, in 647, Gregory, the exarch of Africa, launched a rebellion against Constans and declared himself emperor of Africa. Gregory was a committed Chalcedonian, and religious motives may well have triggered his break with Constantinople. But his rebellion soon failed. In 648, the Arabs, who were sweeping westward along the African coast after taking Egypt in 646, defeated and killed Gregory before the walls of Sufetela. The Arabs withdrew upon receiving a huge war indemnity, and the exarchate of North Africa was temporarily restored to Byzantine control under Gennadius—only to be lost again in 665.

A second chain of events began in late 647 or early 648, when Emperor Constans II and Patriarch Paul II issued the *Typos* (*Edict* or *Regulation*), which annulled the hated *Ekthesis*, but resembled it in trying to silence all debate about the number of Christ's energies or wills. Threats of punishment were included in the text—threats that Constans would later put into grim effect.

The precise dates of events are uncertain, but the publication of the *Typos* appears to have prompted Pope Theodore to formally depose Patriarch Paul (although he had no way to remove him from power) and to announce the convening of a papal council at the Lateran Palace to galvanize resistance to the imperial heresy. Maximus and Anastasius the Monk had been in Rome since 646, and probably helped to organize the council. Theodore died on May 14, 649, before the council could meet, but his successor, Martin I, who was equally committed to the anti-monothelite cause, pushed ahead with plans. When the council convened in October 649, 105 bishops plus some Greek-speaking monks from southern Italy and Sicily attended. The council condemned the *Ekthesis* and the *Typos*, upheld the doctrine of the two wills of Christ, anathematized Patriarch Sergius I (d. 638), Patriarch Cyril (d. 642), Patriarch Paul II, and the once and future Patriarch Pyrrhus, and urged Constans to renounce his heresy.

This brings us to the third chain of events: When Martin was chosen as pope in 649, he had blithely failed to ask Constans to confirm his election. This insult, plus the convening of the Lateran Council, infuriated the emperor. Thus, he ordered Olympius (r. 649–52), the new exarch of Ravenna, to arrest Pope Martin. But Olympius switched his allegiance to the pope and offered him protection instead. Then, in 652, Olympius took the still more fateful step of rebelling against Constantinople. He marched to Sicily, intending to engage either the Byzantine garrison or a band of marauding Arabs, but died soon thereafter of a plague that was ravaging his troops. His rebellion died with him, and Constans appointed Theodore I Calliopas (r. 653–66) as the new exarch of Ravenna (a post he had previously held in 645–46).

This sparked the fourth and fifth chains of events—parallel, but of different lengths. The shorter of the two involved Pope Martin. Theodore Calliopas arrested Martin on June 17, 653 and remanded him to Constantinople, where he arrived on September 17, 653. His trial began on December 20, 653, and his guilt was a foregone conclusion. The reigning ecumenical patriarch, Paul II, was then on his deathbed: he had taken no part in the proceedings, and despite his doctrinal disagreements with Martin, groaned with disapproval when he heard of Martin's conviction.[24] Martin was stripped of his papal insignia, imprisoned for several months, and then exiled to Chersonesus in the Crimea, where he died some months later. During his exile, but before his death, he was succeeded by Pope Eugenius I (r. 655–57). Constans was eager to mend fences with Rome and confirmed Eugenius' election, and the new pope obligingly took no formal stand against monotheletism. Eugenius was succeeded, in turn, by Pope Vitalian (r. 657–72), who formally recognized the legitimacy of Peter, the new ecumenical patriarch (r. 654–66).[25]

The fifth chain of events—the story of the arrest, trials, exile, torture, and deaths of Maximus, Anastasius the Monk, and their colleague, Anastasius the Apocrisiarius—was longer and more complicated than the fourth, stretching over eleven years, but the result was much the same. A full account of the events is necessary for a thorough understanding of Maximus' prison literature. Maximus and Anastasius the Monk were apparently arrested by Theodore Calliopas at about the same time as Pope Martin, that is, in June 653, and taken to the capital.[26] But their trial was delayed until May 655. An eyewitness account of the proceedings indicates that several charges were lodged against them, but the only one that

---

24. Paul II died on December 23, 653, and was succeeded on January 9, 654 by Pyrrhus, who thus succeeded in returning to the patriarchal throne after his deposition in 641. He died six months later.

25. This account of Martin's trial is indebted to Howard-Johnston, *Witnesses*, 158.

26. Howard-Johnston, *Witnesses*, 160, states that in 654 Maximus "made his way to the city at the opening of the navigation season," apparently of his own free will—though why he should have gone there is not explained—and was only arrested after his arrival. This conflicts with Louth's claim that Maximus was arrested by Theodore Calliopas and sent to Constantinople under guard. See Louth, Introduction to Maximus, *Maximus*, 18.

could be made to stick was their opposition to monotheletism. The prisoners' "guilt" was patent, and they were sent into exile—Maximus to Bizya in Thrace (modern Vize, Turkey, about a hundred kilometers northwest of Constantinople) and Anastasius to Perberis (an unknown location, but probably also in Thrace). Yet Constans still hoped that a combination of pressure and flattery might convince Maximus to capitulate. In August 656, Maximus was visited by three officials from the government, which ended amicably, though without agreement on the contested issues. Several weeks later he was transferred to a monastery near the capital, interviewed again, and when no progress was made, sent to Perberis, though not to the same prison in which Anastasius the Monk was being held. The lockup in Perberis lasted from late 656 until 662, during which time at least one more visit to Maximus by imperial officials took place. By spring 662 Constans' patience was gone, and he had Maximus, Anastasius the Monk, and Anastasius the Apocrisiarius[27] brought to the imperial palace. All three were anathematized, along with Martin and Sophronius posthumously. Maximus and the Apocrisiarius had their tongues and right hands cut off and were paraded in disgrace through the streets of Constantinople. Then all three were exiled to Lazica on the southeastern shore of the Black Sea (modern Georgia) and imprisoned in separate fortresses: Maximus at Schemaris (near modern Tsageri), Anastasius the Monk at Scotoris; and Anastasius the Apocrisiarius at Bucolus. Anastasius the Monk died on July 22 or 24, 662, either during his transfer to Suania (modern Svaneti) or shortly after his arrival there. Maximus died at Schemaris on August 13, 662. Anastasius the Apocrisiarius, despite his terrible wounds and his frequent transfers from one prison to another, survived his captivity, was freed in 664, and settled in Thousoumes, at the foot of the Caucasus Mountains. In 666, he somehow fashioned a prosthetic device from twigs to replace his dismembered hand, and using this device, he managed to compose a letter to another member of Maximus' inner circle, Theodosius of Gangra. He died on October 11, 666, nearly two years before the letter was finally delivered.

The aftermath of these chains of events can be told briefly. In 663, Constans travelled to the West, probably to supervise operations against

---

27. Anastasius the Apocrisiarius, who had served as the papal representative in Constantinople during the pontificate of Theodore I, may have been arrested as early as 648 for opposing the publication of the *Typos*. He was exiled to Trebizond on the Black Sea, but transferred to Mesembria, a coastal city in Thrace (modern Nesebur, Bulgaria) in 655. He was summoned to Constantinople in 662 for the final showdown.

the Arabs, who, from their base in North Africa, were raiding Italy and Sicily. After being welcomed in Rome by Pope Vitalian, Constans marched south, crossed to Sicily, and established his new capital in Syracuse. Five years later, he was murdered in his bath by an attendant, and the throne passed to his eldest son, Constantine IV. The latter had been co-emperor since 654 and had been administering the eastern provinces from Constantinople since Constans' move to Syracuse. Constantine IV (r. 668–85) was apparently a wiser—and luckier—ruler than his father. He organized an effective defense of "New Rome" and its environs against the huge naval force sent against him in 672 by the first Omayyad Caliph, Muawiya. The final victory came in 677, when the Byzantines first successfully used "Greek fire" against their enemies and temporarily halted Arab expansionism. Constantine was also more doctrinally orthodox than his father, or at least realized that because Egypt and Syria were gone forever, monotheletism no longer had any propaganda value—nor had it ever been very popular in the Byzantine heartlands, much less their Western possessions. Accordingly, in 678, Constantine IV launched a series of theological consultations to restore unity to the imperial church. These eventuated in the convocation of the Sixth Ecumenical Council (Constantinople III), which sat from November 7, 680 until September 16, 681, with 174 bishops in attendance, and with Constantine himself presiding over many of the sessions. Pope Agatho (r. 678–81) sent words of greeting and commendation; the two-wills doctrine was formally promulgated; Pope Honorius and four ecumenical patriarchs—Sergius I, Pyrrhus, Paul II, and Peter—were anathematized, together with various other monenergist and monothelite ecclesiastics and the usual rogues' gallery of heresiarchs from earlier centuries. Maximus the Confessor is not mentioned in the Council's proceedings, the memory of his torture and exile by the reigning emperor's father being a politically sensitive matter, but Sophronius is explicitly commended. The Council's *acta* were eventually signed by the newly elected Pope Leo II (r. 682–83), and peace was temporarily restored. Unfortunately, the differences between the Greek and Latin branches of the imperial church were growing, and the failure of the so-called Quinisext Council of 692 to resolve them foreshadowed the Photian Schism of the ninth century and the Great Schism of the eleventh. Moreover, monotheletism itself was briefly and abortively revived by Emperor Philippikos Bardanes (r. 711–13) and the ecumenical patriarch, John VI (r. 711–15). But whatever the vagaries of subsequent church history may have been, Maximus the Confessor was vindicated at the Sixth Ecumenical Council, and today is regarded as a father of both the Eastern Orthodox and Roman Catholic Churches.

The Prison Literature of Maximus the Confessor

Seven closely related documents constitute Maximus' prison literature. Pauline Allen and Bronwen Neil have recently published a critical edition of these documents under the title, *Maximus the Confessor and His Companions: Documents from Exile* (hereafter cited in-text as *MCC*).[28] But only three of the seven documents in the dossier require a close reading. One is a transcript of his first trial, one is a transcript of a series of conversations that took place between Maximus and various representatives of the imperial government about a year after the first trial, and one is a short letter by Maximus himself. These three texts give us insight into why and how Maximus mounted his heroic resistance. The other four documents were written by members of Maximus' inner circle: they provide important information about the exile of Maximus and the Anastasii and about the subsequent resistance of the Maximian party to Constans' government, but, with one exception, they do not tell us much about Maximus himself, his religious convictions, or his carceral experience.

Record of the Trial (MCC 48–74)

This document, often known by its Latin title, the *Relatio Motionis*, is an eyewitness account by someone sympathetic to Maximus and Anastasius the Monk of their first trial,[29] which took place in the imperial palace in May 655.[30] The editor of the Greek *Life* incorporated the *Record* almost verbatim into his narrative but incorrectly treats it as the transcript of the second trial, which was held in 662 and which ended

---

28. This superb volume contains the original Greek texts with the editors' English translations on facing pages, as well as a thorough analysis of the historical background and manuscript history, extensive notes, maps, and other helps. Citations will begin with the paragraph number of the document referenced, followed by *MCC* and the page number.

29. Toward the end of his account, the writer states: "This was what was done and said, as much as can be remembered" (§13, *MCC* 72–73). This comment alerts us to the possibility that there may be gaps, redactions, and editorial flourishes in the *Record* which are now undetectable.

30. In addition to the Allen and Neil translation of the *Record*, see "The Trial of Maximus" in Maximus, *Selected Writings*, 15–31.

in the harsh punishments described above.[31] (No record of the second trial survives. Whether the editor's mistake was accidental or done for literary effect is impossible to determine.)

From its opening paragraph (§1, *MCC* 48–51), the *Record* indicates that the trial of Maximus and Anastasius the Monk was really a verdict in search of a charge that could be made to stick. As soon as they landed in Constantinople, they were hustled, naked and barefoot, to separate guardhouses. After a delay of some months, Maximus was taken, apparently without Anastasius, to the palace, "where the senate had assembled and a great crowd besides," and was abruptly accosted by the finance minister "with great anger and frenzy." This bullying was meant to intimidate the prisoner and to impress the government's intentions upon the assembly, while allowing Constans himself to retain his royal dignity and aplomb. And the minister's opening question is instructive: "Are you a Christian?" Maximus naturally assents to this, whereupon, after some further give and take between them, the minister demands, "And how, if you are a Christian, can you hate the emperor?" One might have expected Maximus to draw one of two obvious distinctions here. He might have differentiated between his personal feelings for the emperor as a man and monarch and his principled dissent from imperial policy; or he might have objected that his loyalty to God overrode his responsibilities as a Roman citizen. Instead, Maximus replies, "And what's the evidence for that? After all, hatred is a hidden disposition of the soul (*diathesis psychēs*) just as love is too." This is not only a shrewd legal maneuver—for of course psychological states are not prosecutable offenses—but also a way of exposing the fraudulence of the proceedings. For if anybody can be said to have given publicly observable evidence of disordered emotions it is the finance minister himself, just moments before.[32] But the minister either ignores or fails to understand that Maximus has just skewered him, and he proceeds to lodge the first real charge of the trial, namely that Maximus had committed treason many years earlier, by

---

31. §§51–65 in the *Life* follow §§1–12 in the *Record* almost verbatim. But whereas the concluding paragraph of the *Record* (§13) describes the prisoners' exile to Thrace and exhorts the reader to imitate their perseverance, the concluding paragraphs of the *Life* (§§66–73) describe the ordeal they suffered seven years later. The *Life* also incorrectly presumes that it was Anastasius the Monk who, like Maximus, was mutilated at the conclusion of the second trial, whereas we know from other sources that it was the Apocrisiarius who suffered that punishment.

32. On Maximus' psychology, see Blowers, "Gentiles," 57–85; Blowers, "Dialectics and Therapeutics," 425–51; Farrell, *Free Choice*.

trying to dissuade Peter, a Byzantine general stationed in Africa, from sailing to Egypt to oppose the Arab invasion.[33] It is worth noting that Maximus' alleged crime is said to have taken place during the reign of Heraclius, Constans' grandfather, suggesting that his opposition to imperial policy, or his "hatred" of the royal family, was longstanding. Maximus asks that the incriminating letters that had supposedly passed between the general and himself be produced and offers to "submit to the punishments decreed by the law" if they can be. The minister admits not only that he cannot document his charge, but that he had been relying on camp rumors. Why, then, asks Maximus, did no one at the camp bring this accusation forward at the time? By now it is clear that the charge that Maximus had conspired with the Arabs is bogus. So why has the minister accused him of treason? Is it a matter of personal animus? No, concedes the minister, he and Maximus had never met before that moment. To which Maximus turns to the senate and says, "You must judge whether it's just to have such accusers or witnesses brought forward," and quotes Matthew 7:2: "'By the judgment you judge you shall be judged, and by the measure that you measure, it shall be measured unto you,' said the Lord (*theos*; lit. 'God') of all."

Maximus' next accuser is Sergius Magoudas ($2, *MCC* 50–53), whose charges are equally serious and equally specious. He claims that nine years earlier—that is, in 646—Maximus had supported the abortive rebellion of Gregory, exarch of Africa. By that time Maximus had already gone from Carthage to Rome. His alleged "support" of Gregory consisted of his having "beheld a dream" (*etheōrēsen onar*) that augured well for the rebellion.[34] In this dream, some of the angels of heaven—those in

---

33. The finance minister asserts that this alleged crime took place "twenty-two years ago," that is, in 633. This is odd, for although the Arab armies were on the doorstep of Syria by that date, they did not reach Egypt—where Peter is supposed to have been sent—until December 639. The discrepancy can be explained in any of three equally unsatisfactory ways: (1) Peter might have been sent in 633 to strengthen Byzantine defenses in Syria, instead of Egypt. But that does not explain why the finance minister accuses Maximus of betraying "Egypt, Alexandria, Pentapolis, Tripolis and Africa," rather than Syria and Palestine, to the enemy. (2) Peter might indeed have been sent to Egypt in 633. But that was long before it was known that Syria and Palestine would fall. (3) Some early scribe may have incorrectly assumed that *Record* was a transcript of Maximus' second trial. For "twenty-two years" before that trial, which took place in 662 would have been 640, just when Byzantine reinforcements were needed in Egypt. But if so, the scribe did *not* correct the other dates mentioned in the *Record*, all of which presume that trial was in 655.

34. Allen and Neil translate *etheōrēsen onar* as "had a vision in his sleep." Berthold, in Maximus, *Selected Writings*, 18, renders it as "saw a vision in his sleep." I prefer

the East—promised victory to "Constantine Augustus" (i.e., Constans II), while others—those in the West—promised victory to "Gregory Augustus," with the latter prevailing over the former. Maximus was supposed to have told this dream to Pope Theodore, who then sent a monk to Gregory with the encouraging news. Upon hearing Sergius' accusation, the finance minister, who had just been humiliated in debate, shouts out, "God has sent you to this city to be burnt (*kauthēsōnai*)." Maximus responds first to the mercurial minister, perhaps hearing in his threat an echo of 1 Corinthians 13:3, in which the apostle asserts that "giving his body to be burned" (*kauthēsōmai*) would be futile if he lacked love.[35] "I give thanks to God," says Maximus, "who cleanses me of my voluntary sins by means of involuntary chastisement." He then drops another biblical quotation: "Woe to the world because of scandals. For it is necessary that scandals come, but woe to the man through whom scandal comes" (Matt 18:7). For Maximus, the real question is not whether he can escape with his life from this judicial farce, but whether he can use this trial as an opportunity for self-purification, that is, whether he can love his accusers in a manner befitting a true Christian.

Maximus then goes on to expose the absurdity of Sergius' charge on both procedural and substantive grounds. With respect to due process of law, Sergius has made a grave charge without producing either living witnesses or documentary evidence. He has not only indulged in inadmissible hearsay; he has artificially inflated the supposed political gravity of this dream by claiming that the angels were divided into two "crowds" or "factions" (*dēmoi*), as if Maximus were suggesting that heaven itself had been riven by the same civil war that briefly beset the empire. But if so, the dream was hardly prophetic, because "Gregory Augustus" lost the war. Moreover, Maximus, who has spent years reflecting on the dynamics of the will, has no trouble spotting the fallacy of using

---

"beheld a dream," partly because the verb *theaomai* ("to behold") is a bit more formal than *horaō* ("to see") and partly because, in Greek, *onar* typically refers to a dream while asleep, in contrast to *hypar*, which refers to a waking vision. But, as noted above (41n49), the distinction between dreams and visions, both in language and in people's actual experience, cannot always be drawn with precision.

35. Ancient New Testament manuscripts and various patristic writings differ over whether 1 Corinthians 13:3 should read, "hand over my body that I may be burned (*kauthēsōmai*)" or "hand over my body that I may glory (*kauchēsōmai*)." There are good arguments for both, but the former is found in many Eastern Christian sources, including Maximus the Confessor. See Metzger, *Textual Commentary*, 563-64. Hence my conjecture that Maximus is alluding to this verse in his response to the angry finance minister.

a dream in a court of law—even supposing there was reliable evidence that he had seen such a dream, which there wasn't, and even supposing the dream had come true, which it hadn't. "A dream is something which is not under the control of the will (*aproaireton*). The law punishes only actions which are under the control of the will (*proairetika*), if, that is, they are done in defiance of it" (§2, MCC 52–53). Sin is voluntary action contrary to divine law; crime is voluntary action contrary to human law. But dreams are not voluntary actions at all and therefore cannot be used as evidence either of sin or of crime. Some of the senators realize that Sergius' hollow accusation has given Maximus the upper hand in the debate. One chides Maximus for "teasing" the assembly, but Maximus vehemently denies this, only expressing regret that he has lived long enough to experience such "monstrosities" (*phasmatōn*; lit. "apparitions"). But another senator, Epiphanius, remarks that Maximus would be fully justified in "teasing" them, if the charges against them are as unfounded as they appear. There is a subtle play on words here, for the Greek word for "teasing" (*paizō*) is etymologically related to the word for child (*pais*) (§2, MCC 52–53). It is not that the "old man" (*gerōn*) is treating the senators like children; it is that the senators are behaving childishly in their treatment of the old man.

Having failed to prove Maximus guilty of treason, the government now accuses him of disrespecting the emperor. A third witness is produced, Theodore Chila, who asserts that he had once heard Maximus speak contemptuously of Constans (§3, MCC 52–55). Maximus replies that he had only spoken once in his life with Theodore; that he did so on that occasion in obedience to a written order by the government; and that a third participant in that conversation was Theocharistos, a priest who was the brother of the then reigning exarch of Ravenna. Maximus does not explicitly deny Theodore's charge but implies that under the circumstances it was scarcely plausible that he would have disparaged the emperor. And he offers to take the consequences of having done so, if the charge can be corroborated by Theocharistos, whose reliability the government can scarcely deny. But it is not corroborated.

The government's fourth witness, Gregory the son of Photinus, tries a similar maneuver (§4, MCC 54–59). He testifies that, in a three-way conversation between Maximus, Anastasius the Monk, and himself, he heard Anastasius—not Maximus himself—assert that the emperor "shouldn't be considered a priest"—or more literally, and more damningly, that the emperor "isn't worthy (*axiōthē*) to be a priest" (§4, MCC

54–55). One hears here an echo of what Eastern Christian congregations customarily exclaim when a priest is ordained: *Axios! Axios! Axios!* ("He is worthy!). It appears that Gregory is accusing Anastasius—and only by implication his master—of having denied that Constans was personally worthy to assume the priestly prerogatives that Byzantine emperors enjoyed. But Maximus wants to show that a theological principle is at stake here, not personal hostility toward Constans. He then throws himself to the ground before the assembly and asks permission to review the entire conversation to which Gregory has referred to explicate that principle. He then describes the elaborate courtesy that he had shown Gregory when he arrived at his cell: "When I saw him, as is my custom, I threw myself down on the ground (*erripsa emauton eis tēn gēn*) and welcomed him respectfully (*prosekunēsa autōi*; lit. 'venerated him'). And I kissed him and said to him after we had sat down: 'What is the reason for the welcome arrival of my master?'" (§4, MCC 54–55). The force of these words cannot be lost on the senators, for Maximus has just prostrated himself before *them* and is delivering his present speech from a prone position. Maximus is about to deconstruct their understanding of the principle of caesaropapism: that itself may incur their rage. But he won't concede that he is contemptuous of the emperor or his emissaries.

Maximus explains that Gregory had informed him that he had come to heal the rift between the imperial and papal parties, and that he, Maximus, had inquired about the terms on which "his divinely crowned Serenity has ordered the union to come about." Gregory had replied that the emperor was insisting on papal compliance with the terms of the *Typos*, and Maximus had indicated that such compliance was "impossible." Gregory had reminded him that the *Typos* did not require universal assent to monotheletism but had only closed public debate on the question of the number of Christ's energies and wills. To which Maximus had retorted that silencing the truth is the same as annulling it, and that allowing oneself to be silenced by the government on matters of non-negotiable dogma would be tantamount to consenting to government-sponsored heresy.[36] Compliance with the *Typos* would entail the implicit repudiation of the Nicene Creed. Then, after showing his theological

---

36. As we shall see in chapter 3, Thomas More tried unsuccessfully to argue almost the exact opposite, claiming that in the eyes of the law, "silence implies consent," and therefore that his refusal to endorse the marriage of Henry VIII to Anne Boleyn could not legally be construed as evidence of his opposition to it.

warrant for this shocking claim,[37] he had reminded Gregory that during the Arian crisis of the mid-fourth century, the fathers had often opposed the emperors, "saying plainly that it is the mark of priests to make an inquiry and to define on the subject of the saving teachings of the catholic church." Gregory had then asked, "Isn't every Christian emperor also a priest?" To which Maximus—and Maximus *himself*, not Anastasius—had replied in the negative, carefully distinguishing between the appropriate badges and functions of imperial authority and those of priesthood, and appealing to the manner in which the diptychs are recited during the Byzantine liturgy: "During the holy anaphora at the holy table, after the high-priests and priests and deacons and the whole clerical rank, the emperors are remembered with the laity when the deacon says: 'And the lay-people who have fallen asleep in faith, Constantine, Constans, and the others'" (§4, *MCC* 58–59).[38] Maximus' rehearsal of this conversation is met with angry shouts from the gallery: in denying that emperors possess clerical authority, he has "split (*eschisas*) the church." No, he replies, the unity of the church depends on its members' willingness to adhere to the teachings of Scripture and the fathers. His own longstanding opposition to imperial monotheletism is neither schismatic nor treasonous. It is the logical consequence of his loyalty to the doctrinal standards of the earlier councils, which both sides of the present controversy accept. If the stability of the Byzantine state depends on the unity of the church, if the unity of the church depends upon unanimous assent to its doctrinal standards, if the emperor lacks the authority to interpret those standards, and if his unauthorized interpretation has proven false, then it is the imperial government itself that is guilty of schism, heresy, and treason.

The only way the government can salvage its rapidly disintegrating case against Maximus is to cast doubt upon his churchmanship and his orthodoxy. He is dismissed from the senate chamber, and his disciple, Anastasius the Monk, is brought in and asked why his master

---

37. Maximus' argument here is extremely compressed, and its validity depends on several assumptions that are expounded only elsewhere in his writings. He claims that the Creed attests to one God in three persons, and that the creative and redemptive activity of God is single not triplex. Thus, the will must be a property of *human nature*, not of *human persons*—or in the case of the Triune God, a property of the *one* divine nature, and not of the *three* divine persons. Thus, compliance to the *Typos* would amount to silent endorsement of monotheletism, which regards the will as a property of the human person, not of human nature—or in the case of Christ, a property of his theanthropic person, not of his two natures, considered separately.

38. The Constans mentioned here is Constans I (r. 337–50), the youngest son of Constantine the Great and a stout supporter of Nicene Orthodoxy.

had "distressed" (*thlipsantos*, lit. "squeezed" or "pinched") Pyrrhus, the recently deceased patriarch of Constantinople (§5, *MCC* 58–61). Anastasius replies in a soft voice, "Nobody honored Pyrrhus as my superior did." He is ordered to speak up, but refuses: the narrator notes that he is simply practicing suitable monastic modesty—and not, we are led to assume, that he is intimidated by the hostile audience. But the senators take his modesty as insubordination and have him severely beaten. Then he and Maximus are sent back to prison, with an escort of several high officials, including Menas, a priest who was apparently serving as a theological consultant to the senate during the trial, and Epiphanius, who had earlier in the day come to Maximus' defense. Along the way, Menas accuses Maximus of Origenism, which had been condemned at the Fifth Ecumenical Council (Constantinople II, 553). There is some plausibility to this charge, for themes from Origen and his fourth-century follower Evagrius Ponticus do appear in Maximus' writings, though always carefully corrected.[39] But Maximus promptly anathematizes "Origen and his teachings," whereupon Epiphanius informs Menas that this last-ditch effort to discredit Maximus has thereby collapsed. The two monks are now led to the guardhouse.

That evening, Maximus is visited by two officials, Troilus the patrician and Sergius Eucratas (§§6–9, *MCC* 60–67). Both are well-disposed to him, speak courteously, and seem genuinely interested in the disputed theological issues, although, as politicians, their overriding concern is church unity and civil peace. They ask about Maximus' dispute with Pyrrhus ten years before, and Maximus recounts the story. Then they ask if he is in communion with Constantinople, and he says no, explaining that the government's efforts to conciliate the monophysites without angering the Romans by promulgating a series of official decrees and resorting to repressive measures had come to nothing. In some consternation, they ask if he thinks that he is "the only one who'll be saved, and everyone else will be lost." He replies by comparing himself first with Shadrach, Meshach, and Abednego (Dan 3:1–30), who adhered steadfastly to their faith without "passing judgment" on anyone else, and then with Daniel himself, who "chose to die and not to backslide from God, and to be flayed by his own conscience (*mastigōthēnai syneidēseōs*) in the matter of the transgression of natural law" (Dan 6:1–28). Then he adds, "To the best of my ability I'll choose to die rather than have on my conscience

---

39. See, Louth, Introduction to Maximus, *Maximus*, 65–72, and Thunberg, *Microcosm and Mediator*, passim.

the worry that in some way or other I have suffered a lapse with regard to belief in God" (§6, *MCC* 60–63). These remarks take us to the very heart of Maximus' principled stand against imperial policy. But it is important to observe that Maximus is not asserting the autonomy of the individual conscience or the incorrigibility of private opinion. His conscience is tethered to the orthodox faith: he has no "teaching of his own" (*dogma idion*) (§6, *MCC* 60–61).[40] What makes him unable to accept both the imperial heresy and the imperial edict that prohibits public dissent to it is what he regards as the airtight logic that leads from the dyophysitism of Chalcedon to the dyotheletism of the recent Lateran Council.[41]

Troilus and Sergius do their best to break the impasse. They point out the recent arrival in the capital of representatives from the newly installed Pope Eugenius, who, as we have seen, was more conciliatory toward Constans than his four predecessors. Maximus refuses to believe that Rome will ever endorse monotheletism, but insists that if that unthinkable eventuality should occur, it would displease the Holy Spirit—and certainly not budge him from his allegiance to the teachings of the church fathers. The two officials ask if "it is altogether necessary to speak of wills and activities on the subject of Christ," to which Maximus gives the expected answer and another synopsis of the dyothelite position. They tell him that they agree with his position, and given Sergius Eucratas' pro-Chalcedonian surname, this seems plausible.[42] But they implore him not to "distress (*lypēsēs*) the emperor," who is only seeking peace within the empire. Once again, Maximus throws himself to the ground. "The good and pious master shouldn't be distressed (*lypēthēnai*) by my lowliness. I say this because I cannot distress (*lypēsai*) God by keeping

---

40. In connection with the dogmatic disputes of the seventh century, Chadwick, "Moschus and Sophronius," 74, observes: "Men were not believers in one or two natures because they had reached a conclusion after careful consideration of the intricate questions at issue in the Christological debate. They held different theological positions because of a sense of allegiance to their own communion, to their own party, so that the least concession or deviation from the acknowledged polemical position of the group seemed like ambiguity, or compromise, or a failure of integrity, or 'trampling on one's conscience.'" This may have been true of most people in that era, and it certainly sheds light on the attitudes of many of Maximus' most dogmatic accusers, but it applies only partially to Maximus himself. He certainly displays fierce "allegiance to his own communion," but he no less certainly had given "careful consideration" to the theological issues at stake and insisted during his trial on riveting his accusers' attention to those issues.

41. Cf. the discussion of Maximus' "Chalcedonian logic" in Louth, Introduction to Maximus, *Maximus*, 49–51.

42. See n12 above.

silent about what he himself ordered to be said and confessed" (§6, *MCC* 62–65). In this exchange the Greek verb *lypeō* is used three times. This word means, as Allen and Neil rightly render it, to "distress" or "give pain to." Yet the related noun, *lypē*, is used in Eastern Orthodox spiritual writings to mean contrition or "godly sorrow."[43] If there is an echo here of that sense of the word, then the officials are imploring Maximus not simply to stop making a nuisance of himself, but to refrain from forcing Constans to repent publicly. Maximus shows by his prostration and his ingratiating words that he has no wish to humiliate the "good and pious master" (*agathos kai eusebēs despotēs*),[44] although he would certainly rejoice if Constans abjured his heresy. But nothing will induce Maximus to grieve God by renouncing his opposition to the *Typos*.

The conversation turns to more pleasant matters, "Scripture, nature, and grammar" (§8, *MCC* 64–67). Sergius recalls past times when he visited Maximus for instruction. But the purpose of the present visit—the need to convince Maximus to stop "distressing (*lypeis*) everyone" by "causing many people to be separated from the communion of the church here"—is close to the surface. Maximus insists that he has not publicly advocated separation, and that those who have followed his example are simply obeying the dictates of *their* consciences. Yet the widespread disobedience to the *Typos* throughout the empire has injured the emperor's reputation. Maximus suggests that Constans do with respect to the *Typos* as Heraclius did with respect to the *Ekthesis*, namely, to repudiate it as the work of nefarious "ecclesiastical and state officials." Troilus and Sergius shake their heads at the insolubility of the problem, "exchange obeisances" (*proskynēthentes kai proskynēsantes*) with the saint and depart "very cheerfully" (*hilarotētos*) (§9, *MCC* 66–67).

A week or so later, Maximus and Anastasius are brought back to the palace, and the disciple is interrogated first (§10, *MCC* 68–69). This time he speaks, not with monkish modesty, but "with great outspokenness" (*parrēsias*), a term used frequently in the New Testament to indicate daring Christian witness (Mark 8:3; John 16:25; 2 Cor 3:12; 7:4; Phil 1:20; etc.). He reproaches one of his accusers for gross immorality, reaffirms his anathema of the *Typos*, and "fearlessly" claims

---

43. See the Glossary in Nikodimos and Makarios, *Philokalia*, 2:387, s.v. "Sorrow."

44. Allen and Neil translate *eusebēs* as "orthodox." But "pious" would be the ordinary rendering, and it seems preferable, as Maximus' point all along has been that while Constans may be personally virtuous, he endorses heresy. Berthold, in Maximus, *Selections*, 24, translates the phrase, "good and pious lord."

to have written a short treatise against it. Anastasius is then dismissed, and Maximus is brought in (§11, *MCC* 68–71). Troilus, who has recently established good relations with the prisoner, urges him to "speak the truth" and promises that he will be treated mercifully if he does. Maximus understands this to mean that he must "confess" to treason, which he simply cannot do. Yes, he *has* anathematized the *Typos*, but no, he has *not* anathematized the emperor—and he refuses to concede the government's claim that the one implies the other. Another official asks why is he not in communion with Constantinople, if the diptychs pronounced in the liturgy assert the authority of the ecumenical councils to which he professes allegiance? He replies that it is because the church of Constantinople has decreed things inconsistent with those councils. "Why," asks the finance minister, "do you love the Romans, and hate the Greeks?" To which Maximus replies, "We have a commandment not to hate anybody. I love the Romans because we share the same faith, whereas I love the Greeks because we share the same language" (§11, *MCC* 70–71). This is the most succinct, eloquent, and poignant summary of Maximus' predicament in the *Record*. The government interprets Maximus' opposition to its religious policy as disloyalty to the state, whereas Maximus, who regards that policy as mistaken, opposes it on the grounds of religious devotion and genuine patriotism.

Further discussion ensues (§12, *MCC* 70–73), in which the government denies the validity of the acts of the Lateran Council of 649 because its president, Pope Martin, has been deposed. Maximus denies that Martin's deposition was canonical and asserts that in any case the acts of the council concur with the teachings of Martin's predecessor, Theodore, whose pontifical authority was unquestionable. The council's acts are therefore valid.

With this the trial ends, the government having succeeded in proving only what was never in dispute, namely that Maximus and Anastasius had anathematized the *Typos* on doctrinal grounds, and that the government regards their refusal to accept it as treason (§13, *MCC* 72–74). The two prisoners are then sent to separate prisons in Thrace, "without provisions, without clothing, without nourishment, deprived of all resources for living," and situated too far from the coast for their friends to visit them easily or send them supplies. The author concludes the *Record* by listing the specific tribulations they were made to endure: "hunger, thirst, nakedness, bonds, prisons, guards, captivity, scourging, a cross, nails, vinegar, bile, spitting, slapping, buffeting and mockery, and suffering and different types of death." This inventory of woes obviously recalls the passion of Christ and ends with the edifying promise of the "radiant resurrection" of all who, like Maximus and Anastasius, steadfastly endure persecution for Christ's sake.

Dispute at Bizya (*MCC* 75–119)

This document is a transcript by an unnamed eyewitness of several conversations that took place between Maximus and several officials in Constans' government in late summer, 656, about a year after the first trial. As he did with the *Record of the Trial*, the author of the Greek *Life* has incorporated the *Dispute* almost verbatim into his narrative, correctly noting that it took place after the first trial.[45] However, as we have noted, the *Life* treats the transcript of what was really the first trial as if it were the transcript of the second, which took place in spring 662, and it incorrectly treats the conversations between Maximus and Constans' deputies at the prison in Bizya, as if they took place long after the first trial and just prior to the second. The *Life* thus implies that because the result of these conversations was unsatisfactory to the government, Maximus and Anastasius were brought to the capital for their second trial, the verdict and sentence of which were foregone conclusions. In fact, the conversations recorded in the *Dispute* represent an early phase in what was to become a protracted but unsuccessful campaign by Constans to get Maximus to come to terms.

The *Dispute* opens with a brief address by the transcriber to his readers (§1, *MCC* 76–77), whom he regards as those "who persevere in right belief." He admonishes them to use the "accurate knowledge of these matters," which his transcription will supply, to "glorify God," and expresses the hope that his work will forestall "the enemies of the truth" from circulating false versions of these conversations, versions that would portray Maximus either as a traitor to the state or as a hairsplitting theologian with no sympathy for the monothelites' legitimate religious concerns and

---

45. §§26–49 in the *Life* follow §§3–14 in the *Dispute* closely, aside from some minor textual discrepancies. But neither the introductory paragraphs in the *Dispute* (§§1–2), nor what appears to be its original conclusion (§15) are included in the *Life*. The paragraphs that now conclude the *Dispute* (§§16–17) must be a scribal postscript, as they describe events surrounding the second trial, which took place six years later. These extra paragraphs in the *Dispute* bear only a general resemblance to the concluding paragraphs of the *Life* (§§66–73).

with no awareness of the complexities of the ecclesiastical and geopolitical situation. As it turns out, the transcriber's own account of these conversations shows Maximus to be an exceptionally skillful dialectician and learned patrologist, although there is somewhat less evidence of his patriotism here than in the *Record of the Trial*. But what the transcriber hopes his readers will find edifying is not simply the force of Maximus' arguments, but his complete immunity to the flattery, bribery, and threats used by his visitors. Once again, the government is made to look desperate and underhanded precisely because it is unorthodox.

The first conversation takes place on August 24, 656 (§2, *MCC* 76–77). Three visitors from Constantinople arrive at Maximus' prison in Bizya. These are Theodosius, bishop of Caesarea in Bithynia, representing the ecumenical patriarch, and the two consuls for that year, Paul and another Theodosius, representing the emperor. But this first conversation is dominated by theological matters, and although the presence of the consuls is a solemn reminder that political considerations are not far from the surface, they have almost nothing to say until the very end. The bulk of the dialogue is between the prisoner and the bishop.

Theodosius opens the conversation with what seems like a perfectly sincere expression of courtesy and concern. "How are you, my lord Father?" he asks. Maximus replies: "As God preordained before all ages a way of life for me in his providence, that's how I am" (§3, *MCC* 76–77). Theodosius is understandably puzzled by this. "How can you say that? Did God preordain our individual destinies before all time?" Maximus then draws a distinction between divine predestination (*proorismos*) and divine foreknowledge (*prognōsis*), arguing that God predestines those things that happen to us but that are beyond our control, whereas he only foreknows our "acts of volition (*ekousia*), that is to say, [our] virtues and vices" (§3, *MCC* 78–79). Although this distinction is not elaborated in much detail, Maximus is not simply indulging in academic shoptalk. He is giving a theological rationale for the attitude he is taking toward his own situation and for his obdurate opposition to imperial policy. His belief that God has providentially ordered his "external" circumstances makes him patient in suffering, while his belief that God holds him accountable for his own conduct and character gives him strength in the face of imperial pressure. "The cause of the kingdom of heaven is the keeping of the commandments, just as the cause of eternal fire, too, is transgressing them" (§3, *MCC* 78–79). Yet this is not only a matter of personal spiritual discipline for Maximus;

it is closely related to the very reason that he is incarcerated, namely his commitment to the theological anthropology of Chalcedon, which he takes to be indispensable for an account of human conduct consistent with Scripture. The human will is a function of human nature, and the freedom of the human will is not only the *sine qua non* for human agency, but the condition of possibility for the union of the divine and human natures of Christ. If human beings lacked moral freedom, they would not need salvation, nor could they receive it. And if Jesus lacked moral freedom, he could not have been the Savior of the race, for his obedience to the Father would have been a charade.

Theodosius pronounces himself edified by Maximus' reflections, though in doing so he implicitly concedes the point at issue. Then he presses on to his main business, which is to urge Maximus to "accept our offer and make the whole world happy." Constans will free Maximus if only he will enter communion with the see of Constantinople on the terms of the *Typos*. For Maximus this is impossible, for he regards any concession to monotheletism as apostasy. His unflinching opposition to the empire's doctrinal innovations is grounded in soteriological considerations. If Christ does not have a genuinely human "activity" (*energeia*), then "even if he wants to, he cannot show mercy, because the activity of his blessings has been removed, if indeed without natural activity nothing which exists remains to have an activity or to perform" (§3, *MCC* 82–83). This makes explicit the point of Maximus' earlier distinction between divine predestination and divine foreknowledge, for it is only insofar as Christ is fully human and possesses all the proper "activities" of human nature, that the mercy he shows to sinners can be regarded as a free moral act. Theodosius admits that he himself regarded the publication of the *Typos* as an "evil event" at the time but chides Maximus for breaking communion with the ecumenical patriarchate on account of it. After all, the *Typos* does not oblige people to affirm that Christ has but one will; it only prohibits people from disputing how many wills he has. And this prohibition is intended to restore peace to the troubled empire. "Don't accept as ratified teaching what happened on account of an arrangement" (§3, *MCC* 84–85).

The Greek word Theodosius uses for the imperial "arrangement" is *oikonomia*. A few moments before, Maximus had used this same word when discussing the distinction between the doctrine of the consubstantiality of the three persons of the Trinity ("the language of *theologia*") and the doctrine of the saving work of Christ ("the language of the *oikonomia*") (§3, MCC 82–83). Although neither interlocutor remarks on the fact that they have used the same word in very different senses, Maximus clearly regards the imperial "arrangement" as a disaster. Not only had the *Typos* failed to establish peace, but it had implicitly drained the Christian message of its salvific import. Unsurprisingly, Maximus is unmoved by Theodosius' argument. The government may no longer be publicly enforcing monotheletism, but by failing to repudiate the heresy, it has failed to ratify what Maximus takes to be an inescapable corollary of Chalcedonian orthodoxy and has thereby made it impossible for him to "make the whole world happy" by capitulating. At this point, Maximus makes another agonized prostration[46] and tells Theodosius, "Whatever you order to be done to your servant, do. I will never be in communion with those who accept [the *Typos*]" (§3, MCC 86–87).

The bishop and the two consuls are "frozen" (*apopagentes*) by this, but they soon thaw out sufficiently to make a stunning offer: if Maximus returns to communion with Constantinople, Constans will cancel the *Typos* (§4, MCC 89–101). Maximus is wary of this and is unwilling to proceed unless the government likewise repudiates the *Ekthesis* and those patriarchs who had endorsed it, namely Sergius, Pyrrhus, and Paul II, all of whom had been condemned at the recent Lateran Council. Theodosius replies that that council had been convened without imperial consent (to say the least!), and therefore the emperor cannot reasonably be expected to submit to its religious authority. Thus, the stalemate continues: from Maximus' standpoint, all the government's efforts to break the impasse come to nothing. The *Ekthesis*, which openly promulgated monotheletism, was replaced by the *Typos*, which only prohibited opposition to it; now the government wants to replace the *Typos* with . . . what? Revoking a gag order may permit public dissent, but it still does not constitute the formal repudiation of the new heresies and does not realign the government and the patriarchate with the Definition of Chalcedon.

This triggers a convoluted discussion of whether the validity of an ecclesiastical synod depends on its having imperial consent. Maximus insists not. He mentions several synods that were held at the behest of heretical emperors, which issued teachings that the universal church

---

46. The Greek phrase used here (and again in §14) for Maximus' gesture, is *balōn metanoian*, an idiom that literally means "throwing a penance." Allen and Neil render it, "on bended knee," but I suspect that a prostration rather than a genuflection is meant. Cf. *Report of the Trial* §7, MCC 64–65, where *rhipsas heauton* clearly means, "He threw himself on the ground." I am indebted to my colleagues, Drs. Owen Ewald and Stamatis Vokos, for helping me to make sense of this curious expression.

subsequently anathematized, and several others that were held over the objections of heretical emperors, which issued teachings that the universal church has since upheld. Theodosius finally shows his hand and adduces several patristic quotations that seem to support the imperial contention that in some sense Christ must be said to possess a single *energeia*, for otherwise he must be thought to have acted at odds with himself. But Maximus is not one to be beaten at this game and proceeds to show that the bishop's quotations have been falsely ascribed to orthodox fathers and really come from notorious heresiarchs. Theodosius, who had earlier been "frozen" by Maximus' words, is now "boiling with rage" (*thumōi zesas*) (§4, *MCC* 90–91). Even a quotation taken from one of the biblical commentaries of the great Cyril of Alexandria—Maximus suspects it to be a monophysite interpolation but accepts its authenticity for the sake of argument—doesn't bear the sense that Theodosius supposes. Or at least it must be understood in light of the conventional interpretive "rules" (*nomoi*) of the church (§4, *MCC* 92–93), which do indeed prevent us from imagining that Christ suffered from psychic conflict or moral indecision, but which do not permit us to explain the harmony of his character and the consistent godliness of his actions as a result of any abridgment of his human nature. Theodosius insists that that is precisely the point of the monenergist/monothelite position, and it begins to look as if the dispute turns more on how one counts Christ's wills than on how one understands his person and work, for on this there seems to be substantial agreement. Theodosius can't see why one must count the wills at all! But Maximus is adamant: the concept of a will is logically entailed in the concept of a nature; to deny the reality of distinct human and divine wills and activities in Christ is to deny, at least by implication, the Chalcedonian doctrine of the hypostatic union.

Maximus reinforces his point by "taking the book of the Acts of the holy and apostolic synod of Rome" (i.e., the Lateran Council of 649) and showing that the duality of wills and activities is there regarded as theologically non-negotiable (§4, *MCC* 96–99). Theodosius the consul now enters the discussion for the first time: he takes this book from Maximus and obligingly reads out all the patristic citations given in support of the dyothelite case. Bishop Theodosius is almost ready to capitulate, although the fact that the council fathers had anathematized several patriarchs by name understandably gives him pause. And Maximus is unwilling to accept the bishop's promise to support the council's doctrinal stance until he sees an official government dispatch to Rome acknowledging that its *acta* have been accorded binding legal force. He also wants proof that the names of the anathematized patriarchs have been stricken from the diptychs in the liturgy of the church of Constantinople. Bishop Theodosius suspects that he will be sent to Rome to negotiate the formal reconciliation and implores Maximus to accompany him. At first, Maximus demurs, suggesting that Anastasius the Apocrisiarius, being a former papal official, would be better suited for the mission. But Theodosius says that he and Anastasius have quarreled in times past, whereupon Maximus agrees to make the journey (§4, *MCC* 98–101).

For a moment, all seems well. There are tears of joy, embraces of friendship, and prayers of thanksgiving all around, and the four men engage in a mutually edifying discussion of the faith. But Theodosius the bishop suddenly asks Maximus, "By the Lord, don't keep me in the dark: don't you say in any way at all that there is one will, one activity in Christ?" (§5, *MCC* 100–101). Is this a serious theological question? Or is it a bit of playful banter uttered in the cheery glow of restored friendship? Or is it an expression of sudden misgivings over having conceded too much to the unyielding saint? Whatever Theodosius meant by his question, Maximus takes it seriously and answers it with another lecture on the dyothelite position. But his emphasis on the duality of Christ's natures, wills, and activities sounds suspiciously Nestorian to Theodosius (§6, *MCC* 102–5). Maximus then offers a highly refined exposition of the Neo-Chalcedonian position, which hinges on the use of the technical terms, "mutual interchange" (*epallagē*) and "mutual interpenetration" (*perichōrēsis*), to explain how the distinctive properties of Christ's two natures are preserved inviolate and expressed flawlessly in his person (§6, *MCC* 102–5).[47] This prompts Theodosius to request an elaboration of Maximus' earlier claim that when persons act, they act "naturally" rather than "hypostatically," that is, according to their nature (or in Jesus' case, according to his two natures) rather than according to their individual characters (§7, *MCC* 104–5). From a modern perspective, Maximus' answer seems unconvincing, as it sidesteps the crucial question of what makes each person truly herself—and no one else. But Maximus is not interested in what makes Peter uniquely Peter, and Paul uniquely Paul. Rather, he is interested in what it is that Peter and Paul have in common with each other and with all other human beings, and in what it is that makes all human beings

---

47. On the meaning of *perichōrēsis* in the Eastern fathers generally, and in Maximus in particular, see Crisp, "Problems," 119–40; Harrison, "Perichoresis," 53–65; Prestige, *God in Patristic Thought*, 282–301; Scalise, "Perichoresis," 58–76.

different from all other kinds of living creatures. Those characteristics that all individuals of a particular kind share collectively constitute their "nature" (*physis*) or "essence" (*ousia*), and as different as Peter and Paul may be from each other as persons, the commonalities of their human nature differentiate them both from angels and apes. Moreover, it is because he shares all the constitutive characteristics of human nature—conspicuously including *thelēma* and *energeia*—that Jesus can rightly be regarded as truly and fully human, and it is because he manifests those characteristics with unblemished perfection that he can serve as our "advocate with the Father." Once again, Maximus' theological anthropology is of a piece with his Christology and soteriology.

That settled, Maximus' visitors embrace him and Theodosius confirms that the emperor will post a supplicatory rescript (*paraklētikēn*) to Rome (§8 *MCC* 104–7). Maximus replies, "Of course he will do so, if he wishes to be an imitator of God (*mimētēs tou Theou*) and to be humbled and emptied with him for the sake of the common salvation of us all, considering that if the God who saves by nature did not save until he was humbled willingly, how can the human being, who by nature needs to be saved, either be saved or save when he has not been humbled." This extraordinary remark stitches together three passages from the New Testament: Ephesians 5:1, Philippians 2:7–8, and Jude 3. We saw earlier that Maximus has no wish to humiliate Constans personally or deny his imperial authority, but here he suggests, in delicate passive infinitives, that Constans allow himself to be "co-humbled" (*syntapeinōthēnai*) and "co-emptied" (*sygkenōthēnai*) with Christ (§8, *MCC* 104–5). Constans will demonstrate his worthiness to wear the imperial purple by imitating the meekness of the King of Kings, for whose garments the mocking soldiers gambled (cf. Mark 15:16–24). Theodosius expresses the hope that God will remind him to use this trope when he faces Constans. After giving Maximus "a pitiful amount of money . . . and a tunic and a cloak," the three delegates depart. Almost immediately, the bishop of Bizya, who has been lurking nearby, takes away the new tunic (§8, *MCC* 106–7).

On September 8, 656, the consul Paul, who had been silent in the previous interview, returns to Bizya with orders to move Maximus "with much honor and coaxing" to a monastery in the suburbs of the capital, probably the Monastery of St. Theodore near Rhegium[48] (§9, *MCC* 106–7). There Maximus is visited by Bishop Theodosius and

---

48. On the disputed identity of this monastery, see *MCC* 182n38.

the patricians Epiphanius and Troilus, all three of whom have shown themselves to be well-disposed toward him (§10, *MCC* 106–9). But things don't go well. Troilus asks Maximus, "Will you do what the emperor orders, or not?" Maximus wants to know what the orders are before he agrees to obey them. He already suspects that the emperor has not agreed to the terms negotiated at the previous meeting. The officials display annoyance, and Maximus offers to obey any imperial order "concerning any matter whatsoever which will be destroyed and brought to nothing with this age" (§10, *MCC* 108–9). That, of course, is just what an ecclesiastical dogma is *not*, and Troilus is ready to storm off in fury. Theodosius, chagrined that the promises he had recently made to Maximus at Bizya have not been honored by Constans, now implores Maximus to communicate with Constantinople on the terms of the *Typos*, both for the sake of civil peace and for the sake of the high honors that the emperor has promised to bestow upon him in exchange for his compliance. Maximus sadly reproaches the bishop for having sworn a promise on the Gospels that he proved unable to keep but reiterates that he cannot in conscience consent. Enraged, Troilus and Epiphanius begin to physically assault the old man, but Theodosius restrains them, remarking ominously that "canonical matters (*kanonika pragmata*) are settled another way" (§11, *MCC* 110–11).

The conversation resumes uneasily (§12, *MCC* 110–15), with Epiphanius blustering that he and the other two visitors "are more Christian and orthodox" than Maximus, because they are not only convinced dyothelites but also obedient citizens, who recognize the political necessity of the "arrangement" (*oikonomia*) mapped out in the *Typos* (§12, *MCC* 110–11). Troilus adds that Maximus is free to "believe in his heart" whatever he wishes, but in politics one must be willing to compromise. But for Maximus to profess anything that contradicts his beliefs would be to violate his conscience and subject himself to the same anathemas that he has pronounced against the imperial heresy and the ancient heresiarchs, Arius and Apollinaris, upon whose teachings he thinks the new heresy depends. Exasperated at the interminability of the dispute, the three visitors exit for lunch, after which "they went in angrily to the vigil of the exaltation of the precious and life-giving cross" (§12, *MCC* 114–15). The editor's sarcasm is hard to miss.

Early next morning, the same three officials return, strip Maximus of his remaining possessions,[49] and inform him that he and his two disciples will be exiled and incarcerated in separate dungeons (§13, *MCC* 114–15). They even threaten to depose the present pope and his retinue, although this may be empty bluster, as Eugenius is proving more cooperative with Constans than his four predecessors. Maximus is briefly taken to Selymbria (modern Silivri, about sixty-five kilometers west of Constantinople), where rumors circulate among the soldiers that he has blasphemed the Mother of God (§14, *MCC* 114–17). But upon learning of this libelous accusation, Maximus prostrates himself and expresses his Marian devotion in heartfelt and unequivocal terms. The soldiers are moved to tears and a senior officer has to whisk him away from the camp, lest there be mutiny in the ranks at the injustice being done to him. There Maximus stays for a couple more days, receiving visits from friends, until he is finally taken to Perberis, where he is held for the next six years.

The concluding paragraph of the original text of the *Dispute* informs us of a spurious report that had circulated in the capital according to which Maximus had been offered yet another deal, which he might have accepted but for a disturbance among the monothelites in the capital (§15, *MCC* 116–17). Several manuscripts add a doxology at this point, and some include an appendix that briefly describes Maximus' second trial (§§16–17, *MCC* 116–19). This second trial occurred in spring 662, nearly six years after the events recorded in §§1–15, with the Anastasii present as co-defendants. The full transcript has not survived, but we know that it eventuated in the harsh punishments described above.[50]

Letter of Maximus to Anastasius the Monk (*MCC* 120–23)

On April 18, 658—two years into his six-year incarceration at Perberis, Maximus wrote a letter to Anastasius the Monk, who was being kept at a different facility in the same town. This is the only document from the saint's own pen included in the dossier of his prison literature, and the

---

49. It is difficult to know exactly what personal effects Maximus had been allowed to keep during his imprisonment. *Dispute* §8 and *Report* §§8 and 13 imply extreme penuriousness, but the fact that he had a copy of the *acta* of the Lateran Council on hand at the beginning of his interrogation at Bizya (§4, *MCC* 98–99) suggests otherwise. Perhaps the editors "embroidered" these accounts in places to underscore the saint's learnedness and Christlikeness.

50. For details, see *MCC* 183–85nn52–62.

only thing he wrote between his arrest on June 17, 653 and his death on August 13, 662 that has survived.

Maximus writes that on the previous day he had been visited by representatives of Peter, the current patriarch of Constantinople, who had mockingly asked him what church he belonged to, and had then recited each member of the traditional Pentarchy—with Constantinople, significantly enough, being given pride of place. Rome, listed next, had by that time capitulated to Constans, and had thus implicitly withdrawn its support for Maximus. The other three patriarchates, Antioch, Alexandria, and Jerusalem, were now under Arab control and played no direct role in the ecclesiastical affairs of the empire.[51] In short, Peter had notified Maximus that he was now in communion with no recognized seat of ecclesiastical authority, and therefore ought to give up his "strange path" (*xenēn hodon*), return to the fold, and avoid further suffering (*MCC* 120–21). But for Maximus, exile and imprisonment have changed nothing, even though he is now being threatened with formal anathematization and death. At Bizya, he had refused to capitulate for fear of earning the same papal anathematization that had been meted out to the monothelites at the Lateran council of 649.[52] But now that Rome and Constantinople have been reconciled, Maximus is left with no base of ecclesiastical support. Yet, as he tells his disciple, he still refuses to betray the church fathers and will rely on whatever divine providence has decreed. In relaying this information, he encourages Anastasius to "increase [his] prayer and petition to God" and to pass the word on to whomever of their party he may be in contact with (*MCC* 122–23).[53]

Other Documents in the Prison Dossier (*MCC* 124–75)

There are four more documents in the Maximian prison dossier: a letter by Anastasius the Monk to the Italo-Greek monks of Cagliari, a city on the island of Sardinia (*MCC* 124–31); a letter by Anastasius the

---

51. Cf. *MCC* 185n4.

52. *Dispute* §4, *MCC* 98–99.

53. The letter ends with a Latin coda by an unnamed secretary, indicating that Anastasius had ordered its transcription and circulation. But the coda refers to the fact that "the seed of piety" remains "at least in older Rome." If the date of the letter is 658, this seems odd, given Pope Vitalian's recent rapprochement with Constans and Peter. If, however, the date of the letter is 655, as Sherwood, *Date-List*, 62, suggests, the coda makes more sense; but then the letter itself doesn't fit the role it seems to play in the prison dossier as a whole.

Apocrisiarius to Theodosius of Gangra, another member of the Maximian party (*MCC* 132–47); the so-called "Commemoration" of Theodore Spoudaeus, still another supporter of Maximus (MCC 148–71); and an anonymous diatribe against the people of Constantinople for their collusion with the emperor's brutal treatment of Maximus and the Anastasii (*MCC* 172–75). These documents provide valuable information about the three heroes' ordeals and the continued resistance of the dyothelite party to the imperial heresy, but with one minor exception they give us no new insights into Maximus' character and convictions. The exception is in the letter of Anastasius the Apocrisiarius, where we learn that during his final confinement in Lazica, Maximus had seen "a divine vision," which correctly predicted the date on which God would "take him up" (Letter of Anastasius the Apocrisiarius to Theodosius of Gangra, §5, *MCC* 136–37). Aside from this detail, the other documents in the dossier may be passed over without further comment.

Maximus' Theological Convictions[54]

We are now in a position to summarize and analyze the religious convictions that animate the prison literature of Maximus the Confessor.

1. The Christian conscience is bound by the testimony of the apostles and the orthodox fathers, and by the doctrines and canons promulgated by the ecumenical councils

This is clearly a Type A conviction. For Maximus, a Christian is not free to believe whatever "religious" ideas happen to be intellectually convincing or emotionally appealing to her as an individual, if such ideas contradict the apostolic faith. Rather, her conscience is "formed" by her heartfelt profession of the Creed, her concurrence with the decrees of the ecumenical councils, her participation in the liturgical life of the

---

54. This section of the chapter owes much to Haldon, "Ideology and the Byzantine State," 87–91. Haldon describes the predicament faced by the emperor, who "had to maintain and promote a cult in which his dependence upon divine authority was explicit, and yet at the same time promote his own political authority, which was threatened and even by-passed by those very aspects of this cult or symbolic system which stressed divine support, divine mediation" (88). In contrast, my aim is to describe the religious convictions and practices that undergirded Maximus' resistance to an emperor who was faced by that predicament. See also Howard-Johnston, *Witnesses*, 157–62.

community, and her practice of the customary spiritual disciplines of the church (prayer, fasting, almsgiving, etc.). Accordingly, she is not free to accept any doctrinal innovations that contradict the "common faith" (cf. Titus 4), even if these are propounded by the state church. The church of the present age depends for its legitimacy in the eyes of God and commands the loyalty of its members only to the extent that it is demonstrably faithful to the teachings of the apostles, the fathers, and the councils. Thus, Maximus' conscientious objection to the policies of the imperial church was not driven by the idea that he had a right to his own opinion, but by his commitment to the orthodox faith.

2. Because Jesus Christ possesses both divine and human natures, and because the will is a function of the nature (not of the person), we must conclude that he possesses both divine and human wills

This, too, is a Type A conviction, a specification of Conviction No. 1. The claim that Christ possesses two natures in one person is an irrevocable and non-negotiable church dogma, having been "defined" by an ecumenical council. And the claim that Christ possesses two energies and two wills is a logical corollary of that dogma, because what we mean by "energy" and "will," respectively, are implicit in what we mean by "nature" (and *not* what we mean by "person"). Accordingly, this corollary, too, is irrevocable and non-negotiable. The fact that monenergism and monotheletism failed to heal the ecclesiastical and political schism in the Byzantine Empire was not the reason that Maximus opposed them. Rather, his opposition was theological: he saw that their moral psychology was confused, based on mistaken understandings of "nature" and "person," and therefore that they unwittingly negated the orthodox doctrines of the person and work of Christ. It is not that the Byzantine authorities *denied* the Definition of Chalcedon. They were as committed to it as Maximus was—or at least they understood themselves to be unable to rescind or amend it. But they were also desperate to reestablish communion with the monophysites of the East, who flatly rejected the Definition, but who wielded economic and military power which the empire needed. Hence the efforts of the Byzantine government to "interpret" the Definition in a way that honored the monophysites' concern to uphold the integral personhood of Christ. What Maximus saw—and what he saw to be implicit in what the Definition affirmed—was just what it was that had to be integrated: not only the divine and human natures, but also their respective natural properties, among which were their respective energies and wills.

3. Although a Christian state is responsible for supporting the orthodox church, it has no authority to promulgate new doctrines for the sake of political advantage or to force the state church to do so

This Type A conviction also follows from Conviction No. 1, but it brings into sharper relief the fact that the specific context in which Maximus bore Christian witness against the state was a state that professed to be Christian and collaborated closely with a state church. Now, even in "Christian" states such as seventh-century Byzantium, there is often some tension between the civil and ecclesiastical authorities. Caesaropapism is not theocracy. But the need for cooperation is evident to all, and therefore the danger of the cooptation of the church by the state is great. This was the situation in which Maximus found himself: he was a prominent citizen of an imperiled state, and a leading theologian of a coopted church. And he took his stand against both—against the state, for soliciting the church to make unwarranted adjustments to longstanding doctrine for the sake of perceived political advantage, and against the church for succumbing to state pressure. The fact that the government believed that the stability and security of the empire depended on such doctrinal adjustments could not persuade him to yield. He certainly did not advocate—and no one in that age could even have imagined—the "separation of church and state" for the sake of protecting either the purity of the church or the consciences of private citizens. Nor did he deny that such a thing as a "Christian empire" should exist. But he insisted that what keeps a Christian empire truly Christian is the fidelity of the state church to the apostolic faith, and on that basis, he could insist that ecclesiastical leaders must firmly resist the temptation to formulate Christian doctrine in accordance with perceived political expediency.

4. In a Christian state, principled resistance to state-sponsored heresy is the highest form of patriotism

This conviction belongs to Type B, despite following logically from Conviction No. 3. We saw that during his trial, Maximus was asked why he loved the Romans and hated the Greeks, to which he replied: "We have a commandment not to hate anybody. I love the Romans because we share the same faith, whereas I love the Greeks because we share the same language." This reply alerts us to the fact that Maximus was not only a Christian confessor but a loyal Byzantine citizen. Precisely because the Byzantine Empire thought of itself as a Christian state, its legitimacy depended on its fidelity to the Christian faith. Accordingly, a Byzantine citizen who had grounds for believing that his country had fallen into heresy was conscience-bound to protest, not only to preserve the purity of the faith, but also to defend the moral rationale upon which the state rested. The tragic irony of the seventh century was that the state's promulgation of heresy discredited it in the eyes of many of the faithful without bringing any political advantage. The lesson was that "arrangements" that jeopardize the faith ultimately jeopardize the interests of the state as well, and conversely, that conscientious opposition to such arrangements, while surely infuriating to the government, is the best way to serve the commonweal.

5. The Christian who resists the state and/or the state church must display humility and courtesy toward those civil and ecclesiastical officials who are sent to bring pressure to bear on his conscience

Type B. A conspicuous feature of the way in which Maximus interacts with the representatives of the government and the church who had been sent to secure his capitulation is his self-effacing, deferential, and scrupulously courteous attitude. He greets them with the titles of respect and the gestures of obeisance that are customary in Byzantine court etiquette, and when he is forced to say something that he knows will agitate them, he often humbly prostrates himself before them. He makes his arguments patiently and thoroughly, carefully marshaling the biblical and conciliar evidence in support of his case. He never loses his temper, even when they lose theirs, and he is as calmly unfazed by their threats as he is politely unmoved by their bribes. There is no reason to suspect that these courtesies are disingenuous, but it is important to recognize that they show that his dissent against state policy is not driven by disrespect for the emperor or the patriarch. Had he resisted the blandishments of his interrogators in a rude, angry, contemptuous, or rebellious spirit, he would have given them reasonable grounds to suspect that his refusal to "make the whole world happy" was driven by a desire to destabilize or delegitimize the government. He must have known that courtesies alone would not resolve the impasse. But he must also have realized that any high-handedness on his part would have caused them to dismiss his position as mere obstinacy or personal spleen and would have contradicted the gospel for which he contended. The monk's task is to be a source of edification *for* the world while still being a sign of contradiction *to* the world—and that requires, among other things, good manners and simple human decency.

But courtesy in bearing witness to the apostolic faith does not mean "flexibility" in formulating the doctrines constitutive of that faith. However courteously Maximus may have treated the imperial emissaries, his commitment to the apostolic faith, as elaborated by the post-Nicene Eastern fathers, was unshakable. Nothing would make him "flay his conscience" or equivocate on his principles for the sake of political or ecclesiastical "arrangements."

CHAPTER 3

Thomas More

Introduction

THE STORY OF THE career of Thomas More (1478–1535), of his eventual fall from royal grace, and of his arrest, imprisonment, trial, and execution, has fascinated students of English political and ecclesiastical history ever since those events occurred. Excellent biographies of More abound, and we leave it to those works to tell the full story.[1] But to understand the writings More produced during his imprisonment in the Tower of London, we must briefly narrate some of the most salient background events that eventuated in his arrest and that shaped the religious and political convictions that suffuse those writings and the rhetorical strategies he used to articulate them; we shall then offer a thumbnail sketch of his life and character.

Historical and Religious Background

On November 14, 1501, a marital alliance was struck between the Kingdoms of England and Spain. Arthur Tudor, Prince of Wales, eldest son of King Henry VII of England, married Princess Catherine of Aragon, the daughter of Queen Isabella I of Castile and King Ferdinand II of Aragon.

---

1. Those on which I have drawn most heavily are: Ackroyd, *Life*; Harpsfield, *Life and Death*; Marius, *More*; Martz, *Search*; Roper, *Life of More*, 195–254; Stapleton, *Life and Martyrdom*.

But the marriage lasted less than five months. On April 2, 1502, Prince Arthur died, having, according to Catherine's testimony, been unable to consummate the marriage. Henry, still hoping to maintain his advantageous alliance with Spain, determined to marry the newly widowed princess to his younger son, the future Henry VIII. Protracted negotiations between Henry VII and Ferdinand II ensued, pertaining to uncollected dowry payments and uncertainty about the legitimacy of any children who might be born to the couple. Moreover, the permissibility of the marriage was in doubt. Scripture is ambiguous on the matter. Leviticus 20:21 seems to forbid it: "If a man takes his brother's wife, it is impurity; he has uncovered his brother's nakedness; they shall be childless." But Deuteronomy 25:5 seems to command it: "When brothers reside together and one of them dies and has no son, the wife of the deceased shall not be married outside the family to a stranger. Her husband's brother shall go in to her, taking her in marriage and performing the duty of a husband's brother to her." Canon law followed Leviticus, and thus special papal dispensation was needed. Eventually, agreement for the marriage was reached by the monarchs, and approval was secured from Pope Julius II. Henry VII died on April 21, 1509, six weeks before the wedding, which took place on June 11, 1509. Two weeks later, on June 24, the joint public coronation of Henry VIII and Catherine was celebrated.

Securing the succession was one of the chief duties of a late medieval monarch, and because the civil wars and succession crises of the previous century remained fresh in English memory, this was a high priority for Henry. But the ominous warning of Leviticus 20:21 that a marriage between the brother of a deceased man and his widow would remain childless hovered over the young monarchs. A stillborn daughter was born to them in 1510; a son died in infancy in 1511; and two more stillbirths, both boys, occurred in 1513 and 1515. Finally, a daughter, Mary, arrived on February 18, 1516, and although she survived the perils of birth and infancy, she was not the male heir Henry longed for. After the stillbirth of another daughter in late 1518, Catherine was apparently unable to bear more children. But she remained steadfastly committed to her marriage and protective of her own royal dignity and of Mary's legitimacy. Henry, however, was determined to have a lawful male heir to succeed him, and that would require him to divorce Catherine and remarry.

In his early life, Henry had been a pious Catholic and staunch supporter of the papacy. In 1521, he had written a treatise titled *The Assertion of the Seven Sacraments* against Luther, for which Pope Leo X had awarded him the title, "Defender of the Faith." One of his research assistants was the young courtier Thomas More, and at one point Henry proposed forging a political alliance with the papacy. More disagreed, noting that the pope is "a prince . . . and in league with all other Christian princes," such that later events might render such an alliance disadvantageous to England. But Henry was adamant: "We are so much bounden unto the See of Rome that we cannot do too much honor unto it."[2] So, the religious scruples Henry began voicing in early 1527 about the legitimacy of his marriage in God's eyes seem sincere enough, and his later breach with Rome was not due to any longstanding antipathy to the papacy *per se*.

But rationalization with respect to his love life and cold-hearted pragmatism with respect to statecraft were undoubtedly factors in Henry's actions as well. His conscience certainly hadn't prevented him from taking several mistresses from as early as 1518, and by 1527 his amorous attentions were fixed upon one of the women at court, Anne Boleyn. But he faced grievous legal and political impediments to securing a divorce from Catherine before he could marry Anne. In early 1527, Henry had concluded an alliance with Pope Clement VII, King Francis I of France, and several Italian republics. The alliance sought to oppose the growing power of Charles V, King of Spain, Emperor of the Holy Roman Empire—and nephew to Catherine of Aragon. In May 1527, Charles's troops sacked Rome, disinterred and mutilated the body of Pope Julius II, and held Clement VII under house arrest. Thus, Clement was in no position to grant the annulment of the marriage of Henry and Catherine, given that Henry had recently allied himself against the now victorious Charles, given that Catherine was Charles's aunt, and given that the marriage he was being asked to annul had required special papal approval in the first place and had seemed amicable enough for many years.

The person who had managed Henry's foreign policy since 1515, and who, in 1527, was put in charge of the delicate negotiations to secure Henry's divorce, was Thomas Wolsey, archbishop of York and chancellor of England. But the political impasse Wolsey faced was insurmountable, and his diplomatic efforts came to naught. In mid-October 1529, Wolsey resigned the office of chancellor, though he retained his archepiscopal rank. But a little over a year later he was arrested for treason, having been accused by the Boleyn faction of stalling

---

2. Roper, *Life of More*, 235. More told this story in 1534 during one of the interrogations prior to his arrest.

the divorce proceedings several years earlier. He died on November 29, 1530, *en route* to London for trial.

On October 25, 1529, a week after Wolsey's fall, Henry appointed Thomas More as chancellor, knowing that More opposed the divorce, but exempting him from having to participate in the divorce proceedings, perhaps hoping that the promotion itself would induce More to change his mind on the matter.[3] A week later, on November 3, Henry summoned Parliament, which sat intermittently until 1536 and passed the foundational legislation for the English Reformation, which is summarized below. Henry also recruited into his service two men who would help him (as More would not) to secure his divorce from Catherine, to legitimize his marriage to Anne, to renounce the Church of England's obedience to the papacy, and to become, precisely *as* the king of England, the "supreme head" of the church of England. These were Thomas Cromwell, who entered Henry's Privy Council in late 1530, and who oversaw the legislative work of the Reformation Parliament; and Thomas Cranmer, who provided the theological justification for the divorce, and who, as archbishop of Canterbury, secured the acceptance by the English clergy of the schism from Rome.

Thomas More: A Brief Biography and Character Sketch

Let us now summarize the life of Thomas More, giving special attention to those characteristics of his personality that ultimately crystallized into the unshakable convictions that he delineated in his prison writings and for which he died. Even as a young adult, More came to be known as "the man for all seasons." The phrase itself goes back to a comment made by the Roman Emperor Tiberius and recorded by the historian Suetonius. Tiberius, a hard drinker, had spent two days and the intervening night with two boon companions and subsequently rewarded them with prestigious appointments in the government, calling them *iucundissimos et omnium horarum amicos*. Robert Graves translates this phrase as "good fellows at all times of the day or night,"[4] but it might more literally be rendered as "most pleasant friends at all hours." Desiderius Erasmus included this expression in his collection

---

3. Or so More's son-in-law and first biographer, William Roper, implies. See his *Life of More*, 217.

4. Suetonius, *Tiberius* 42, in *The Twelve Caesars*, 130.

of quotable quotes from antiquity, the *Adages* (1500), and subsequently cited it in his most famous book, *Praise of Folly* (1509). Erasmus wrote the latter work in More's home, and its Latin title, *Moriae Encomium*, is a pun on More's name. In the Prefatory Letter of the book, Erasmus says to More: "Your intelligence is too penetrating and original for you not to hold opinions very different from those of the ordinary man, but your manners are so friendly and pleasant that you have the rare gift of getting on well with all men at any time, and enjoying it."[5] Several years later, Robert Whittington alluded to Erasmus' description of More in his *Vulgaria* (1520), but gave it the pithy coinage that has since become familiar: "More is a man of an angel's wit and singular learning; I know not his fellow. For where is the man of that gentleness, lowliness, and affability? And as time requireth a man of marvelous mirth and pastimes; and sometimes of as sad gravity: a man for all seasons."[6]

In 1960, Robert Bolt used Whittington's rendering of the original Latin phrase as the title of his famous play on More's life and included Whittington's full remark about More, just quoted, as the epigraph to the playscript.[7] There is some irony here, because More was no tippler, as Tiberius' two dissipated comrades had been, nor was his meteoric rise in the English government due to crass nepotism. Indeed, in his personal habits More was abstemious and even ascetical.[8] Yet as the remarks by Erasmus and Whittington indicate, More was famous for his personal charm, his ready wit, his ability to adapt himself effortlessly to every situation, and his amicable relations with people of all ranks and stations in society. He knew just what to say and how to act on the most solemn or formal occasions, such as courtroom trials, international trade missions, and delicate diplomatic negotiations, but also on the most festive or informal ones, such as dinner parties and private conversations with

---

5. Erasmus, *Praise of Folly*, 4n4. See also Ackroyd, *Life*, 55. Ackroyd, 421n4, notes that Erasmus had also used the phrase *omnium horarum* of More in one of his letters. Erasmus published many of his letters, so it may have been from that letter, rather than the prefatory letter to *Praise of Folly*, that Wittington borrowed it.

6. I am indebted to my colleague, Dr. Owen Ewald, for his assistance in translating the various renderings of this adage. Ewald surmises that Whittington "seems to be influenced by the Greek *hora*, translated as 'season,' more often than the lookalike Latin word." Personal correspondence, April 6, 2024.

7. Bolt, *Man for All Seasons*, v.

8. Roper, *Life of More*, 224, tells us that he wore a hair shirt throughout his adult life—even during his time in prison—and that he sometimes flagellated himself with whips of knotted cords.

friends. Was he then a protean figure, a moral chameleon? Certainly not—and if he had been, he would not have died the death he did. A paragraph from the Preface to Bolt's play is worth adding to the character sketches from Erasmus and Whittington that we have just examined, as it beautifully captures that two-sidedness of More's character: his smooth adaptability to circumstances that required no moral compromise, and his utter inflexibility when his core convictions were tested.

> [More] became for me a man with an adamantine sense of his own self. He knew where he began and left off, what area of himself he could yield to the encroachments of his enemies, and to the encroachments of those he loved. It was a substantial area in both cases, for he had a proper sense of fear and was a busy lover. Since he was a clever man and a great lawyer, he was able to retire from those areas in wonderfully good order, but at length he was asked to retreat from that final area where he located his self. And there this supple, humorous, unassuming, and sophisticated person set like metal, was overtaken by an absolutely primitive rigor, and could no more be budged than a cliff.[9]

Both sides of More's character described by Bolt emerged early in his life and remained fixed throughout. The laudatory remarks by Erasmus and Whittington focus on his wit and affability because, in his early years, when they were writing about him, his social and professional obligations, far from *contradicting* his core convictions, were usually opportunities for *practicing* them. But even during his years as a young lawyer and courtier, those core convictions were evident to all, and it was precisely because of his deep piety and unimpeachable honesty that he attained professional eminence. In his later years, the obligations of his office and the expectations of his king put his convictions to the harshest test—but they held firm, and without souring his jocularity and charm.

More was born (most probably) on February 7, 1478, to John More, a prominent London lawyer, and Agnes Graunger More. As a child he attended St. Anthony's School in London, and between the ages of twelve and fourteen, he served as a page to John Morton, archbishop of Canterbury and chancellor of England. Morton loved the boy and prophesied a great future for him. In 1492, More "went up" to Oxford, where, as a budding devotee of Renaissance humanism, he studied Greek and Latin. He left in 1494 before taking his degree and began the study of law, first at the Inns of Chancery (1494–96) and then at

9. Bolt, *Man for All Seasons*, xii.

Lincoln's Inn, one of the Inns of Court (1496–1501). In 1501, he qualified as an "utter barrister." But his legal studies had not dampened his enthusiasm for "the new learning." In 1499, while still a law student, he entered the circle of leading London humanists, John Colet, William Grocyn, and Thomas Linacre, and first became acquainted with Desiderius Erasmus, who was visiting England at that time.

Humanism in northern Europe and England was devoted not only to the study of classical antiquity, but also to ecclesiastical reform. Colet electrified London in 1497 with a series of sermons on Paul's Letter to the Romans, using the latest philological techniques, and Erasmus' *Enchiridion of the Christian Knight* (1501) denounced commercialism, ceremonialism, and superstition, and called for the reform of church and society through the study of Scripture and the purification of personal and public morals. More made his own contributions to this program of reformist Christian humanism in his translations of several of the satires of Lucian (1506) and especially in his masterpiece, *Utopia* (1516). But for More, advocating the reform of the church was a sincere expression of his devotion to the faith, and from 1501 through 1504 he lived as a guest in the London monastery of the Order of Carthusians, an order famed for the severity of its asceticism and its unyielding fidelity to its founding principles and practices. More attended their liturgies and contemplated taking monastic vows and becoming a priest.[10]

Eventually, however, he decided to pursue his legal practice and to establish a family. In January 1505 he married Jane Colt, who bore him four children in the next six years. Shortly after her death in 1511, he married Alice Middleton, a propertied widow seven years his senior. They had no children of their own, but More was a loving stepfather to Alice's daughter by her previous husband, and she was a dedicated stepmother to his four children by Jane Colt. For many years, the More household was simultaneously a hive of religious devotion, a busy model of Renaissance educational pursuits, and a popular hub of London social life.

All the while, More's career as an attorney was thriving, and the string of offices to which he was appointed (some of which he held concurrently) is astonishing: under-sheriff of London (1510); master of requests, i.e., judge in the Court of Requests or "Poor Man's Court" (1514); member of diplomatic missions to Antwerp (1515), Calais (1517, 1520), Bruges (1521), and Cambrai (1529); member of the

---

10. For a general account of More's religious sensibilities and practices, see Marc'hadour, "Thomas More's Spirituality," 125–59.

Council of the Star Chamber (i.e., the King's Council) (1516); undertreasurer of the Exchequer (1521); knight of the realm (1521); knight of the shire (i.e., member of Parliament) for Middlesex and speaker of the House (1523); high steward of Oxford University (1524); high steward of Cambridge University (1525); chancellor of the Duchy of Lancaster (1525); member of the King's Privy Council (1526); and finally lord high chancellor (1529). Throughout his public career, More was known for his honesty and discretion; his complete immunity to bribes and coercion; his eloquence of speech; his swiftness in rendering judgment, together with an eagerness to settle lawsuits out of court whenever possible.[11] Yet his steady rise to public prominence and political power did not diminish his sense of humor. In 1525, a bawdy poem titled *The Twelve Mery Jests of Wyddow Edyth* was published: part of the action takes place in the More household, and the poem may have been composed by More himself. A year later, the London printer John Rastell, More's brother-in-law, published *A Hundred Merry Tales*: many of the stories were probably written by More himself.

Yet when Protestant ideas began infiltrating England from the Continent after 1517, More became one its most outspokenly dogmatic opponents. In addition to assisting Henry VIII with the *Assertio Septem Sacramentorum* (1521), More published in rapid succession the *Response to Luther* (1523), the *Letter to [Johannes] Bugenhagen* (1526/27), *A Dialogue Concerning Heresies* (1529; against William Tyndale), *Supplication of Souls* (1529; against Simon Fish), a *Letter against [John] Frith* (1532), *The Confutation of Tyndale's "Answer"* (1532), the *Debellation of Salem and Bizance* (1533), and *The Answer to a Poisoned Book* (1533). His language is often sharply satirical, sometimes ferocious, and occasionally crude or savage. In January 1530, barely two months after becoming chancellor, he issued a proclamation against heretics. He subsequently authorized their surveillance and arrest, and on occasion personally undertook their interrogation. He abstained from torturing the prisoners, but he acquiesced in—and perhaps approved of—the burning of several heretics in 1530–31. However, in March 1532 his persecution of Protestants was curtailed by Thomas Cromwell, the rising star in Henry's government, who found the anti-papal writings of some of them helpful in the furtherance of the king's efforts to secure his divorce from Catherine. More now realized that his refusal to endorse the divorce

---

11. The most exhaustive study of More's legal and political life remains Guy, *Public Career*.

proceedings, the restriction of his ability to protect and preserve the ancient faith, his increasing marginalization within the government, and the decline of his own physical health, rendered his position untenable. On May 16, 1532, he resigned his chancellorship, pledging to dedicate the rest of his life to his studies and religious devotions.

Perhaps the simplest way to illustrate the increasingly dire situation in which More found himself from early 1532 until his death on July 6, 1535, is to list some of the major parliamentary and ecclesiastical enactments that took place during that period. Also included in this list, and shown in italics, are two key dates in More's life during this period:

- February 1532: Parliament passes the *Act in Conditional Restraint of Annates*, restricting payment by the appointee to a church "benefice" of the first year's revenue from that post to the pope.
- March 18, 1532: The House of Commons publishes its *Supplication against the Ordinaries*, itemizing numerous grievances against the Church of England. The "ordinaries" (i.e., the English bishops) publish their *Answer* in late April 1532, promising not to promulgate or execute any ordinance unless by royal consent.
- May 15, 1532: The Convocation of Canterbury issues the *Submission of the Clergy*, accepting the right of the king to give consent to the passage of church laws. This is formally ratified into law by Parliament as the *Submission of the Clergy Act 1533* and given royal assent on March 30, 1534.
- May 16, 1532: *More resigns as Lord Chancellor. Henry tells More, "For your service you have done me, you will find me a good and gracious lord . . . ."*
- November 14, 1532: Henry VIII secretly marries Anne Boleyn. A second wedding ceremony, formalizing the marriage, takes place on January 25, 1533.
- March 30, 1533: Thomas Cranmer is consecrated as archbishop of Canterbury. (Pope Clement VII had officially approved Cranmer's appointment in hopes of placating Henry and preventing schism.)
- April 7, 1533: Parliament passes the *Act in Restraint of Appeals*, declaring that England was an ancient "empire," which owed no allegiance to foreign princes or potentates (including the pope), forbidding the appeal of the rulings made in English courts to "higher"

courts outside England (particularly Rome), and thereby giving the king of England supreme judicial power over the English church.

- May 23, 1533: Cranmer declares the marriage of Henry and Catherine null and void.

- May 28, 1533: Cranmer declares the marriage of Henry and Anne good and valid.

- June 1, 1533: Coronation of Anne Boleyn as Queen of England. (More's absence from the festivities infuriates Henry.)

- March 30, 1534: Parliament passes the *First Succession Act*, declaring Henry's marriage to Catherine of Aragon invalid, rendering their daughter Mary illegitimate, and establishing Elizabeth Tudor, who had been born to Queen Anne on September 7, 1533, as the rightful heir to the throne.

- March 30, 1534: Parliament passes the *Act Concerning Ecclesiastical Appointments and Absolute Restraint of Annates*, stipulating that English bishops would henceforth be selected by the king, and transferring the payment of annates to the crown.

- April 5, 1534: Convocation of Canterbury rules that no pope can set aside the divine law that forbade a man to marry his deceased brother's wife.

- April 12, 1534: *More is summoned to appear before a royal commission at Lambeth Palace and ordered to take the oath of succession. The next day he answers the summons but refuses to take the oath. He is held at Lambeth Palace until April 17, when he is imprisoned in the Tower of London.*

- November 3, 1534: Parliament passes the *Second Succession Act*, requiring all English citizens to swear to uphold the *First Succession Act* of March 30.

- November 3, 1534: Parliament passes the *[First] Act of Supremacy*, making the reigning monarch of England the "supreme head" of the Church of England. This act, like the *Acts of Succession*, included an oath, which all subjects of the Crown were required to swear.

- December 18, 1534: Parliament passes the *Treasons Act*, making it a capital offense to deny—or even "to maliciously will, wish, or desire to deny"—to members of the royal family their "dignity, title, or name of their royal estates."

- Late 1534/early 1535: Parliament issues an *Act of Attainder* against More "for intending to sow sedition" by his refusal to take the oath of succession.

As mentioned above, on April 13, 1534, More met with the royal commission that had been set up to assure universal compliance with the *First Succession Act*, which had been passed two weeks earlier. The commission included Thomas Cranmer, the archbishop of Canterbury; Thomas Cromwell, Henry's principal secretary; Thomas Audley, the new lord chancellor; and William Benson, the abbot of Westminster. A person's compliance with the act involved swearing an oath to honor and obey it, but oddly, the exact wording of the oath had not been specified in the text of the act itself.[12] When More read the act, he detected its legal ambiguity and refused to swear to it. As he later explained to his daughter, Margaret Roper, he told the commissioners: "My purpose was not to put any fault either in the act or any man that made it, or in the oath or any man that sware it, nor to condemn the conscience of any other man. But as for myself in good faith my conscience so moved me in the matter, that though I would not deny to swear to the succession, yet unto the oath that there was offered me I could not swear without the jeoparding of my soul to perpetual damnation."[13] Abbot Benson suggested that his personal conscience ought to yield to the collective wisdom of the Parliament, but More replied—in words reminiscent of things Maximus the Confessor had said on the evening after his first trial—that he was not "bounden to change [his] conscience, and conform it to the council of one realm, against the general council of Christendom."[14] These remarks did not satisfy the commission—indeed, they infuriated Cromwell, who by now was the virtual puppet master of Parliament. More was confined to Lambeth Palace for the next four days, in hopes that seeing other prominent subjects of the king cheerfully signing the oath would soften his resolve. It did not. On April 17, 1534, he was remanded to the Tower of London, where he was held until his death on July 6, 1535.

His cell was one of those reserved for prisoners of high rank. It was pentagonal in shape, had a vaulted ceiling nearly twenty feet high, and a floor space of about 360 square feet. Its slit windows overlooked the

---

12. Powicke, *Reformation in England*, 54n1; Ackroyd, *Life*, 378. This oversight was corrected on November 3, 1534, with the passage of the *Second Act of Succession*.

13. Letter to Margaret Roper, c. April 17, 1534, in More, *Last Letters*, 57–58.

14. Letter to Margaret Roper, c. April 17, 1534, in More, *Last Letters*, 60.

Thames River. It was furnished with a table, a chair, and a pallet bed. One of his servants was allowed to stay with him for the duration and attend to his needs.[15] A letter written to Margaret several weeks after his arrest carries an editorial superscription indicating that it had been "written with a coal,"[16] but within a short time he was allowed to have writing materials and books in his cell. These he put to extraordinarily good effect, writing two full-length books, the conclusion of a book he had begun earlier, and numerous letters, prayers, and devotional works. Writing was his consolation and pastime and the way he steeled his resistance to the pressures being brought to bear on his conscience.[17]

After the passage of the *Treasons Act* (December 18, 1534), which declared that opposition, even in one's private thoughts, to all the newly enacted royal prerogatives was "malicious" and therefore a capital offense, and the passage of the *Act of Attainder* against him personally (late 1534 or early 1535), which declared that his refusal to subscribe the oath of succession was intended "to sow sedition," More's properties were confiscated and he was placed in closer quarters in the Tower. On April 30, 1535, More was called before the royal commissioners. But whereas the earlier interrogations had focused on his views on the *Acts of Succession*, the emphasis now shifted to his views on the *Act of Supremacy*. Yet the moral validity of the *Acts of Succession*, if not their legality *per se*, depended on the *Act of Supremacy*. For only the church *could* sanction Henry's divorce and remarriage; only an autonomous English church *would* do so; and the autonomy of the English church presumed the royal supremacy. More replied to the commissioners' inquiry as follows:

> In good faith I had well trusted that the King's Highness would never have commanded any such question to be demanded of me, considering that I ever from the beginning well and truly from time to time declared my mind unto his Highness, and since that time I had, I said, unto your Mastership Master Secretary [i.e., Cromwell] also, both by mouth and by writing. And now I have in good faith discharged my mind of all such matters, and neither will dispute King's titles nor Pope's, but the King's true faithful subject I am and will be, and daily I pray for him and for all his, and for you all that are of his honorable

---

15. Ackroyd, *Life*, 365–66.
16. Letter to Margaret Roper, April/May 1534, in More, *Last Letters*, 62.
17. See Ahnert, "Writing in the Tower of London," 183–92; Zim, "Writing Behind Bars," 304–8.

Council, and for all the realm, and otherwise than thus I never intend to meddle.[18]

When pressed that his refusal to cooperate with the commission's demands was having the effect of stiffening public resistance to the recent *Acts*, More answered: "I am the King's true faithful subject and daily beadsman and pray for his Highness and all his and all the realm. I do nobody harm. I say none harm. I think none harm, but wish everybody good. And if this be not enough to keep a man alive, in good faith, I long not to live."[19]

On June 3, 1535, More was again summoned before the royal commission and asked to swear the oath to Henry's supremacy of the English church. Again, he refused, after which his reading and writing materials were taken from him—partly as punishment for his continuing refusal either to approve the succession and the supremacy or to explain his objections to them, and perhaps partly to hinder his preparations for the formal trial that was now inevitable. Nine days later, on June 12, three men appeared in his cell to remove them. While two of them packed up his library, the third, Richard Rich, solicitor general for England and Wales, an old acquaintance of More's, engaged him in lawyerly conversation. Several accounts of this conversation survive: they differ in some details but generally agree on what Rich later said at More's trial.[20] And the key point of Rich's (perjurious?) testimony was that More had claimed that Parliament had no more legal authority to declare the king of England the supreme head of "the church" than it did to declare God not to be God. Such a statement, if it had been made, would have violated the *Treasons Act* by implying that the king's supremacy was not legally valid.

It is doubtful that More allowed himself to be beguiled into making such a statement, having spent the previous two years keeping mum on such matters, and having long had a dim view of Rich's personal integrity. Moreover, even if More did make the remark, it was made during a discussion of hypothetical legal cases and was not intended as a direct avowal of his own opinion. Accordingly, it was not legally actionable. Furthermore, the question arises as to what More meant by "the church."

18. Letter to Margaret Roper, May 2 or 3, 1535 in More, *Last Letters*, 113.

19. Letter to Margaret Roper, May 2 or 3, 1535 in More, *Last Letters*, 114. Note: a "beadsman" is someone who prays for another. See the Glossary in More, *Last Letters*, 195.

20. Roper, *Life*, 244–48; Harpsfield, *Life*, 53 (abstracted from Roper); Linder, "Trial of Thomas More."

The English Parliament might grant Henry the headship of the church in England, but it obviously had no jurisdiction over the church universal. Thus, if More was referring to the latter, he was simply asserting that Parliament lacked a degree of legal competency that no one thought it possessed, and so his assertion could not be deemed treasonous. But whether Rich deliberately misrepresented what More actually said or misconstrued what he meant, his testimony provided the evidence that Henry and Cromwell needed to convict him.

More's trial took place on July 1, 1535. There were four main counts against him. The first three were soon dropped; the fourth, on which the court proceeded, was that during More's conversation with Richard Rich on June 12, 1535, More had admitted that the king might be accepted as the *de facto* head of the church in England but had denied Parliament's competence to award him that title. The evidence for this depended entirely on Rich's testimony, as the other two men who were in More's cell when the fateful conversation took place pled that they were too busy with More's books to pay it close attention. More denied both the accuracy of Rich's testimony and its pertinence as evidence of his malice against the king. He insisted that he had never voiced his actual views on the competence of Parliament to grant Henry's status as head of the church in England or, therefore, on the consequent validity or invalidity of that headship. But the jury found Rich's testimony credible and declared that, irrespective of the context of the conversation, the only "church" which had any bearing on the case was the English church. It therefore found More guilty of denying the king's ecclesiastical authority.[21]

As the jury was about to render judgment, More asked permission to address the court. He began by stating unequivocally the belief that he had so long kept to himself, namely that "no temporal prince" might presume to arrogate to himself the "spiritual preeminence" which "Christ himself had given only to the See of Rome."[22] He then pointed out that the recent parliamentary legislation pertaining to the English church was directly contrary to various unrepealed laws of England—including Magna Carta itself—and to the king's own

---

21. See Derrett, "Trial of Sir Thomas More," 449–77, for a thorough analysis of the indictment, the evidence, the courtroom interactions, and the ultimate significance of the trial for English jurisprudence. See also Fenlon, "Thomas More and Tyranny," 453–76; Hauerwas and Shaffer, "Hope Faces Power," 456–79; "The Paris Newsletter Account of More's Trial and Execution."

22. Roper, *Life*, 248.

coronation oath. And he reminded the court of the historic dependency of the English church upon the papacy, a dependency that stretched back to Pope Gregory I and his emissary, Augustine of Canterbury, in the seventh century. Although More did not name Henry in his speech, the clear implication of all this was that the king ought to have known better than to detach the English church from papal obedience, when he himself had once highly honored the pope and when the pope had once highly honored him as the "Defender of the Faith."

More's own attitude toward the papacy had matured over the years—and as he was quick to point out, it was King Henry himself who first convinced him, as early as 1521, that the primacy of the papacy was "begun by the institution of God."[23] By 1534 he certainly accepted the divine origin and primacy of the papacy,[24] but his chief reason for doing so seems to have been a deep concern for the spiritual unity and institutional indissolubility of "Christ's universal Catholic Church," of whom the pope was the both the symbol and the guarantor.[25] He spoke little about the personal prerogatives and worldly powers of the pope himself. And when reprimanded by Cromwell for "stiffly sticking" to his private convictions instead of going along with the "bishops, universities, and best learned" of England in regards to the royal supremacy, More appealed not directly to the papacy but rather to the general testimony of the bishops and saints of the church—who greatly outnumbered the royal apologists of England—as the shaper of his Christian conscience: "But if I should speak of those which already be dead, of whom many be now holy saints in heaven, I am very sure it is the far greater part of them that, all the while they lived, thought in this case that way that I think now. And therefore am I not bound . . . to conform my conscience to the council of one realm against the general council of Christendom."[26]

These arguments failed to sway the court, and the chief justice of the King's Bench, Sir John Fitzjames, cautiously, perhaps reluctantly, concurred with the jury's prior verdict: "My lords all, by Saint Julian . . . I must needs confess that if the act of Parliament be not unlawful, then is not the indictment in my conscience insufficient." Cromwell was apparently not satisfied with this string of qualifications and double negatives and registered a far more pointedly worded verdict. More was granted

23. *Letter to Cromwell*, March 5, 1534, in More, *Last Letters*, 53.
24. Ackroyd, *Life*, 228, 270–71; Marius, *More*, 457.
25. Roper, *Life*, 248.
26. Roper, *Life*, 249–50.

the privilege of dying by beheading, which was regarded as the least brutal of the various means of executing someone for treason. With his case now definitively lost, More made one last short speech:

> More have I not to say, my lords, but like as the blessed apostle Saint Paul, as we read in the Acts of the Apostles, was present and consented to the death of Saint Stephen, and kept their clothes that stoned him to death, and yet be they now both twain holy saints in heaven, and shall continue there friends forever, so I verily trust, and shall therefore right heartily pray, that though your lordships have now here in earth been judges to my condemnation, we may yet hereafter in heaven merrily all meet together, to our everlasting salvation.[27]

In these few words, More limns what I shall call his "eschatology of communal merriment," and shows that the two sides of his character—his human warmth and his serene faith—have been fused and thoroughly integrated.

We observe this same integration of character on the day of his death, July 6, 1535, as he was being conducted from his prison cell to the place of his execution. To Sir Thomas Pope, a member of the King's Council and More's own "singular friend," who was responsible for conveying Henry's orders about the execution and was moved to tears by More's composure, More remarked: "Quiet yourself, good Master Pope, and be not discomforted. For I trust that we shall, once in heaven, see each other full merrily, where we shall be sure to live and love together in joyful bliss eternally." To Sir Edmund Walsingham, the official from the Tower who had escorted him to the steps of the scaffold, he quipped: "I pray you, Master Lieutenant, see me safe up and, for my coming down, let me shift for myself." And, after putting his head on the block and commending himself to God in prayer, he "turned to the executioner and with a cheerful countenance spake thus to him: 'Pluck up thy spirits, man, and be not afraid to do thine office. My neck is very short. Take heed therefore though strike not awry, for saving of thine honesty.'"[28] We see

---

27. Roper, *Life*, 250. Harpsfield, *Life*, 57, who depends heavily on Roper, quotes this speech verbatim, but adds a final sentence: "And thus I desire almighty God to preserve and defend the King's Majesty and to send him good counsel." This is probably Harpsfield's own composition, but even if fictive, it underscores More's unswerving devotion to his king and wryly suggests that Henry has become the victim of the foolish fanaticism of his courtiers.

28. Roper, *Life*, 253–54. On August 4, 1535, *The Paris Newsletter* ran a brief article on More's trial and execution. It states that his last words were the prayer that those

here gallows humor of the most exquisite kind—levity about the force of gravity that is about to claim his severed head—combined with sincere, if delicately ironic, compassion for an old friend performing a hated task and for the axman performing his grisly duty. These pithy and poignant comments serve as interpretive clues to his prison writings.

The Prison Literature of Thomas More

In studying the surviving prison literature of Perpetua and Maximus, we were able to bore deeply into a few relatively short texts. This approach will not be possible with the Tower writings of Thomas More. More was a voluminous writer throughout his adult life, and his literary output did not slacken during his incarceration. Thirteen letters (or fourteen, as explained below) to his family and friends from this time survive; he also wrote two full-length books, and an array of prayers, meditations, self-exhortations, miscellaneous comments on Scripture, and notations in the margins of his prayer book.[29] A close reading of all this material will be impossible. Instead, our aim will be to highlight some of the main religious convictions that animate these writings and the rhetorical strategies he used to keep his spirits up, to maintain his resistance to the relentless efforts by the royal commission to cajole, tempt, or threaten him into capitulation, and to express his confidence that despite his trials and sufferings, he was safe in the hands of a gracious God.

---

attending his death would "pray to God to give the King good counsel" and the affirmation "that he died [the King's] good servant, and God's first" (§7). None of the earliest biographies of More—Roper (1557), Harpsfield (1557/58), and Stapleton (1588)—quotes this line, nor does the *Newsletter* mention the witty remarks recorded by the earliest biographers. The precise lines between historical fact, family lore, and hagiographical embroidery are impossible to draw at this point, and I shall proceed on the assumption that More *did* say everything that he is recorded by the various earliest sources to have said, even though none of those sources ascribes all of those sayings to him.

29. More also wrote, in Latin, a *Treatise to Receive the Blessed Body of Our Lord, Sacramentally and Virtually Both* during his incarceration (see More, *Complete Works*, 13:189–204). Although the *Treatise* is classified among More's "Tower Works," and although it illuminates his sacramental piety, we shall not deal with it here. It appears to have been intended as the third section of his *Treatise on the Passion*, which he wrote in English prior to his arrest, and tells us little (at least directly) about the convictions for which he was incarcerated or his experience of incarceration, which are our primary concerns here. See Martz, Introduction to More, *Complete Works*, 12:lxxix–lxxxvi, and Haupt, Introduction to More, *Complete Works*, 13:cxxxvi–cxl.

Prison Correspondence, April 1534–July 1535

Alvaro de Silva's splendid edition of *The Last Letters of Thomas More* (hereafter cited in-text as *LL*) includes twenty-four documents, and we shall follow his numbering.[30] The letters are arranged chronologically, though some of the dates of composition are approximate, having been determined from internal evidence by More's early editors. Twenty-three were written in English and one in Latin. Nos. 7, 10, 23, and 24, all quite short, are said in the editorial superscriptions to have been "written with a coal," indicating that at the time of their composition More lacked proper writing materials. Of these, Nos. 7 and 10 were written at the very beginning of his time in lockup,[31] and Nos. 23 and 24 within a day or two of his death. Nos. 1–5 are not "prison literature" at all, having been written before More's arrest. In these communications—four of them to Cromwell and one to King Henry—More tries to allay the suspicions that were steadily mounting against him.[32] Eight of the letters (Nos. 6–8, 16, 17, 20, 22, and 24) are addressed to More's eldest daughter, Margaret Roper, detailing his own situation and offering consolation to his frightened family. One short note (No. 10) was sent, via Margaret, to "all his friends," requesting material assistance for himself during his incarceration. Two letters (Nos. 13 and 14) were sent to Dr. Nicholas Wilson, a fellow prisoner in the Tower; one (No. 19) went to Stephen Leder, a

---

30. The text of the letters in this collection is "a modernized version of the edition by Elizabeth F. Rogers, *The Correspondence of Sir Thomas More*" (*LL* viii). De Silva often allows Tudor terms that would be unfamiliar or confusing to modern English readers to stand, but then supplies a modern English equivalent in a footnote. In several quotations below, I have placed de Silva's footnoted rendering in brackets beside More's original.

31. Letters No. 6, 8, and 9 seem too lengthy and carefully composed to have been scrawled on scrap paper with a bit of charcoal. Yet No. 6 was certainly written *before* No. 7. And No. 10 *may* have been written at the same time as No. 7 but incorrectly sequenced by the editors, so that it belongs before Nos. 8 and 9. If so, then it seems that More had writing materials at the time of his confinement in the Tower, which were removed shortly thereafter, but then quickly returned to him, only to be removed again over a year later by Richard Rich and his two cronies.

32. This fact reminds us that, far from courting martyrdom, More did everything he could, short of violating his conscience, to avoid it. Between the time of his resignation from the chancellorship and throughout his months in the Tower, he avoided saying or doing anything that could be held against him as treasonous, and he used every legal means at his disposal to be acquitted of that charge. See Marius, *More*, 470–71 (cf. 485–86 and 517–18), who expatiates on the "insoluble mystery" that hangs over More's martyrdom, that is, on how much he did to avoid it, and yet how carefully he prepared himself to face it, once he was convinced that it was inevitable.

Carthusian priest, denying the rumor that he, More, had surrendered to the commission's pressure; and one (No. 23), composed in Latin, was sent to the Italian banker Antonio Bonvisi, expressing gratitude for their long friendship and for Bonvisi's steadfast and generous support. Finally, the collection includes six letters written by other members of More's family to various recipients: two (Nos. 9 and 15) by Margaret Roper to More, offering consolation; one (No. 11) by More's step-daughter, Alice Alington, to Margaret, explaining a disturbing conversation she had had recently with Thomas Audley, the new lord chancellor; one (No. 12) by Margaret (but probably co-authored or ghost-written by More himself) replying to Alice Alington; and two (Nos. 18 and 21) by More's wife, Lady Alice More, one to Cromwell and one to King Henry, defending her husband's innocence and soliciting material support after the confiscation of family property. We will make no further reference to the seven letters that Thomas and Alice More wrote to Cromwell and Henry, or to More's letters to Wilson, Leder, Bonvisi, and "all his friends." These express friendly consolation, or self-exoneration, or the need for assistance, depending on the addressee and the occasion, but tell us little about More's religious convictions or carceral experience. Our primary focus will be on More's exchanges with Margaret Roper and Alice Alington, which elucidate his personal piety, his defense of the inviolability of conscience, and his eschatology.

The first letter we shall consider, Letter No. 6, was written by More to his daughter Margaret on April 17, 1534, the day of his imprisonment in the Tower (*LL* 57–61). It gives a detailed account of his interrogation at Lambeth Palace four days earlier, and recounts the various tactics used by the members of the royal commission to induce him to swear the oath of succession: First, they offered him friendly words of persuasion; then they applied peer pressure by showing him a list of the "names of the lords and the commons which had [already] sworn." Next, they forced him to watch a group of those who had already signed the oath engaging in light-hearted, self-congratulatory conversation (More calls the scene a "pageant"). Finally, they stoop to furious browbeating. But More resolutely refuses to sign the oath as it had been formulated in the *Second Act of Succession*, although he does make three offers: first, to "swear to the succession itself" (which was *fait d'accompli* by this point); second, to explain in writing his refusal to swear the oath, if doing so would not "offend his Highness, nor put [himself] in the danger of any of his statues"; and third, presuming he were allowed to fulfill the first two conditions, even to swear the principal oath itself, if anyone could explain its provisions in a way that "satisfied his conscience." But, as he tells Margaret, when the commissioners refused these offers, he brought the interrogation to an end in these words:

> Surely as to swear to the succession I see no peril, but I thought and think it reason, that to mine own oath I look well myself, and be of counsel also in the fashion, and never intended to swear for a piece ["part"], and set my hand to the whole oath. Howbeit (as help me God), as touching the whole oath, I never withdrew any man from it, nor never advised any to refuse it, nor never put, nor will, any scruple in any man's head, but leave every man to his own conscience. And methinketh in good faith that so were it good reason that every man should leave me to mine. (*LL* 61)

More's second surviving prison letter to Margaret Roper (No. 7), is dated "April-May? 1534" by More's early editors (*LL* 62–63). As noted above, it is quite short and is one of those "written with a coal." More writes to assure his daughter—and, through her, his whole family, and his former secretary, John Harris—that he is "in good health of body, and in good quiet of mind," and that he has "no more of worldly things" than he needs or desires (apart, perhaps, from writing materials, which must have been given him shortly thereafter). He exhorts his family "to make . . . merry in the hope of heaven," prays that Christ will keep him "continually true faithful and plain," and indicates that he has no desire to live a long life. But the fact that he is "content to go . . . tomorrow," if need be, and that he does not wish anyone to "have a fillip" ["flick a finger"] on his account does not imply that he is depressed or suicidal. These sentiments, conventional as they may seem for someone trying to convince his family not to worry overmuch about him, are significant for our purposes, as they help elucidate More's eschatology. He understands "merriment," not only as something that the residents of heaven enjoy together, but also as something that believers here below may and should enjoy together now. Merrymaking is a Christian duty, and no less serious a duty for being a pleasure and a blessing. Indeed, it is never more important a duty to perform than when one is facing tribulation, because it implies that the state of a Christian's soul is finally governed not by one's immediate earthly circumstances but by one's trust in God's promises. Letter No. 7 thus adumbrates some of the themes he will develop at great length in his *Dialogue of Comfort*, which he writes later that year.

Letter No. 8, also addressed to Margaret and dated May 1534, must have been drafted shortly after No. 7, and presumably after More had a stock of quills, ink, and stationery (*LL* 64–65). But it is much darker in tone, for he is responding to a "lamentable letter" that he has just received from her, in which she urges him to take the oath. More avers that he no longer cares much what other people think of him, but he cares greatly that his family continue to support his "respect unto [his] own soul." And that means they must respect his decision not to take the oath, and not to tell anyone why he will not take the oath. Yet he acknowledges the terrible predicament he and they are in. For although his refusal to say why he would not swear the oath may provide some protection from being charged outright with treason, his very refusal to swear it might itself eventually be deemed treasonous. That, in turn, could put his family in danger—a thought which is a "deadly grief" to him. But he ventures to hope that King Henry will eventually show "tender favor" to his family and come to see that his refusal to swear the oath does not reflect any treasonous thoughts but is due to his fear that violating his conscience would incur God's displeasure and thus disqualify him from "the endless bliss of heaven."

Shortly after receiving this letter from her father, Margaret replied with Letter No. 9 (*LL* 66–67). She never directly apologizes for her earlier efforts to convince him to take the oath. Instead, she asserts in rather fulsome language the "comfort" that she and the whole family had always taken in his "life past and godly conversation, and wholesome counsel, and virtuous example," and were now taking in the "continuance of the same, but also a great increase by the goodness of our Lord to the great rest and gladness of your heart devoid of all earthly dregs, and garnished with the noble vesture of heavenly virtues" (*LL* 66–67).

Letter No. 11 was written by More's stepdaughter, Alice Alington, to his daughter, Margaret Roper, on August 17, 1534 (*LL* 69–71). It was prompted by a disturbing conversation she had had recently with Thomas Audley, the lord chancellor. Audley had visited the Alington estates, and this was initially deemed a good sign, for it hinted that he was positively disposed toward More. But Audley's bonhomie appears to have been, if not overtly disingenuous, at least part of a strategy to beguile More's family into pressuring him to capitulate, and thus to save the government, and More himself, a great deal of trouble. To convey this advice (or warning), Audley tells Alice Alington two Aesop-like fables. The first is intended to emphasize the futility of opposing inflexible moral principle to the exigencies of Tudor *Realpolitik*. The second is meant to illustrate how one who professes to follow one's conscience can easily "interpret" the facts of a morally problematic situation in such a way as to justify one's self-interest without admitting to oneself that one has really surrendered one's principles. And because, for Audley, acting in one's self-interest is inevitable, one would be more prudent, and in a sense even more honest, simply to surrender one's principles whenever they conflict with one's self-interest, instead of indulging in pointless self-deception. After telling the first of these fables, and before telling the second, Audley comes straight to the point: "I would not have your father so scrupulous of his conscience" (*LL* 70). Alice is understandably alarmed, and perhaps a bit scandalized, at all this, and is unsure how to answer. But she immediately realizes how important it is for More to hear what has transpired, and because Margaret alone of the More family has permission to visit him in the Tower, Alice recounts Audley's ominous message in a letter to her. She closes with a pious exhortation that her stepfather should trust God as "the comforter of all sorrows, [who] will not fail to send his comfort to his servants when they have most need" (*LL* 71).

Letter No. 12, which purports to be Margaret's reply to Alice, but which, as its superscription suggests, and as most modern authorities agree, More himself largely coauthored, is dated by the editors as August 1534 (*LL* 72–89).[33] It is one of the most important documents for our purposes in all of More's prison correspondence, for its powerful defense of the inviolability of the conscience and for the insights it yields into the state of his mind four months into his incarceration. In the opening paragraph, Margaret (as putative sole author) tells Alice that she had shown their father her letter, partly to assure him of Alice's "loving labor taken for him," and partly to warn him, on the basis of Audley's message, "that if he stand still in this scruple of his conscience (as it is at the leastwise called by many that are his friends and wise) all his friends that seem most able to do him good either shall finally forsake him, or peradventure not be able to do him any good at all" (*LL* 72). There is plenty in the letter to indicate how much More has appreciated the good service that Alice has done him in prudently conveying Audley's message and in counseling him to rely upon God's comfort. And he gives thanks for the fact that she has proven herself, not only in this case, but over many years, to be as devoted to him

---

33. For details on its authorship and contents, see Ackroyd, *Life*, 377; Curtwright, "More as Author," 1–27; de Silva, editor's note in More, *Last Letters*, 166; Marius, *More*, 466–68; Martz, Introduction to More, *Complete Works*, 12:lxi.

as his natural children by his first wife (*LL* 75). But most of the letter is Margaret's recounting of her father's response to Audley's complaint that More is "so scrupulous of his conscience." To unpack More's response to Audley's charge, we must make a brief foray into the use of the words "scruple" and "conscience" in Tudor English.

In classical Latin, the word *scrupus* meant "sharp stone." Its diminutive form in late Latin, *scrupulus*, meant "pebble," but also took on a moral connotation, referring to a nagging worry or doubt, perhaps on analogy with the experience of getting a piece of grit in one's shoe.[34] The word passed into medieval French as *scrupule*, which also could mean either a stone or a moral qualm. The word apparently entered English, via French, in the fourteenth century as "scruple," though in its oldest known uses it carries yet another shade of meaning, that of a small unit of weight, such as an apothecary's measure. According to the *Oxford English Dictionary*, its earliest known appearances as a moral term in published English sources occur in 1526 and 1534—and the second of these is the very letter we are presently discussing, where it refers to a worry that greatly exceeds the objective seriousness of a possible moral failing.[35] Thus, Audley regards More's refusal to swear to the succession and supremacy as absurd—a gesture of negligible moral significance which is causing political trouble for the government and unnecessary suffering for himself. More will reply that in expecting him to swear to what he does not believe—especially when he has not committed treason either by publicly denying the succession or the supremacy or by inducing others to do so—the government is asking him to destroy himself by violating his own conscience.

The word "conscience," too, requires some careful lexicographical explanation. According to C. S. Lewis's detailed study of the complex and nuanced history of the term, "conscience" had two distinct senses in

---

34. *Cassell's Latin Dictionary*, 540, s.v. *scrupus* and *scrupulus*.

35. *Oxford English Dictionary*, s.v. scruple (noun1) and scruple (noun2). The citation given in the entry for noun2 reads: "'Though men... say it is no conscience but a foolish scruple.' T. More, *Wks*, 1435/1." The reference is to More, *English Works*, which was published in 1557 by More's nephew, William Rastell, during the reign of Queen Mary I. In that edition, Alice Alington's letter to Margaret Roper of August 17, 1534, is printed on pp. 1433-34, and Margaret's reply on pp. 1433-43. The latter letter also includes the phrases "but a scruple" and "right simple scruple," both referring to a qualm of conscience disproportionate to the actual gravity of a putative sin or crime. I am indebted to Steve Perisho for his assistance in locating this information.

early Tudor English.[36] The first sense, which Lewis calls the "indicative," simply referred to an opinion that a person might hold. A good example of the term being used in the indicative sense is the hypercautious judgment rendered by Chief Justice Fitzjames during More's trial: "If the act of Parliament be not unlawful, then is not the indictment in my conscience insufficient." As Lewis states, "Fitzjames is giving a judge's reply; *conscience* must mean 'opinion.'"[37] This sense of the term is now obsolete. But the second, or "imperative," sense is in common use today. It refers to a person's "moral compass," her capacity to differentiate right from wrong, good from evil, virtue from vice. In Catholic moral theology, for one to act voluntarily against the dictates of one's conscience—say, for the sake of personal advantage—is to commit grave sin, or as More puts it in Letter No. 6, to "jeopard one's soul unto damnation" (*LL* 58). As Lewis points out, in the prison literature of Thomas More, the indicative and imperative senses of conscience often mix and interpenetrate. We have already seen the example Lewis cites of such a "mixed usage." At his trial, when More states that he is "not bounden to change [his] conscience, and conform it to the council of one realm, against the general council of Christendom,"[38] he seems to be using the term both in reference to a religious conviction that he holds and in reference to an obligation that he cannot voluntarily evade. He regards the pope of Rome as the head of the universal church and therefore denies that Henry can be the rightful head of some schismatic "church of England." But the government is demanding that he "conform his conscience" (i.e., change his mind) about this and signify his conformity by swearing the oaths of succession and supremacy. Yet to do so would be to forswear himself; it would be to break God's law to escape punishment for breaking a human law. As Lewis remarks: "In this passage the indicative (Henry is not the head of the Church in England) and the imperative (Thou shalt not forswear thyself) are so closely linked both in logic and in emotion that the double meaning is almost inevitable."[39]

---

36. Lewis, *Studies in Words*, 181–213. See also Cummings, "Conscience and the Law in Thomas More," 463–85.

37. Lewis, *Studies in Words*, 203–4.

38. See Roper, *Life*, 249–50, which Lewis is following. According to Letter No. 6, *LL* 60, More had made an almost identical comment during his interrogation by the royal commissioners on the eve of his arrest.

39. Lewis, *Studies in Words*, 203.

In Letter No. 12, and indeed, throughout More's prison correspondence, "conscience" usually bears both the indicative and the imperative senses. That is, when More speaks of his conscience, he is speaking of religious convictions that he holds on good authority and for good reason, and that he feels duty-bound not to surrender.[40] As we are using the term in this volume, "convictions" are identity-shaping opinions: to alter (or to be coerced by someone else into altering) a conviction is to become, in an important sense, a different person.[41] Accordingly, one has a duty to oneself not to alter one's convictions—and therefore one's very selfhood—unless one has overriding rational grounds for doing so. An opinion that one would willingly change for the sake of short-term advantage would not count *as* a conviction. Conversely, there is something morally admirable about the willingness to change an identity-shaping conviction if—but *only* if—overriding evidence is available to warrant the change. And as we have noted, More told the government that he *would* swear the oaths *if* anyone could dispel his objections with rationally persuasive and legally relevant evidence.

But given his "adamantine sense of himself," More's deep-rooted convictions were not easily malleable. And whereas Audley supposed that More was being foolish for allowing himself to be imprisoned for the sake of a "scruple," More now replies that failing to obey his conscience—grounded as it is in the collective wisdom of the church—would be a far greater foolishness, because it would imperil his soul. On that basis, he deconstructs the two fables that Audley had told Alice Alington and then proceeds to tell a tale of his own—really an allegory of his own present situation. It is the story of an "honest man" by the name of Company, who was serving on a jury of twelve in a trial of an alleged criminal. Company said little during the jury's deliberations—until, when the rest were ready to render verdict, he informed them that he disagreed with their view of the case. The other jurors tried to sway him for the sake of "good company." But he turned their pun upon his name upside down. He told them that God would eventually send them to heaven for voting their conscience—but would send him to hell for voting against his conscience for the sake of "good company." And if Company could not join his fellow jurors in heaven, would they willingly join him in hell "for company's sake?" (*LL* 79–81). Then comes the moral of the story. He tells Margaret: "He that

---

40. On More's use of the term "conscience," see also de Silva's introduction to More, *LL* 8–13, and Cummings, "Conscience and the Law in Thomas More," 463–85.

41. See Introduction above.

thinketh against the law, neither may he swear that law lawfully made, standing his own conscience to the contrary, nor is bounden upon pain of God's displeasure to change his own conscience therein, for any particular law made anywhere, other than by the general council or by a general faith grown by the working of God universally through all Christian nations" (*LL* 83). More will make no attempt to sway his fellow citizens to his view of the succession and the supremacy, but neither will he be swayed by political pressure to contradict the *sensus fidelium*.

To capture the full significance of Letter No. 12, it is important to observe that More is not merely debating with Audley, via his daughters, about the claims of conscience. He is also debating with his own family, who cannot yet reconcile themselves to the sacrifices he is making for his conscientious objection to the oaths. As we have seen, he rebuts Audley's arguments with withering, if somewhat archly expressed, logic; but he responds to his family's anguished love with gentle humor. He wryly compares Alice with the serpent in the garden and Margaret with "mistress Eve" for tempting him "to swear against his conscience, and so send him to the devil" (*LL* 73–74). Later he cracks a joke at his own expense: "[What] this name of mine ... signifieth in Greek, I need not tell you. But I trust my Lord reckoneth me among the fools, and so reckon I myself, as my name is in Greek. And I find, I thank God, causes not a few, wherefore I so should in very deed" (*LL* 77). Later still, when telling the story of Company, he gently mocks his own legal profession—and the legal proceedings being used against him—by referring to "a quest of twelve men, a jury as I remember they call it, or else a perjury" (*LL* 80). And he ends the letter with his signature eschatology: "And I right heartily pray both you and them [i.e., his family and friends], to serve God and be merry and rejoice in him. And if anything hap to me that you would be loath, pray to God for me, but trouble not yourself: as I shall full heartily pray for us all, that we may meet together once in heaven, where we shall make merry for ever, and never have trouble after" (*LL* 89). Both sides of More's character are on full display in this letter.

Letter No. 12 also contains a remark that illuminates More's attitude toward his imprisonment: "As yet [the king] hath taken from me nothing but my liberty (wherewith, as help me God, his Grace hath done me so great good by the spiritual profit that I trust I take thereby, that among all his great benefits heaped upon me so thick, I reckon upon my faith my prisonment even the very chief)" (*LL* 88). Of course, More may have written this in the expectation that it would be read by the authorities. If so, then it may be intended not only as an honest report of his mental state but also as evidence that he bears no malice toward his king. Nevertheless, the full paragraph in which this sentence appears is an extended confession of his "lewdness" [wickedness] in which he interprets his incarceration not as punishment for a crime but as a self-imposed penance for his sins, serving "for release of my pain in purgatory" (LL 88).

In Letter No. 16, addressed to Margaret and dated simply 1534 (*LL* 99–103), More briefly reiterates some of the major themes that he had so fully elaborated in Letter No. 12, but the focus here is his relationship with King Henry. This leads him to clarify two points that had not come out so clearly in the earlier correspondence. First, More insists that he remains Henry's loyal subject, despite his inability to endorse the new laws that have redefined royal authority. He expresses this terrible conundrum with lapidary clarity: "Before the world . . . my refusing of this oath is accounted an heinous offense, and my religious fear toward God is called obstinacy toward my Prince" (*LL* 100). Although the exact date of this letter is uncertain, it appears to have been written in late autumn 1534, by which time More fully expected to be executed for his stand. Second, he acknowledges the conflict in his own soul between his fear of death and his devotion to duty, but he thanks the Spirit for granting him "mastery" over his fear and for enabling him to see his situation as "a case in which a man may lose his head and yet have none harm, but instead of harm inestimable good at the hand of God" (*LL* 102).

Letter No. 17 is also addressed to Margaret and dated by the early editors simply to 1534, presumably rather late in the year (*LL* 104–7). It is More's reply to a letter she had recently sent to him. Her letter has not survived, but we know its essential content from the quotes he includes in his response and from his extensive interaction with the issues she has raised. Margaret is no longer playing "mistress Eve" by urging her father to save himself. Rather, she is resigned to the fact that his stand makes his eventual execution increasingly likely, and shares with him her "frailty," that is, her anguish and fear. He, in turn, says little more about his conscientious opposition to the new laws; he dwells, instead, on his own "faint heart." One sentence from his letter encapsulates this epistolary exchange: "That you fear your own frailty, Marget, nothing misliketh ["displeases"] me. God give us both twain the grace to despair of our own self, and whole to depend and hang upon the hope and strength of God" (*LL* 105).

Nearly half a year elapses before the next surviving letter by More to Margaret was written. This letter, No. 20, is dated May 2 or 3, 1535 (*LL* 112–15), and it documents the interrogation to which More had been subjected on April 30 by five members of the Royal Council, including Cromwell and Richard Rich. More tells Margaret that Cromwell had relayed Henry's demand that he give his opinion of the royal supremacy, to which he replied that he had repeatedly done so in private conversations with the king prior to his arrest and had been assured that he would never be required to do so formally and publicly. "And now," he had told the Council, "I have in good faith discharged my mind of all such matters, and neither will dispute King's titles nor Pope's, but the King's true faithful subject I am and will be, and daily I pray for him and for all his, and for you all that are of his honorable Council, and for all the realm, and otherwise than thus I never intend to meddle" (*LL* 113). After having been dismissed from the room, and then recalled and reminded of his duties to his sovereign, he had assured the Council that he wished "none harm" and reiterated his loyalty to the king. The Council had then told him that Henry would be informed of his silence, had warned him that nothing good would come of it, and had sent him back to his cell. He concludes by assuring his family and friends of his prayers, soliciting their prayers for him, and expressing his "trust in the goodness of God," which, whatever might happen in this world, would ultimately be "for the best" (*LL* 115).

Letter No. 22, also addressed to Margaret, was penned a month later, on June 3, 1535 (*LL* 118–22). Earlier that day he had been interrogated by Audley, Cromwell, Cranmer, and two other members of the Council. But on this occasion, the Council had added a slightly new twist to their old drill: More was told either to "confess [the royal supremacy statute] lawful ... or else to utter plainly [his] malignity" (*LL* 119). In short, the Council would henceforth construe his continuing silence as evidence of malicious and treasonous opposition to the statues. But, as More related to Margaret, he had told the Council that his silence on matters pertaining to recent English legislation was not due to any malice on his part toward anyone but was grounded in his obedience to the laws of "the corps of Christendom." It was thus "a very hard thing" for the Council to compel him to choose between violating his conscience to save his life and abiding by his conscience to save his soul, but he was bound to choose the latter course (*LL* 120). And then it was More's turn to thicken the plot. Because of his faith, he had virtually assured his execution, but he did not regard himself as a martyr—or at least not what the early church would have called a "voluntary martyr," that is, someone who baited the government into killing him to earn immediate entry into heaven. The church had condemned this attitude as prideful and presumptuous, and More was determined to be guilty neither of a sinful eagerness for death nor of the sinful repudiation of his convictions (*LL* 121).

On July 5, 1535, one day before his execution, More, using a piece of charcoal from the fire in his cell, wrote Letter No. 24 to Margaret (*LL* 127–28). Absent are the themes so prevalent in his earlier correspondence. Here he is saying goodbye, one by one, to the members of his family, expressing his love and sending along a few small personal items—a handkerchief, a writing tablet—that he had kept with him during his confinement. He gives some last-minute instructions about the disposition of family property. He commends Margaret's "daughterly love and dear charity," as well as the "natural fashion" of his son, John More. But his faith remains firm, and his eschatological hope still shines through: "Fare well my dear child and pray for me, and I shall for you and all your friends that we may merrily meet in heaven" (*LL* 128).

A Dialogue of Comfort Against Tribulation, 1534

The first of the two books Thomas More wrote during his incarceration was *A Dialogue of Comfort Against Tribulation*.[42] Its title page carries the first of the many instances of dry humor sprinkled throughout it. We read that it was "made by a Hungarian in Latin and translated out of Latin into French and out of French into English" (*DCT* 15). On the face of it, this is nonsense. It was made by an Englishman in English. But why disguise his identity? Only the nationality of the author—not even a pseudonym—is given. And the English text purports to be a translation of a translation of the original. Is this elaborate subterfuge intended to fool the prying eyes of any royal officials who might intercept the manuscript? Perhaps, but anyone familiar with More's thought and style would immediately recognize him as the author. Or was More poking fun at the

---

42. References in this subsection are to Mary Gottschalk's modern English rendering. I have also consulted More, *Complete Works*, Vol. 12 from which Gottschalk herself worked. Citations to the Gottschalk translation will be abbreviated *DCT* and given in-text for convenience. However, in any quotations given below in which the verbal resonance and/or semantic nuances of More's Tudor terminology seem to have been lost in translation, I will add the original wording in an explanatory note.

cloak-and-dagger atmosphere then prevailing in the English government and judicial system? Perhaps, but given the times, that would have been dangerous, as the people whose self-importance and officiousness were being mocked were those best situated to retaliate against their mocker. Or was More simply suggesting by this subtitle that the two great themes of the book—the unavoidability and universality of human suffering and the proper Christian way to face it—transcend all boundaries of nationality and language? That seems the likeliest explanation.

Whatever coded message the subtitle is meant to convey, the fact that the putative author is Hungarian is significant. The *Dialogue* purports to take place in the wake of the three great battles of the Hungarian-Ottoman War: The Siege of Belgrade (1521), the Siege of Rhodes (1522), and the Battle of Mohács (1526). The Ottomans had decisively won all three; the young king of Hungary, Louis II, had been killed at the third; two rivals for his throne were then fighting each other; and the Kingdom of Hungary now expected to be invaded and occupied by the armies of the sultan and absorbed into the Ottoman Empire. The Hungarian people, decimated and demoralized by the war, were terrified of what vassalage to the Turks would entail and feared that unless they renounced their Christian faith and converted to Islam, they would be martyred or enslaved. This is the *mise-en-scène* of More's book—the very immediate "tribulations" that the Hungarian people were undergoing in the year or two after Mohács (*DCT* 17–23). How might they find "comfort" in this dire situation?[43]

Only two characters appear in the *Dialogue*: The first is Vincent, a frightened young man, who wonders whether death or captivity is to be preferred. The second is his saintly uncle, Anthony, full of years and now near death, but still eager to engage in edifying conversation and willing to dispense the advice that Vincent craves. Their names are clearly significant, although the text does not directly explain them. "Anthony" presumably alludes to the great fourth-century Egyptian desert father, the prototypical Christian monk, whose life had been one long battle with

---

43. More knew the political, military, and religious situation in Europe well from his days in government service, and the *Dialogue* should therefore not be read "allegorically," as if every mention of a historical person or event refers in coded terms to something else, say, a person or event in More's personal experience. It may, however, be read "analogically," given that many striking parallels are observable. So, when the Ottoman sultan is discussed, it is truly Suleiman the Magnificent who is meant—yet it may also be an indirect allusion to Henry VIII. For a full discussion of this point, see Manley, Introduction to More, *Complete Works*, 12:cxx–cxxxv.

trials, temptations, privations, and dangers, and whose *Vita* and surviving letters offer counsel on triumphant self-mastery via faith in Christ.[44] "Vincent" means conqueror, and that is just what the young man in the *Dialogue* eagerly desires to be—not over the Turks, for that is impossible, but over his own fears of captivity, torture, apostasy, and death.

Before examining the religious message of this book, it is important to note why More chose the dialogue as the literary genre best suited to communicate it. As a youth, he had often participated in plays and pageants, and in his various professional roles as attorney, trade negotiator, courtier, diplomat, member of Parliament, and royal counselor, he had engaged in lively debate every day. Two of his earlier works used this genre, namely, *Utopia* (1516) and the two-volume *Dialogue Concerning Heresies* (1529). And Letter No. 12 of August 1534 purports to be a verbatim transcript of a conversation between himself and Margaret Roper. The form is well suited for the elaboration of radically differing points of view, and for the raising and answering of both highly abstract and deeply personal questions. Here the genre is used to portray the giving and receiving of timely—and timeless—spiritual edification.

Yet there is a profound sense in which the *Dialogue of Comfort* is also a monologue, an extended exercise in self-encouragement. For the two characters in the story represent the two sides of More's character as they had developed and gradually coalesced throughout his lifetime. Vincent is the polite young man that More himself had been decades earlier: deferential to his elders and yet self-assured in their presence; full of big questions and eager for solid answers; devoutly religious but admirably suspicious of his own ability to put pious formulas into concrete practice. Anthony is the elderly sage that More has now become: sick in body but sharp of mind; wise from wide experience but not prone to sentimentality or nostalgia; brimming with biblical citations, exempla from classical antiquity, and personal anecdotes; sober but not solemn; witty and wittily self-critical of his own wittiness. Vincent poses

---

44. More's wit, and perhaps also his wistfulness, is once again displayed in his literary artistry. For St. Anthony the Great had spent many years walled alone into an abandoned Roman military fortress (see Athanasius, *Life of Antony* 40–43), just as More himself was locked in the Tower of London. In his early years More seriously considered joining the Carthusians, a religious order whose monasteries are designed to maximize the eremitic seclusion of the brethren. And Roper, *Life*, 211, tells us that "because he was desirous for godly purposes sometime to be solitary, and sequester himself from worldly company, a good distance from his mansion house [in Chelsea] builded he a place called the New Building, wherein there was a chapel, a library, and a gallery." There he spent his Fridays "in devout prayers and spiritual exercises."

the questions that inevitably arise in times of trouble, and Anthony gives the theologically orthodox answers—answers that More certainly *does* believe, and which are now enabling him to comport himself with that dignified mirth, lawyerly cunning, and Christian fortitude for which he had always been known.[45]

The conversation between uncle and nephew takes place on two separate days, with a day or two intervening between them, and with a break for lunch separating the morning and afternoon sessions on the second day (*DCT* 87).[46] The book is thus divided into three parts. Each part has a preface that establishes the basic theme of that part, followed by numerous chapters of widely varying lengths in which that theme is developed. Part One of the book corresponds to Day One of the conversation and comprises slightly less than a quarter of the book. Part Two corresponds to the morning of Day Two and comprises just over a third. Part Three corresponds to the afternoon of Day Two and comprises nearly half. In Parts One and Two, Vincent mentions a host of tribulations to which human beings are subject, and Anthony offers time-tested Christian wisdom on how to respond to them. Part Three focuses on the religious persecution that threatens to befall the Christian people of Hungary—and which, of course, threatens Thomas More himself. But persecution is different in two crucial ways from the other kinds of tribulation that human beings face: first, it is inflicted not by misfortune or the frailty of the flesh but by the malign intent of enemies; and second, it can often be avoided, or at least mitigated, if its victims cooperate with their enemies' demands. The reader of the *Dialogue* knows from the book's opening pages that a discussion of the Christian response to persecution is where the entire conversation is heading, and is forced to ask, with ever-growing urgency, whether and how the sage advice Anthony is dispensing along the way for life's other troubles will apply when people are forced to choose between apostasy or death.

45. I am focusing here on the ways in which the *Dialogue* reflects More's own interior monologue and his efforts to steel himself against his fears, doubts, and temptations. But he undoubtedly had other prospective audiences in mind as well: family and friends, general readers, and government officials. See Manley, Introduction to More, *Complete Works*, 12:cxx–clxiv.

46. In his Introduction to More, *Complete Works*, 12:lxvi, Martz compares the conversations between Anthony and Vincent in the *Dialogue* to the conversations between More and Margaret in the Tower, rather than projections of More's internal dialogue. Martz's reading seems to me at least as plausible as my own, and yet I doubt that we are really disagreeing, insofar as Margaret was in many ways More's alter ego (as he was hers).

Part One of the *Dialogue* opens when Vincent pays a visit on Anthony and asks for more of the "good help, counsel, and comfort" that the elderly gentleman has always offered his family (*DCT* 17–18), but which is especially timely in their country's time of chaos. Anthony responds by offering "an antidote against the poison of the despairing dread that might arise from the occasion of a terrible tribulation" (*DCT* 22). This antidote is no mere palliative. Suffering is an inescapable feature of life: it must be faced squarely. Yet through faith in God, suffering can become the occasion for "an increase of merit" and personal sanctification (*DCT* 42). We should "realize that God has sent it for our own good, and so be moved to thank God for it" (*DCT* 83). Conversely, earthly prosperity is spiritually dangerous, by tempting us to self-satisfaction and complacency. Yet Anthony is neither valorizing suffering for its own sake nor condemning earthly felicities. Rather, he is warning us against making this "wretched world . . . our home," and encouraging us to "sow now, in this world, so that in the next world we may reap . . . and have in heaven a merry, laughing harvest forever" (*DCT* 52). Etymologically, the word "comfort" means "with strength," and the kind of strength that Anthony offers Vincent comes from faith in the gospel message, which offers victory over both the fear of tribulation and the allurements of prosperity: "Comfort, Nephew, is understood properly . . . not as a present pleasure with which the body is delighted and tickled for the time being, but rather, as the consolation of a good hope, a hope that people take in their hearts, of some good coming toward them" (*DCT* 76).

Part Two opens with Vincent expressing concern that his uncle might have been exhausted at the end of their previous talk. But Anthony assures him that their talk had been invigorating for him and goes on to point out that "although we spoke of sorrow and affliction, what we chiefly thought about was not tribulation itself, but rather the comfort that can arise from it" (*DCT* 87–88). This sets the agenda for today's discussion, an inquiry into the three kinds of tribulations: "something willingly taken on, something willingly endured, and something impossible to get rid of" (*DCT* 94). But as Anthony observes, they had sufficiently covered unavoidable tribulations in their previous conversation (*DCT* 94–95), and sufferings that people voluntarily take on themselves for the sake of spiritual gain (i.e., penances) do not require comfort from others at all (*DCT* 95–96). Thus, the morning's conversation focuses on those tribulations we willingly endure. There are two distinct but closely related kinds: temptations and persecutions (*DCT* 106–7). Most of Part Two is devoted to temptations, and these are further subdivided into four types: fear (including impatience, faintheartedness, and suicidal ideation) (*DCT* 112–58), pride (*DCT* 158–66), worldly busyness (*DCT* 166–86), and open persecution. (At this point, the logical structure of Anthony's argument gets a bit muddled,[47] for temptation had earlier been distinguished *from* persecution, but here persecution is listed as a fourth *type* of temptation.) The rest of the morning is devoted to fear, pride, and busyness.

Part Three corresponds to the afternoon of Day Two, after Anthony has had lunch and a nap. The conversation opens by returning to the problem of the anticipated Ottoman takeover: How will Christians respond to persecution and the specific kinds of temptation that it occasions? One passage, which obviously parallels More's own experience of the tactics used by the Royal Council to induce his capitulation, is worth quoting at length: "In this persecution against the Christian faith, he [the devil or his servant, the Ottoman sultan] uses . . . not only the allurements of peace and quiet (attained through deliverance from pain and death) and some other pleasures of this present life, but also, in addition to all that, the terror and the infliction of intolerable pain and torment" (*DCT* 199). Anthony stoutly asserts—as More himself had asserted to Margaret in Letter No. 16—that "no tribulation can do the soul any harm at all unless the soul, because of some inordinate love and affection that it bears to the body, consents to slide from the faith and thereby harms itself" (*DCT* 201). Anthony inventories the "goods of fortune" that can be taken away by a persecutor, such as "worldly riches, offices, honor, and authority," but insists that in each case the loss is negligible to those who endure it without apostatizing (*DCT* 204–5). After all, time will inevitably take these worldly goods from us anyway, but heaven and hell are forever. Then he

---

47. Marius remarks that "the *Dialogue of Comfort* rambles gently from topic to topic like a boat afloat on a placid sea and moved by soft waves" (*More*, 472). And at one level, the work certainly does bear all the marks of an intimate and informal conversation between a family patriarch and a doting nephew, laced as it is with familial reminiscences, amusing anecdotes, and frequent expressions of affection and concern. But underneath all the banter, digressions, and yarn-spinning, the lawyerly cast of More's mind comes through: his flair for sharp definitions, careful distinctions, and tight reasoning—and what Protestant readers might deem the legalistic elements of his faith—his defense of penances, good works, and purgatory (*DCT* 47–51, 100), his criticisms of solifidian antinomianism (*DCT* 106), and his casuistic discussion of how "a difference in circumstances greatly affects" the way Christians should obey the moral prescriptions of Scripture (*DCT* 180–81). Martz puts this well: "This combination of dialogue and argument, conversational ease and underlying design, is entirely characteristic of the [author] himself and the literary style exhibited in all his Tower works" (Introduction to the *Complete Works*, 12:lxxxix).

shifts to the punishments that a persecutor can inflict, such as torture, enslavement, imprisonment, and execution. His response is to relativize these miseries by reminding those who suffer them, first, of the pains of hell they must endure if they betray their faith, and then of "the marvelous joys of heaven" they will enjoy if they stand strong (*DCT* 292).

Throughout the *Dialogue*, Vincent frequently reiterates his weakness and self-doubt, and he occasionally wonders whether Anthony's theological reasoning, sound as it is, will suffice to brace him if he should fall victim to persecution. And Anthony constantly sympathizes with Vincent's worries and offers kindly reassurances. But in the closing pages, Anthony issues a bracing and decisive challenge: Vincent must prepare himself for any eventuality, both by means of orthodox arguments and by the assiduous practice of "spiritual exercise" (*DCT* 293), i.e., by constantly meditating on Christ's passion (*DCT* 297); by fasting, prayer, and almsgiving (*DCT* 303; cf. 293); by remembering Christ's commandment to love one's enemies (*DCT* 304); and by the "deep consideration of the joys of heaven" (*DCT* 305). Yet he interjects a warning, too: preparing oneself to *face* martyrdom when it cannot be honorably avoided is Christian prudence, but craving to undergo it, and baiting one's enemies into inflicting it, is "a proud, presumptuous attitude," which a Christian must avoid (*DCT* 302). Anthony's advice to Vincent is, of course, More's advice to himself.

Three of the religious convictions that animate the prison letters drive the *Dialogue of Comfort Against Tribulation* as well. But in the *Dialogue*, More is not arguing for the validity of these convictions *per se*. Rather, he is assuming their validity and using them to fortify himself. He is not trying to persuade the government to leave him in peace or his family to accept his decision to refuse the oaths. Instead, he is erecting a defensive barrier for himself against the temptation to succumb to the government's threats and inducements. He is distinguishing between the true comfort that results from spiritual integrity and the easy comfortableness that would follow from timorous submission to the state. These three convictions are as follows:

First, the central task of one's moral and spiritual life is to achieve "clearness of conscience" (*DCT* 41, 42, 43, 44, 45, 151, 180, 183). But in the *Dialogue*, conscience never refers to the opinions one holds (Lewis's "indicative" sense of the term), as it sometimes does in More's other writings, but always to one's moral compass alone (the "imperative" sense). Furthermore, in the *Dialogue*, one's moral compass functions less as a guide to future conduct and more as the judge and monitor of one's present moral status, as determined by one's past conduct. This shift in connotation can be explained by remembering that the rhetorical objective of the *Dialogue* is to enable the author, now engaged in self-encouragement rather than dispute with others, to receive divine comfort in the face of persecution. People's capacity to receive strength from God in the face of unavoidable tribulations will depend "on how clear or sin-encumbered their conscience is" (*DCT* 41). In fact, the longest sustained discussion of conscience in the book pertains to the problem of moral scrupulosity (*DCT* 117–26; cf. 135), that is, to the problem of a *weak* conscience. This is defined as "an obsessive preoccupation with God's rigorous justice, in order to keep [people] from the comforting remembrance of God's great, mighty mercy and thus make them do all their good works wearily, without any consolation or enthusiasm" (*DCT* 119). True, "a conscience a little too constricted is certainly better than a conscience a little too permissive," for such scrupulosity reduces the number and severity of one's sins (*DCT* 119). But it also prevents one from experiencing God's grace, on which one's true comfort depends. The aim is to achieve moral balance: to be conscientious enough to act virtuously and yet humble enough to know one's weaknesses and to accept God's mercy.

Second, More's eschatology of communal merriment is also prominent in the *Dialogue*, as his comments about having a "merry laughing harvest" in heaven (*DCT* 52) and similar remarks (*DCT* 54, 98, 294–95) indicate. But here, too, a subtle shift is detectable. In the prison correspondence, More admonishes his family and himself to be merry *now*, in exuberant defiance of their present misfortunes and in expectation of their future joys in heaven. But the situation Anthony and Vincent face is somewhat different: they foresee religious persecution, but exactly when and how it will strike remain uncertain. It is difficult to merrily defy a danger that one anticipates with anxiety but cannot define with clarity. So, divine comfort in this situation is allaying one's worst fears before tribulation actually materializes. Anthony's strategy is to lighten the gloom with striking literary images and amusing stories.[48] He states: "We come together now to talk of as serious and sad things as anyone can think of, and yet we start off by telling frivolous, silly stories. Really, Nephew, as you know quite well, I am by nature far too fun-loving. I

---

48. In his Introduction to Gottshalk's translation of the *Dialogue*, Wegemer catalogues forty-three vivid "images" (e.g., God as a mother hen and the Ottoman sultan as a pet dog) and forty-six "stories, examples, and hypothetical situations" (e.g., Cato's suicide and Saul's superstition) (*DCT* 315–17), which lighten the tone of the book.

wish I could as easily correct my fault as know it, but I can hardly control it, old fool that I am. However, I will not be so partial to my fault as to praise it" (*DCT* 91).[49] Of course, Anthony represents More himself, and we hear behind this comment More's lifelong love of puns, practical jokes, tall tales, and "merry jests."[50]

Third, More's insistence on taking comfort from the religious and moral authority of the "whole body of Christendom" (*DCT* 49, 105) or "the common faith of the Church" (*DCT* 137) recurs in the *Dialogue* several times. But here there are three distinct kinds of adversary. First, there are the Muslims, whose power via the Turks had been steadily growing for five centuries, and who were now putting immense pressure on Central Europe. This threat is the immediate occasion of the *Dialogue*. Second, there are apostate Christians, that is, Catholics dwelling in lands immediately threatened by the Turks and now considering conversion to Islam to avoid persecution. Vincent remarks: "There is not a Turk alive who is so cruel to Christian folk as is the false Christian who falls from the faith" (*DCT* 20; cf. 286). Finally, there are the Protestants. Of course, More had long been their fierce opponent, but in the prison correspondence his opposition is expressed indirectly, primarily in reference to the way their ideas were being used to legitimize the royal succession and supremacy. Here he returns to the broader themes of his anti-heretical writings of the 1520s, namely, to what he regarded as the Protestants' novel and erroneous readings of Scripture, their failure to honor the teachings of "the ancient, holy doctors of the Church" (*DCT* 105), the

---

49. The phrase that Gottshalk translates "frivolous, silly stories" is "wanton idell talys." And whereas Gottshalk renders Anthony's confession, "I am by nature far too fun-loving," the original reads "my selfe am of nature evyn halfe a giglot & more" (More, *Complete Works*, 12:83). The self-mockery in these expressions seems much heavier in More's Tudor diction. Anthony is accusing himself of lasciviousness, not merely playfulness.

50. On More's sense of humor, see especially Ackroyd, *Life*, 87–95. See also Erasmus, *Ten Colloquies*, 42, where a character who represents More is said to have "a wonderful sense of humor" and not to be "averse to pranks." The modern reader may bristle, however, at how many of these tropes make fun of women, especially his wife, Lady Alice More (*DCT*, 40–41, 71–72, 88–89, 89–90, 117–18, 123, 131–32, 168, 216–17, 267–68, 270). What to us smacks of sexism in these tales was probably intended as good-natured teasing rather than high-handed scorn. More does include several references to "wise women" in the text (*DCT* 118, 119–22), and his respect for women is attested both in his deep investment in the classical education of his daughters and in the tribute he paid to both his wives in the epitaph he wrote for his own tomb. On More's attitude toward Lady Alice, see Ackroyd, *Life*, 141–50. For the text of his epitaph, see his Letter to Erasmus, June? 1533 in More, *Selected Letters*, 182–83.

"singularity of [their] opinions" (*DCT* 137), and their generally schismatic and antinomian tendencies (*DCT* 106). Yet, dangerous as More still believes Protestant ideas to be, here he holds out some hope that the "Germans," many of whom were Protestants by the late 1520s, might join with Catholic Europe "in the defense of Christendom against our common enemy the Turk" (*DCT* 105).[51]

The Sadness of Christ, Spring 1535

With his trial looming and his execution now likely, More wrote *On the Sadness, the Weariness, the Fear and the Prayer of Christ, Before He Was Taken Prisoner*. This work is often known by the shortened version of its Latin title, *De Tristitia Christi* (*The Sadness of Christ*).[52] It is a verse-by-verse commentary of the story of Christ's agony in the Garden of Gethsemane and his subsequent arrest, as told in Matthew 26, Mark 14, Luke 22, and John 18 (which More harmonizes into a single narrative, though occasionally noting the differences between the Evangelists' accounts). The conventions of its genre and the circumstances of its composition give this work its distinctive characteristics. He is doing here just what, in the *Dialogue*, Anthony had counseled Vincent to do in the face of tribulation, namely, to meditate on the passion of Christ, or rather that portion of the passion narrative that most closely paralleled More's own immediate situation. He draws every conceivable lesson from Christ's actions in the Garden about how a disciple should comport himself in the face of impending martyrdom; he also draws numerous parallels between the behavior of the characters in the story—Jesus' disciples, Judas, the Jewish authorities who bribed Judas into betraying Jesus, and the members of the arresting cohort—and the various forces arrayed now against

---

51. I have been unable to determine whether More was aware that Protestant ideas had begun taking root in Hungary as early as 1528. (For details, see Parsons, "Reformation in Hungary.") No explicit tie-in between the threats posed respectively by the Muslim Turks and the Protestant missionaries is offered in the *Dialogue*.

52. References in this subsection are to Wegemer's edition of More, *Sadness of Christ*: these will be abbreviated *SC* and given in-text for convenience. Wegemer follows Miller's translation of the Latin original in More, *Complete Works*, 14.I:1–681. This latter volume features a photographic reproduction of the Valencia manuscript on even-numbered pages and the running Latin text and Miller's translation on odd-numbered pages. Vol. 14, Part II includes Miller's introduction, an extensive textual commentary, and several useful appendices. Ackroyd, *Life*, 380–82, and Marius, *More*, 483–87, offer briefer introductions to this work.

himself—perfidious royal commissioners, cowardly or corrupt English bishops, and Protestant heretics. More's Christocentric piety, his human anguish over the injustice to which he was being subjected, and his moral indignation at the general course of English politics and religion are all revealed in the tone and content of this work.

More's original handwritten manuscript has survived. It was apparently smuggled out of prison in small sections, and several copies were soon made and circulated privately. An English translation of *De Tristitia Christi* was made by More's granddaughter, Mary Basset, and published in William Rastell's edition of More's *English Works* in 1557.[53] The Latin original appeared in Peter Zangrius' edition of More's Latin works in 1565 under the title of *Expositio Passionis Christi* (*Exposition of the Passion of Christ*).[54] At some point the original manuscript was taken to Spain, where it was placed in the Chapel of Relics of the Royal College of Corpus Christi in Valencia, and forgotten until 1963. The final pages in the Valencia manuscript include More's collection of scriptural quotations and random reflections.[55] These give poignant testimony to his private thoughts and devotional exercises as he wrote the book (*SC* 115–27).

Wegemer offers a useful outline of *The Sadness of Christ*, which we here adapt to our own purposes.[56] The book opens with Jesus and the eleven singing the closing hymn at the Last Supper and then retiring to Gethsemane. More uses the singing of a hymn to chastise the impiety and frivolity of contemporary social occasions. He then discusses the "mysterious meanings" of the place names of the scene (*SC* 3). "Cedron," he says, means "sadness," i.e., the sadness that Christ and all of us must endure in this life; "Olivet" signifies the branch of God's peace that Christ offers to sinful humanity; and "Gethsemane" ("fertile garden") symbolizes the joys of heaven, which Christians will enjoy after they "cross over . . . the valley of tears and stream of sadness" of this life (*SC* 3–4). More praises the eleven for "following" Jesus to this secluded place for prayer and chastises Judas for using his knowledge of Jesus' habits to betray him (*SC* 5–6). More then exhorts his readers to imitate the pious practices exemplified by Jesus and assures them that "if we set out to make a habit of doing the least little bit of good . . . God will soon set us forward a great way on the path of virtue" (*SC* 6). The aim of the book

53. More, *English Works*, 1277–1349.
54. More, *Omnia Latina Opera*, 118–32.
55. See More, *Complete Works*, 14.I:626–91.
56. See his Introduction to *SC*, xv–xvi.

is thus established from the start: to contrast the pious attitudes and actions of Christ with the weakness and failure of his disciples and to warn the readers against imitating the failures of the latter.

More next develops the overarching theme of the book, namely, Christ's "sadness, grief, fear, and weariness." He catalogs the terrors that Christ anticipates, and that do indeed follow in the Gospel stories: "the treacherous betrayer, the bitter enemies, binding ropes, false accusations, slanders, blows, thorns, nails, the cross, and horrible tortures stretched out over many hours" (*SC* 7). But More also imagines that Christ "was tormented by the thought of His disciples' terror, the loss of the Jews, even the destruction of the very man who so disloyally betrayed Him, and finally the ineffable grief of His beloved mother" (*SC* 7). One immediately thinks of More's letters, which often reflect the anguish he feels for his family's sufferings. And he emphasizes that Christ's sorrows and fears were *real*, functions of his human nature, which were by no means mitigated by his deity (*SC* 8). He then goes on to discuss martyrdom, which he now realizes is his own inevitable fate. While expressing admiration for those Christians who "rushed to their deaths eagerly and joyfully, triumphing over tyrants and torturers" (8), More again insists, as he had done in the *Dialogue*, that Christians need not feel shame over their human fear of death and are free to escape martyrdom if they can do so without denying Christ. In short, Christ's agony in the Garden, along with his courageous confrontation of Judas and his posse, is both a genuine reflection of his human nature and personal character and a paradigm for his disciples (*SC* 9–17).

The third section is devoted to Christ's prayer in the Garden and its application to the Christian devotional life. More sharply contrasts the intensity and concentration of Christ's devotional practice with the "negligence, sloth, or apathy, [or rather with] the feeblemindedness, the insanity, the downright blockheaded stupidity with which most of us approach the all-powerful God" (18). He differentiates the humble, face-to-the-ground posture assumed by Christ from the "careless and sprawling deportment of our bodies" at prayer (*SC* 19). This moralistic finger-wagging goes on for several pages. Wegemer states that this section is "marked by More's characteristic humor and wit" (*SC* xvi), but his satirical portrait of indolent piety, even if it is intended partly as self-mockery, seems harsh, a far cry from the "merry tales" that animate the *Dialogue*.

More's reflections on prayer extend into the fourth section of the book, which juxtaposes Christ's intense concentration on and humble submission to God's will with the disciples' persistent sleepiness. More uses Christ's repeated demand that his disciples watch and pray with him to advocate a synergistic moral theology, arguing that instead of "effectually wishing" their wakefulness, as he might have done, Christ accorded them the freedom "to cooperate with the promptings of His inward assistance" (SC 34). But their failure to do so was culpable and contributed to their disgrace. This section also includes a passage that reminds us of Maximus the Confessor: More argues that just as Christ has two natures, divine and human, so he has two wills, and despite his human desire to escape death, his human will "was in such complete conformity with the will of the Father that no disagreement was ever found between them" (SC 37). This leads More to reiterate and expand his argument that true Christian courage in the face of death consists in the obedient performance of one's duty, whether that is accompanied by "fear and trembling" or heroic defiance. More then draws an unflattering comparison between the eleven apostles and their latter-day successors, the bishops, many of whom seem "sleepy and apathetic in sowing virtues among the people and maintaining the truth" (SC 46).

The fifth section deals with Christ's treatment of Judas Iscariot. More begins by noting that Christ "was captured only because He, and He alone, wished to be taken" (SC 65) and thereby refutes any suggestion that Christ was merely the helpless victim of the scheme of his traitorous disciple and the Jewish and Roman authorities. Having made that point, More begins extracting moral lessons from the story of Judas's perfidy. That the Gospels remind us that Judas was "one of the Twelve" teaches "all who exercise high public office" not to glory in their titles but to concentrate on their duties (SC 67). That Judas had carefully instructed his posse to arrest only the one whom he would kiss is taken to show the extent of the traitor's greed and malice, as if Judas were afraid that Jesus might escape in the scuffle and thus prevent him from earning his thirty pieces of silver (SC 68–69).[57] That Judas had been present earlier at the Supper gives More the opportunity to inveigh against the Protestant practice of distributing the Eucharist in both kinds and the Protestant denial of the real presence (SC 70–71).[58] And that Judas had used the kiss,

---

57. More here follows Mark 14:10, which asserts that the chief priests "promised to give [Judas] money," presumably *after* the arrest had been made, rather than Matt 26:15, which suggests that they paid him in advance.

58. For a lengthier account of More's mature views on the Eucharist, see his *Treatise on the Blessed Body*, in *Complete Works*, 13:191–204.

a sign of friendship, to identify the target of the conspiracy shows how "hateful to God" it is when we "[pervert] the real nature of good things to make them the instruments of our malice" (SC 73–74). But More's tirade against Judas does gives rise to a positive lesson: by addressing Judas as "Friend" at the very moment when Judas was about to betray him (Matt 26:50), Christ taught us "to bear patiently and gently all injuries and snares treacherously set for us; not to smolder with anger, not to seek revenge, not to give vent to our feelings by hurling back insults, . . . but rather to set ourselves against deceitful injury with genuine courage and to conquer evil with good" (SC 72–73). But in the remaining pages of this section (SC 74–84), More is careful to emphasize that the traitor eventually receives his just deserts from God.

More now turns to the story of the severing of Malchus' ear by Peter and of the wound's immediate healing by Jesus. More draws several lessons from this parabolic episode. First, the proper mission of Christ's disciples is to fight "not with [the sword of iron] but with the sword of the word of God" (SC 87), and therefore they are to avoid impetuous and violent zeal, even in the service of the good. Second, the use of the "sword of iron" is the office of "legitimate authority," i.e., the civil magistrate (SC 87, 91). Third, violence by the disciples in defense of Christ is unnecessary, partly because Christ could have summoned overwhelmingly powerful angelic assistance, if he had wished, and partly because these events, however tragic they might seem, are in God's hands and in accordance with Christ's will.

In the seventh section, More draws a twofold lesson from the story of the flight of the disciples, and especially of the unnamed young man mentioned in Mark 14:51–52, who was present at the arrest but fled the scene naked: we should, if possible, avoid situations in which we *might* sin, but if we do find ourselves in such a situation, we should do our best to escape (SC 108–9).

The eighth and final section simply states that the crowd who had come to arrest Christ were not able to do so until all the other events in the Gethsemane story—the Judas kiss, the discomfiture of the search party, the wounding and healing of Malchus, Christ's prevention of retaliatory violence, and the flight of the disciples—had all fully run their course. And this was because Christ himself willed it so (SC 112–14). According to More, this entire story unfolded with the precision of a divinely authored script, and every event therein was charged with profound theological significance and powerful moral relevance.

Instructions and Prayers, April 1534–July 1535

Five short works from More's incarceration also survive—four in English and one in both English and Latin versions. Modern English renderings are included in Wegemer's edition of *The Sadness of Christ*, which we follow here, using the same method of in-text citation. However, we shall follow the sequence in which they appear in Rastell's edition of More's *English Works*, which appears to be correct.[59]

Rastell describes the first two as "Godly Instructions," that is, More's self-admonitions on the practice of Christian virtue in the face of the world's hostility. The earlier of the two, which Wegemer titles "How to Treat Those Who Wrong Us" (SC 142–43), was probably written in late April or early May 1534, about the same time that he wrote Letter No. 7, for it too was written with "no other pen than a coal" (SC 142). Here he seems to be recalling the harsh interrogation to which he had been subjected at Lambeth Palace on the eve of his arrest, and which he had described to his daughter Margaret in Letter No. 6. More tells himself to "bear no malice or evil will to any man living." For malice toward those who are good is evil, whereas malice toward those who are evil, though perhaps quite natural, is harmful only to oneself, for they will either be justly punished by God or will repent and be saved. More adds a characteristic eschatological note, stating that if he and his former enemies are both saved, they will "in time be coupled in eternal friendship" (SC 142). More closes by cautioning himself against bearing against his enemies any "secretly malicious or cruel affection ... under the cloak of a just and a virtuous zeal" and vowing to pray for "such merciful amendment in other folk as our own conscience shows us that we have need of in ourselves" (SC 143).

The second "Godly Instruction," titled "On Saving One's Life" (SC 144–47) by Wegemer, was also written 1534, probably late in the year, by which time he realized that he would eventually be executed.[60] He was thus faced with the choice of avoiding "temporal death" in a way

---

59. References in this subsection are to Haupt's translation of these works, which is included in Wegemer's edition of *The Sadness of Christ*, but which originally appeared in More, *Complete Works*, 13:205–31. See Haupt's introduction to the latter volume, pp. cxl–clxvii, for the publication history of these five works and for his reasons for concurring with Rastell's sequencing. Haupt's extensive textual commentary on them is found on pp. 300–315.

60. A slightly differently worded Latin version is included in the Valencia manuscript of *The Sadness of Christ*; it, too, appears in More, *Complete Works*, 13:209–11.

that displeased God and thereby purchasing "eternal death," or of accepting without complaint a death that could not be avoided without dishonor and thereby winning "the everlasting joys of heaven" (SC 144). His duty was clear, and here he urges himself to muster up the faith and courage needed to perform it.

To understand the third and fourth of these five short writings, we must briefly explain the actual pages on which they were written, and which, like the original manuscript of *The Sadness of Christ*, have somehow survived. Large portions (but not complete copies) of two different devotional manuals, a Latin *Book of Hours* (1530) and a Latin *Psalter* (1522), were at some point bound together into a single volume, which has come to be known as *Thomas More's Prayer Book*. Whether the joining was done before More's imprisonment or shortly after his death and why the missing pages were omitted at the time of the joining cannot be determined with certainty. But there is no good reason to think that More *didn't* have the now bound volume with him in the Tower, and we shall assume that he *did*. And it is certain that he at least had the *contents* of the now bound volume with him in prison, for the pages of both sections carry extensive marginal annotations in his handwriting. It is these annotations that constitute the two short writings with which we are presently concerned.[61]

Rastell titled the first of these "A Devout Prayer, Collected Out of the Psalms of David." As originally published by Rastell, this prayer consists *only* of selected verses from the Psalms, arranged as a single continuous "Imploration for Divine Aid Against Temptation, While Scorning Demons Through Hope and Confidence in God" (SC 128-41). But Rastell's arrangement closely follows indications that More wrote into his *Prayer Book*, so the prayer's design seems to be More's own. And when we interleave the marginal comments that More wrote beside the specific verses he selected for inclusion in the prayer, as Wegemer has done, we have an extraordinarily intimate and powerful window into the prisoner's prayer life.[62]

---

61. See Duffey, *Marking the Hours*, 107-18; Martz and Sylvester, *Thomas More's Prayer Book*, xiii-xlv; Haupt, Introduction to More, *Complete Works*, 13:cxliii-cxliv.

62. For a complete inventory of these correlations, see Martz and Sylvester, *Thomas More's Prayer Book*, 189-202 and Haupt, "Commentary" to More, *Complete Works*, 13:311-13. More's complete selection of verses from the Vulgate, minus his annotations, may be found in More, *English Works*, 1408-16; More, *Complete Works*, 13:214-25. Not all 150 Psalms are represented in the "Devout Prayer," and some of the marginal notes in More's Psalter are to verses that he did not include in that prayer.

Not surprisingly, the psalms of lament draw forth some of More's most poignant remarks. More's comments rarely refer directly to the contemporary socio-political situation or to his dispute with the English government.[63] The "enemies" and "adversaries" about which the Psalmist so frequently complains are understood by More as the demonic forces that assault the soul, and the personal dangers that the Psalmist fears are interpreted by More as temptations to sin. Consider, for example, the following verses from Psalm 3, into which More's annotations of those verses are inserted in square brackets:

> O Lord, how many are my adversaries! Many rise up against me! [the soul recovering from sin] Many are saying of me, "There is no salvation for him in God." But you, O Lord, are my shield; my glory, you lift up my head! When I lie down in sleep, I wake again, for the Lord sustains me. [one who rises from sin] I fear not the myriads of people arrayed against me on every side. [scorning the demons] (SC 128).

More also frequently jots such words as "confidence," "patience," and "tribulation" into the margins of his Psalter, perhaps as ejaculatory prayers that arose as he read, or as reminders to imitate the Psalmist's godly attitude or conduct. Occasionally, however, a verse from a psalm will draw from More a longer meditation. For example, Psalm 38:13, "But I am like a deaf man, hearing not, like a dumb man who opens not his mouth," occasions the following comment: "So should the meek man act during tribulation; he should neither speak proudly nor throw back words badly spoken, but should bless them that speak badly and suffer willingly, either for the sake of justice if he has merited it or for the sake of God if he has not" (SC 135).

More's famous "Meditation on Detachment" was written across the top and bottom of the pages in the Daily Office portion of the *Book of*

---

63. What Duffy describes as More's "reticence" to indulge in autobiographical complaint or political commentary in these notes may be due partly to his concern that his *Prayer Book* might fall into the hands of his captors and be used as evidence against him. Yet More's determination to use his imprisonment as a time of quasi-monastic seclusion in preparation for death would dispose him toward a "spiritual" reading of the Psalter. Moreover, he does occasionally refer to current events in his marginalia, particularly when commenting on verses in the Psalms that he has not included in the "Devout Prayer." For example, he sometimes identifies the Psalmists' enemies as "the Turks" of his own time. But then again, Cromwell could scarcely have held More's animosity toward the Turks against him.

Hours section of his *Prayer Book* (SC 148–50).⁶⁴ It consists of nineteen unrhymed and unmetrical couplets of widely varying lengths, and it summarizes, in language of inexpressibly moving stateliness and solemnity, many of the themes in More's other Tower writings. More writes as a penitent expecting to die and imploring God for the grace to comport himself in a godly manner, that is, to be content with his lot, to be weaned from worldly "business," to repent of his sins and yet to rely on God's pardon, and "to have continually in mind the passion that Christ suffered for me." In view of what we have repeatedly seen of More's sense of humor, we are surprised to read couplets 16 and 17, in which he vows "to abstain from vain confabulations, to eschew light foolish mirth and gladness" and to renounce "recreations not necessary." But here he is referring to the frivolous amusements of this life, not the "communal merriment" of the next. This point is secured by couplet 18, in which he admonishes himself to "think my greatest enemies my best friends," recalling the biblical character of Joseph, whose brothers unwittingly did him more good "with their malice and hatred" than they ever could have done "with their love and favor." The final couplet reads: "These attitudes ["myndys"] are more to be desired of every man than all the treasure of all the princes and kings, Christian and heathen, were it gathered and laid together all upon one heap" (SC 150).

The fifth text, "A Prayer Before Dying" (SC 151–55) was composed in the few days between his trial and his execution. Like the "Meditation on Detachment," it expresses rather conventional yet thoroughly "owned" late medieval Catholic sentiments, but in deeply moving tones of serene confidence. More's superscription indicates that one is to begin by reciting "the Pater Noster, Ave Maria, and Credo." The first paragraph of the prayer itself is addressed to the Holy Trinity and implores divine mercy for "my long-continued sinful life, from my very childhood to the present" (SC 151). He then calls to mind—without committing to paper—the specific wrongs he has done at different stages of his life. Having completed this inventory, he offers a long series of petitions for what he will need to meet his death in a godly manner. The series is impossible to summarize without trivializing or truncating, but two examples of the great psychological and spiritual insight that More has achieved through his long ordeal are noteworthy. First, he differentiates

---

64. The original has no title, and I have followed Wegemer's suggestion. The original text may be found in More, *Complete Works*, 13, 226–27 and 313–14; Duffy, *Marking the Hours*, 114–15.

between two ways of experiencing those emotions that might arise at such a time: fear, sorrow, hope, and "sinful mirth." He might experience them negatively, as terror, self-pity, presumption, and sardonic jocularity. Instead, he vows to do so in a way that is "profitable for my soul," as reverence, penitence, trust, and eschatological merriment (SC 152). Second, he prays for a "longing" to be with God—not to avoid the miseries of this life or the pains of purgatory or hell, nor even to attain the joys of heaven for his own sake, but simply "for a genuine love for You" (SC 153). Then More offers intercessions "for friends" and "for enemies," and concludes with a sentence that encapsulates his lifelong approach to Christian experience and practice: "The things, good Lord, that I pray for, give me the grace to labor for. Amen."

More's Theological Convictions

In sketching Thomas More's life, in describing his character, and in analyzing his prison writings, we have repeatedly noticed how frequently and forcefully he expressed his central theological convictions (aside from those that directly contradicted the ideology of the Henrician Reformation, about which he held his tongue until the very end of his trial). It suffices to summarize the key points here.

1. The conscience of a Christian is bound by the non-negotiable doctrines of the universal church, as articulated in Scripture, the historic creeds, the decrees of the ecumenical councils, the official pronouncements of the papacy, and the vast system of canon laws

This might well be classified both as a Type A and as a Type B Conviction. It fits Type A insofar as it functioned in More's life as that *to* which he gave much of his adult life and, in silent protest against the Henrician Reformation, as that *for* which he was imprisoned and executed. But it fits Type B insofar as his faith in the heritage and authority of the Catholic Church gave him the courage and stamina to withstand the efforts by Henry's government to induce his capitulation. Robert Bolt's statement that More had "an adamantine sense of his own self" might easily mislead us into thinking of More as a prototypically modern individualist, who regarded his own opinions as intellectual private property. But no: More took his stand, not as a mock-heroic political dissenter, who objected to the exercise of royal and parliamentary authority as such, but as a humble and obedient Catholic, who denied that the English government possessed the right to establish a state church in schism from the Roman papacy in violation of England's own laws and ancestral ties to Rome. Such an artificially and uncanonically constructed state church could have no final jurisdiction over the conscience of a Christian citizen. Hence, it might be better to say that what was truly "adamantine" about More was his sense of his religious duties. Yet that sense, in turn, was definitive of his sense of himself.

2. In a state whose laws reflect the teachings of the Catholic Church, one's duties as a citizen are usually morally consistent with one's duties as a Christian, and the faithful performance of one's civic duties is a tangible expression of one's Christian discipleship. But when and to the extent that the state apostatizes, one's duty as a Christian is to withdraw one's support from the state apparatus, while abstaining, if possible, from illegal conduct

This conviction, too, can be classified under both Type A and Type B, and it is, in fact, a direct corollary of Conviction No. 1. Throughout most of More's life, his civic duties did indeed coincide with his Catholic faith, and his extraordinary intellectual gifts and legal skills enabled him to pursue his professional ambitions with a clean conscience. But when the time came that he could not perform his duties as a citizen without violating his conscience, he resigned his office, and ultimately surrendered his freedom and his life. If the *Paris Newsletter* account of More's trial and execution is correct, his last words were that he "died the King's good servant, and God's first." And the tragic irony of More's life was that the very king to whom he had rendered distinguished service, and who had once espoused to him the principle that one's loyalty to God should supersede one's loyalty to one's monarch, decided to punish him for staying true to it. The great eighteenth-century man of letters, Samuel Johnson, once remarked, "Patriotism is the last refuge of a scoundrel."[65] For Thomas More, it was the penultimate duty of the Christian citizen.

65. Entry for Friday, April 7, 1775, in Boswell, *Life of Johnson*, 253. Boswell is careful to add, however, "that [Johnson] did not mean a real and generous love of our country, but that pretended patriotism which so many, in all ages and countries, have made a cloak for self-interest."

3. The Christian life is a journey, in the company of fellow Christians, toward the eternal, merry fellowship of heaven

This is clearly a Type B conviction—not one that ever threatened the English government, but certainly one that marked both More's public and private life, and one that significantly lightened his spirits during his months in the Tower. It is conventional for Christians to speak of the "joys" of heaven, and in his final prayer, More does just that. But More construed the "joys" of heaven as communal celebrations, which would include his former enemies no less than his family and friends. And he construes these celebrations not merely as elevated solemnities, but also—and in a very profound sense—as good fun. We are reminded of the remark made by the heavenly elders to the martyrs in Saturus' vision in *The Passion of Saints Perpetua and Felicitas*: "Go and play!" The merriment of heaven involves having the last laugh—the truly final, eschatological laugh—that we will all have together over the fact that the sins and sorrows and general foolishness of our earthly existence are over forever.

4. But the communal merriment of heaven must be adumbrated in the way we treat others here and now

Again, Type B. With our dearest friends and relations, we may enjoy cheerful conviviality and share productive labor. Indeed, we *must* do so, for sports, games, jests, table fellowship, literary and scientific pursuits, legal proceedings, and honest business dealings are all moral duties, no less than pleasant pastimes or useful activities. Of course, with those who are now our bitterest enemies, such conviviality and cooperation will be temporarily impossible: yet they must nevertheless be treated as our *future* friends—with all due respect, forgiveness, and charity, in anticipation of the general hilarity and togetherness that await us. All of this is but another way of saying the Christian life is not only a journey toward heaven, but also a time of arduous probation, a time for conquering temptations, enduring tribulations, and practicing the virtues, in order to fit us for what awaits.

CHAPTER 4

Martin Luther King Jr.

Introduction

THE IMPRISONMENTS OF MARTIN Luther King Jr. and the form and content of his prison writings differ in five significant ways from those of our other three ambassadors. First, King was imprisoned on many different occasions;[1] he was never behind bars for more than fifteen days at a stretch, usually only for a few; and he never suffered brutal torture or execution at the hands of the state.[2] In contrast, Perpetua, Maximus, and More were all incarcerated but once, though for greatly different lengths of time, and all suffered greatly. Perpetua was in prison for about a week, at the end of which she was executed in the arena. Maximus was in prison for over nine years, was eventually mutilated, and died of his wounds. More was in the Tower of London for about fifteen months, after which he was beheaded.

Second, King's imprisonments, though frequent, were all due to relatively "minor" crimes: traffic violations, contempt of court, and

---

1. Oates, *Trumpet*, 449, refers to the five-day sentence that he and several of his lieutenants served in October 1967 as his nineteenth jailing. As far as I can tell it was his last.

2. In an interview with Kenneth B. Clark, which probably took place in late spring or summer 1963, King stated: "I haven't had any experience of physical violence from jailers, but I have had violence of words from them. Even in Birmingham, for the first few days [i.e., before President Kennedy began intervening on his behalf], some of the jailers were extremely harsh in their statements." King, *Testament*, 333.

various acts of nonviolent civil disobedience against local segregation laws whose injustice and unconstitutionality King was determined to expose. Accordingly, the writings that King produced during his times behind bars were short and—with the obvious and immensely significant exception of his "Letter from Birmingham Jail"—generally lack the personal weightiness displayed in many of the works we have surveyed in this book, which were written in the face of death, and often of a death that might have been averted if the author had capitulated to the demands of the authorities.[3] Even the great "Letter" was written in a single day, about midway through a jailing that lasted but one week. In contrast, Perpetua, Maximus, and More were all arrested on capital charges. Perpetua's diary describes her sufferings, her visions, and her anticipation of death. Only one short letter from Maximus's lengthy imprisonment survives, but we have transcripts of his interrogations which give us vivid and moving records of his "prison voice." More wrote two powerful theological treatises and many deeply moving personal letters and shorter pieces during his time in the dock.

Third, King's specifically *religious* convictions did not place him outside the pale of the dominant forms of Christianity in his own social world. He was raised with what he himself described as the "fundamentalist" beliefs of his African American Baptist heritage but moved to the "left" theologically and politically during his college, seminary, and graduate school years. Yet even in his most politically "radical" late speeches, such as those against the Vietnam War and the endemic poverty of the urban ghettos, he stood well within the boundaries of American Protestant progressivism. So, unlike Perpetua, Maximus, and More, King was not persecuted for holding religious convictions that were objectionable to the national government or the churches of his land. Rather, it was the social, cultural, political, and economic implications that he drew from his religious convictions for which he was persecuted. But although, as a twentieth-century American, he enjoyed constitutional protection from persecution for his convictions *per se*, as a Southern Black living in the Jim Crow Era, many of his civil rights were systematically violated by state, county, and local laws. And as a prominent the leader of the movement

3. King did, of course, have a premonition that he would be assassinated. See, e.g., the concluding paragraphs of his sermons, "The Drum Major Instinct" (February 4, 1968) and "I See the Promised Land" (April 3, 1968), in King, *Testament*, 266–67 and 285–86, respectively. But he was never charged with or imprisoned for a capital crime, and thus none of his prison writings are shaped by the expectation of immanent execution.

that fought for the restoration of those rights, he was constantly watched and frequently incarcerated for his political activities.

Fourth, precisely because many of the local laws that King was imprisoned for breaking were unconstitutional, he could appeal to the federal government for support during his campaigns, although such support was sometimes given reluctantly and tardily. No such appellate authority was available to Perpetua, Maximus, or More.

Fifth, several of King's arrests were quite intentionally instigated by King himself for strategic reasons. Our other three ambassadors understood that imprisonment was the possible consequence of their public stand, and that they could not back down without violating their conscience. But they did not actively *seek* imprisonment for the sake of conscience. In contrast, King put the Gandhian method of "filling the jails" to good use, and he was convinced, despite the occasional misgivings of his lieutenants, that he himself had to undergo imprisonment for the cause. He believed that a mass of nonviolent demonstrators, who voluntarily accepted arrest as a means of dramatizing the injustice of the laws, and who then "transformed [the jail] from a dungeon of shame to a haven of freedom and human dignity" through prayer and song,[4] could exert effective moral pressure on the local authorities and the entire nation. But he also recognized that *leading* his followers to jail was a crucial element of this method, not just because it demonstrated his personal sincerity, but also because, as an increasingly well-known and well-respected public figure, his arrest would capture media attention, embarrass the local authorities, and force the federal government to intervene. Accordingly, King's prison writings are neither edifying self-exhortations, nor apologias for an outlawed theological program, nor explorations of novel theological ideas. Most are prophetic pronouncements, which were intended for wide public circulation, and which advocated specific changes in the legal, political, and social order.

But in one important respect, King's prison pronouncements do resemble the carceral writings of Perpetua, Maximus, and More: they express their author's profound convictions about the nature and purposes of God and about how Christians ought to comport themselves in the face of the ungodliness of their time. For Perpetua, that ungodliness took the form of pagan idolatry; for Maximus, imperial heresy; for More, national apostasy; for King, racial injustice.

---

4. "Address at the Freedom Rally in Cobo Hall, Detroit," June 23, 1963, in King and Shepard, *Call*, Disc 3.

Martin Luther King Jr.: Some Biographical Highlights

Before studying King's prison writings, let us look at some of the major events in his life and offer a cursory assessment of his character, intellectual development, and leadership gifts.[5]

King was born on January 15, 1929, the eldest son of the Rev. Martin Luther King Sr. and Alberta Williams King. "Daddy" King was the pastor of the Ebenezer Baptist Church in Atlanta, Georgia. Alberta was the daughter of Adam Daniel Williams, the previous pastor of that prestigious, middle-class African American congregation. Thus, Martin Jr. grew up in what had long been his family's church. From an early age, he showed himself to be intellectually precocious and spiritually sensitive, and to possess a glorious speaking and singing voice and a way with words. But he also became painfully aware of the injustices and humiliations to which Black Americans in the racially segregated South were subjected, and the story of his life is the story of how he integrated and deployed his academic prowess, his rhetorical gifts, his spiritual longings, and his moral passion.

He was admitted to Morehouse College in Atlanta in autumn 1944 at the age of fifteen, having skipped several years in elementary and high school. He took an array of liberal arts courses, which enabled him to pass through a brief period of adolescent religious skepticism and to reembrace the faith in which he had been reared—minus the elements of fundamentalist dogmatism and fevered emotionalism that had previously alienated him. He received his BA in Sociology from Morehouse on June 8, 1948, and matriculated that autumn at Crozer Seminary in southeastern Pennsylvania. There he immersed himself in the Western philosophical tradition, becoming a devotee of Walter Rauschenbusch, the champion of the social gospel, and an astute critic of Karl Marx's atheistic materialism. He also encountered the teachings of Mahatma Gandhi, whose strategies of nonviolent resistance to racial and political oppression electrified him, and the Christian realism of Reinhold Niebuhr, which alerted him to the depths of evil in the human heart

---

5. The main sources for this sketch are Garrow, *Bearing the Cross*; King, *Autobiography*; Oates, *Trumpet*; and the Chronology and Encyclopedia in the Martin Luther King Jr. Research and Education Institute website. The following biographies also deserve mention: Ansbro, *Making of a Mind*; Bennett, *What Manner of Man*; Branch, *At Canaan's Edge*; Branch, *Parting the Waters*; Branch, *Pillar of Fire*; Lewis, *King*; Miller, *King*. For King's intellectual development, see King, *Autobiography*, chapters 1–4; "Pilgrimage to Nonviolence" in King, *Testament*, 35–40; Oates, *Trumpet*, 3–51.

and in all human societies and institutions. During the summers of his seminary years, he served as assistant pastor at Ebenezer, and regularly preached there during visits home. On May 8, 1951, King received his BD from Crozer, delivered the valedictory address, and won a scholarship to attend graduate school.

He entered Boston University in autumn 1951. There he was introduced to the "Boston personalism" of its faculty, Borden Parker Bowne, Edgar Sheffield Brightman, and L. Harold DeWolf, which deepened his appreciation for the personal character of the Christian God. He also studied the dialectical idealism of Hegel, which assured him that human history, for all the catastrophes and atrocities that have occurred, was moving toward the ultimate realization of universal justice. The themes of his later career reflect the synthesis of the ideas that he assimilated during his education at Morehouse, Crozer, and Boston with the spiritual resources and distinctive modes of Christian witness characteristic of the American Black Church. He continued to serve at Ebenezer during summer vacations and was often invited as a guest preacher in African American Baptist churches throughout the East and South,

Several months after matriculating at Boston University, King began dating Coretta Scott, a student at the New England Conservatory of Music. They were married on June 18, 1953. On January 24, 1954, King preached a trial sermon at the Dexter Avenue Baptist Church in Montgomery, Alabama, and was subsequently called to be its pastor. He began his ministry at Dexter on September 1, 1954, having arranged with the congregation to divide his time between pastoral duties and the completion of his doctoral dissertation. On May 31, 1955, he was awarded the PhD. During these years, he regularly received invitations to preach in Baptist churches and to speak at various civic and academic events, and he began to get involved in the civil rights work of the National Association for the Advancement of Colored People (NAACP).

On December 1, 1955, Rosa Parks, an NAACP activist, was arrested in Montgomery for refusing to yield her seat on a city bus to a white passenger. This event prompted the leaders of the city's Black community to launch a boycott of Montgomery's busses, a boycott that lasted until December 20, 1956, when the U.S. Supreme Court's ruling that segregationist policies on public transit systems was a violation of the equal protection clause of the Fourteenth Amendment took effect. During that year, King served as the president of the Montgomery Improvement Association, which had coordinated the boycott. The creativity, determination, and inspired oratory that he displayed in that role propelled him to national attention, and from that point until his death he was the acknowledged leader of the Civil Rights Movement—or at least of the Southern Christian Leadership Conference (SCLC), which was formed on August 7, 1957, to spearhead the wing of the movement that insisted on the use of nonviolent methods of protest.

On January 31, 1960, King preached his farewell sermon at Dexter Avenue and shortly thereafter moved back to Atlanta to serve as co-pastor with his father at Ebenezer. From this home base, he traveled widely, preaching, raising funds for the SCLC and other civil rights organizations, and participating in various campaigns. In the following section of this chapter, we will look closely at three major civil rights campaigns in which he was involved between winter 1961 and spring 1965, each of which eventuated in his imprisonment and in his composition of writings intended to justify and solicit support for his work. But it behooves us first to mention briefly a few of the key events in the latter years of his life.

On August 28, 1963, during the March on Washington for Jobs and Freedom, King delivered his "I Have a Dream" speech from the steps of the Lincoln Memorial. He helped to pressure the U.S. Government into passing the Civil Rights Act (July 2, 1964) and the Voting Rights Act (August 6, 1965), and on December 10, 1964, he was awarded the Nobel Peace Prize. In the mid-1960s he became increasingly involved in urban renewal work in Northern cities, particularly Chicago (January–August 1966), and in the growing protest movement against the Vietnam War. In February 1968, the Sanitation Workers in Memphis, Tennessee began striking for better pay and working conditions and recruited King's support. On April 3, King delivered his "I've Seen the Promised Land" speech, in which he foresaw "difficult days ahead" for the strikers and appeared to prophesy his own death. The next day, April 4, 1968, while standing on the balcony of his motel room waiting to leave for a dinner engagement, King was shot by a sniper, who was holed up in a boarding house across the street. King's funeral took place on April 9 at Ebenezer, with eight hundred people in the sanctuary, as many as one hundred thousand standing outside, and about one hundred twenty million watching on television.

King's surviving prison writings come from a brief arrest in Atlanta, Georgia (October 1960) and from three of his most notable civil rights campaigns, those which took place in Albany, Georgia (December

1961–August 1962), Birmingham, Alabama (April–May 1963), and Selma, Alabama (January–March 1965).

The Magnolia Tea Room Incident

On October 19, 1960, King was arrested for participating in a sit-in at the Magnolia Tea Room of Rich's Department Store in Atlanta, GA and was taken to the Fulton County Jail, where he refused to post bond. Charges on this offense were soon dropped, but he was rearrested immediately upon release for violating the terms of a twelve-month suspended sentence that had been passed on September 23 for a traffic violation that had occurred on May 4. On October 25, he was sentenced to four months hard labor and transferred the next day to the Georgia State Prison at Reidsville. Thanks to the intervention of presidential candidate John F. Kennedy, King was freed on bond on Thursday, October 27.

Five documents from this episode survive.[6] They are too brief to warrant sustained attention here, but several of the ideas that King elaborates in his later prison writings appear in embryonic form. He states that when persons are willing to undergo the privations, humiliations, and sufferings of incarceration for the sake of conscience, they not only demonstrate the strength of their resolve and the justice of their cause, but also weaken the morale of their opponents, place them on the defensive by subjecting them to media scrutiny, and pressure them to negotiate.

---

6. The five documents from this incident appear in King, *Papers*, Vol. 5: *Threshold*: (1) the draft of a statement to Judge James E. Webb, dated October 19, 1960 (522–24); (2) an eight-point outline for an article to be titled, "Why We Chose Jail Rather than Bail," dated by his editors to sometime after King's October 1960 arrest (the article was apparently never published) (525); (3) a press release, dated October 21, 1960 (527); (4) a letter to female inmates, dated sometime between October 19 and 23, 1960 (528–29); and (5) the transcript of a televised interview given on October 27, 1960 upon release from Reidsville (535–36). Additionally, he preached a sermon at the Ebenezer Baptist Church on November 6, 1960, titled "Eight Days Behind Bars." This sermon is mentioned in the Chronology for *Papers*, Vol. 5, *Threshold*, 61, but the text is not included either in that volume or in King, *Papers*, Vol. 6, *Advocate*, and apparently has not survived.

The Albany Movement[7]

On November 17, 1961, a coalition of civil rights groups was formed in Albany, GA to desegregate the city's public facilities. Prominent among these groups were the NAACP and the Student Nonviolent Coordinating Committee (SNCC). The SCLC entered the fray about a month later, when the president of the Albany Movement, Dr. William Anderson, invited King to address a rally. King agreed, stipulating that his participation would be limited to a single speaking engagement. But the overwhelming crowd response prompted Anderson to beg King, in front of the whole audience, to lead the march scheduled for the next day. King agreed; but being thrust so suddenly into the limelight triggered widespread resentment among many of the movement's leaders, especially those representing SNCC. Internal squabbles, disagreement about objectives, and poorly coordinated action marked the campaign for the next eight months, and when it collapsed the following summer, little had been accomplished, although, as we shall see momentarily, King was able to find a silver lining in it all.

Another factor that prevented the Albany Movement from gaining traction was the wisdom or shrewdness of the Albany Chief of Police, Laurie Pritchett, who, as Stephen Oates observes, "planned to overcome nonviolent protest with nonviolent law enforcement."[8] Because the local authorities did not resort to overt brutality, and because they generally succeeded in preventing the most overtly racist elements of the population from retaliating violently against the protesters, King was unable to stake out the moral high ground in Albany, as he had done during the Montgomery bus boycott, and as he would do later in the Birmingham and Selma campaigns. Yet the city authorities refused to capitulate to the movement's demands. Over five hundred movement members were already in jail when King addressed the rally on December 15, 1961, and on the following day, when the march took place, over two hundred more, including King and several of his SCLC lieutenants, were locked up for parading without a permit and obstructing the sidewalks.[9] While King and his associates were in jail, his rivals in the movement negotiated a deal with the

---

7. Sources for the following account include: Garrow, *Bearing the Cross*, 173–230; King, *Autobiography*, 151–69; King Institute Encyclopedia, "Albany Movement"; Oates, *Trumpet*, 188–201.

8. Oates, *Trumpet*, 195; cf. King, *Autobiography*, 160.

9. Oates, *Trumpet*, 192.

city. Imagining that a swift victory had been achieved, King allowed bond to be posted on his behalf, only to discover upon his release on December 18 that the "deal" involved few real gains for the movement.

Protests continued intermittently during the winter and spring of 1962, but without King's direct involvement. On July 10, the city court, having found King and his chief lieutenant, Ralph Abernathy, guilty of the charges, sentenced them each to pay a $178 fine or spend forty-five days "on the streets,"[10] that is, doing civic work for the city during the day and spending their nights in the jailhouse. They opted for the jailing, hoping for the media attention that this would arouse. But early on June 13 they learned that their fines had been paid by an unidentified citizen, and they were unwillingly "kicked out of jail."[11] A month later, a court injunction delayed the next scheduled protest march. This was overturned by a higher court, but on July 24 one or two episodes of police brutality occurred at the county jail, which was under the county sheriff's jurisdiction, not Chief Pritchett's. This precipitated a wave of mob violence, causing King to cancel the march and call for a day of penance on July 25. Two days later, King, Abernathy, Anderson, and nine supporters staged a prayer vigil at city hall intending to get arrested. Pritchett once again committed them to the city jail, in the basement of the city hall. They were locked up from July 27 through August 10, when they were given suspended sentences. Upon their release, King and Abernathy halted the campaign and returned to Atlanta, ostensibly to give the city commission a chance to "save face," but knowing full well that the movement, riven by internal dissension and consistently outmaneuvered by the authorities, was dead.

Yet King believed that the Albany campaign had had some worthwhile results. Thanks to their public demonstrations, he said, "the Negro people straightened up their bent backs." Also, thousands registered to vote, a fact that tipped the state's next gubernatorial race in favor of a candidate who was relatively progressive on racial issues.[12] Moreover, King realized that future civil rights campaigns would require sharply focused objectives, careful strategic planning, unity among the leaders,

---

10. King, *Autobiography*, 156–57.

11. King, *Autobiography*, 159. King's remark appears to be an unattributed paraphrase of a joke that Abernathy had cracked at a mass meeting on the evening of their release: "I've been thrown out of many places in my day, but never before have I been thrown out of a jail." Cited in Oates, *Trumpet*, 193.

12. *Playboy* interview, in King, *Testament*, 344; cf. King, *Why We Can't Wait*, 41–42.

and the thorough training of demonstrators in the theory and practice of nonviolence.

Four documents from King's three stays in the Albany City Jail survive: the diaries he kept during his second and third lockups and two articles that appeared in *The New York Amsterdam News*, one written during his second lockup and published three days after his release, and the other written during his third lockup and published eight days after his release.

Jail Diary for July 10–11, 1962[13]

The first of the two jail diaries was written on a spiral notebook, which King either took with him into his cell at the time of his arrest or was given him by Coretta when she visited him later that day. It was apparently intended only for his own use, or at least it was subsequently used by his secretary and his daughter Yolanda for other purposes. The entry for July 10 tells us that King, Abernathy, their wives, and three friends flew from Atlanta to Albany early that morning, were picked up at the airport by Anderson, and driven to Anderson's home for a short strategy session. Their host gave them an overly optimistic appraisal of the Black community's enthusiasm for the movement and its readiness to endure the penalties of public protest. From there they proceeded to the city courthouse for their scheduled mid-morning sentencing on the charges filed back on December 16. King notes that he and Abernathy "could not in all good conscience pay the fine, and thereby chose to serve the time." Immediately after sentencing, they gave a short press conference in the vestibule of the courthouse to explain their actions, and were then taken downstairs to the jail, which King describes as a "dingy, dirty hole with nothing suggestive of civilized society." King and Abernathy were placed together in the same cell, which "was as filthy as all the rest." However, as King notes wryly, Chief Pritchett understood that he could make the deplorable conditions of the jail known to the public and ordered that it be cleaned up immediately. These comments show that although King may not have been *writing* with an eye to publication, he was certainly *acting* for the sake of publicity. He thinks of himself both as a person moved by deeply held personal convictions

---

13. King, *Autobiography*, 156–59, and King, *Papers*, 7:511–16. The diary is in the possession of the King Archive at Boston University.

and as the leader (or at least the guest "celebrity") of a grassroots political campaign, who could use his public stature to embarrass the authorities and to instigate social change—if only, at that point, to secure proper custodial services in the jail. One senses a mixture of worldly-wise amusement and professional pride in the fact that his presence secured these services for all the prisoners, not just himself.

But Pritchett was not to be outdone. First, he declared that King and Abernathy could not work on the streets, ostensibly to prevent angry Whites from assaulting them, but probably also to thwart King's hope to "give some attention to the daily round" of Black prisoners in a Jim Crow jail. King was crestfallen that his political agenda had been stymied, and after only a few hours he was depressed by "the dull monotony of sameness" in the jail. His spirits were lifted by a visit from Coretta that afternoon, although even this joy was dampened by her report that Yolanda had burst into tears upon learning that her father was in jail. He had several other visits that day from movement representatives, who briefed him on developments, but he spent a miserable night, and awoke with a sore back. Things improved the next day, when he enjoyed a good breakfast—thanks to the fact that the food was prepared at a nearby café, not by city employees. He was also cheered to learn that the protest marches were continuing and that the newly arrested sang freedom songs as they were booked. Thus, the unpleasantness of jailhouse life was rendered tolerable by the knowledge that the cause was prospering. There is no record for the next day in the diary, and, as noted above, King and Abernathy were unexpectedly released early on the morning of July 13, when someone paid their fines.

"A Message from Jail," July 21, 1962[14]

On the day after their release, an article by King appeared in *The New York Amsterdam News*, an African American weekly newspaper, explaining why he and Abernathy had gone to jail. The article begins by asserting that the two friends had undergone "careful soul searching" and had kept their commitments to their families, their churches, and the

---

14. Martin Luther King Jr., "Message from Jail," *New York Amsterdam News*, July 14, 1962, 11, 38. An excerpt is printed in his *Autobiography*, 157. King and Abernathy were arrested on July 10 and released early on July 13, but the opening line asserts that the article is being written "*from* the Albany city jail." An editor's note in the *News* indicates that by the time of publication, King had already been released.

SCLC in mind. But it insists that they were driven to their decision by the fact that over seven hundred members of the Albany Movement were still in jail awaiting trial, and it excoriates the "racist tactics" being used against the protestors, few of whom could afford to post bail or pay their fines. "The time has now come," King writes, "when we must practice civil disobedience in a true sense or delay our freedom thrust for long years." The tone of the article suggests that King and Abernathy were increasingly frustrated at their inability to exert much leverage against the Albany authorities or to orchestrate the protests in a way that would lead to concrete gains. Their ire is publicly directed against the city commission, but disappointment over the contentiousness and ineffectiveness of the movement's leaders lurks just beneath the surface. Nevertheless, their resolve is firm, and one important feature of the article is King's refutation of the charge that the Albany Movement "fosters disrespect for the law and encourages 'lawlessness.'" No, he argues, those who practice civil disobedience to unjust laws and who are willing to pay the penalty for their witness are demonstrating "the highest respect for the law," by honoring the principles of social justice that the laws are intended to implement. King concludes by insisting that imprisonment for the sake of justice "transforms the jail into a haven of liberty and freedom." These arguments anticipate points that King will make again in his "Letter from Birmingham Jail" (April 16, 1963) and in his Address at the Freedom Rally in Cobo Hall in Detroit (June 23, 1963).

Jail Diary for July 27–August 10, 1962[15]

In contrast to the first diary, the second quickly became a piece of movement propaganda. It was published in the August 23, 1962 issue of *Jet*, the African American newsweekly, bearing an editorial note boasting that King had written it "exclusively for *Jet* magazine." It appears that the arrangement with *Jet* was made *during* his incarceration, for the entry for July 29 indicates that he had received a visit that day from Larry Still, an associate editor for the magazine. Whether Still imposed any word limits on King is unknown, but the entries get noticeably shorter as the days pass: those for the first five days are fairly detailed,

---

15. King, "Integration Leader Wary of Being Tricked Out of Jail," *Jet* 22, August 23, 1962, 14–21, reprinted in King, *Autobiography*, 160–67, and King, *Papers*, 7:558–66, 568–69, and 589–90.

containing several paragraphs each; those for the last ten days rarely exceed a few sentences in length.

Quite aside from the fact that his diary was destined for publication, King was aware that his imprisonment and his running battle of wits with Chief Pritchett were making the news. On the very evening of his arrest, King was summoned to Pritchett's office, and refused to leave his cell, remembering how, two weeks earlier, he had been prematurely released. Pritchett himself came downstairs and assured his prisoner that there was no trick here, but rather that he had received a telephone call from Lawrence Spivak, the host of the weekly television program, *Meet the Press*, on which King was scheduled to appear on July 29. King states that Spivak "was very upset and literally begged me to come out on bond." King was allowed to consult with his attorney and staff, and it was agreed that Dr. Anderson would post bond and appear on the show, while he himself would remain in jail.

But the entry for the next day informs us that Pritchett had once again come to his cell, this time with the news that money had been sent for his bond and that he, Pritchett, was obliged to release him. King's reply illustrates the multiple ironies of the situation: "I told him I certainly did not want to be put in the position of being dragged out of jail, but that I had no intention of leaving because I wanted to serve my sentence." King realized that his moral authority depended not only on his willingness to suffer punishment for his cause, but also on the dignity he displayed in his public appearances. To be seen being "dragged out of jail" might have demonstrated his heroism, but it might also have blemished his image. Pritchett, for his part, was taking pains to show King as much courtesy and consideration as possible, partly because of all the media scrutiny, but also out of genuine respect for King. Pritchett had no wish to keep King behind bars, was trying to make his stay as tolerable as possible, and now had legal means to bring his jail time to an end. But he couldn't release his prisoner without aggravating him. It was then that Pritchett informed King of the outbreak of violence at a nearby county jail and of the volatility of the whole situation. King's response was to order his staff to ask the Kennedy Administration to intervene. Apparently, Pritchett made no further effort to eject King from jail.

Most of the remaining entries describe day-to-day events of life behind bars: the sweltering heat of the cells (relieved by occasional trips to the air-conditioned courtroom upstairs), the somewhat erratic meal schedule (relieved by the delivery of "food packages," courtesy of Chief

Pritchett), the devotional services held by King and Abernathy for the other prisoners (with leaders and participants alike all remaining in their cells), and regular visits by family and friends. On the outside, demonstrations continued. King received regular visits from movement leaders, who kept him informed of events. At one fateful strategy session, noted in the entry for July 30, he and his colleagues decided that a four-pronged approach was needed in "the Albany battle," namely legal action in the courts, demonstrations in the streets, an economic boycott, and a vigorous voter registration campaign. But King later realized that a sharply targeted approach would have been more effective than this comprehensive one.

"Why It's Albany," August 18, 1962[16]

Shortly before the end of his third stint in the Albany jail, King wrote a second article for *The Amsterdam News*. He states that he is again writing from his jail cell, and he refers to the prayer vigil on the courthouse steps for which he had been arrested as an event that had taken place "two weeks ago." But the jailing itself was of fifteen days' duration, so he must have composed the article a day or two before his release, and by the time the article appeared in print, King had already been out for a week. Unlike the two jail diaries and the "Message," which were heavily autobiographical, King says almost nothing about himself in this article. Rather, the piece is a straightforward apologia for the Albany Movement. He denies the charge of his opponents that civil rights groups had been engaged in some nefarious conspiracy which had led them to choose Albany as the target of an all-out campaign. But he suggests, somewhat mischievously, that Albany *was*, in a sense, "chosen by destiny" for this dubious honor. By this he means that local demographic and economic factors made it a suitable site for an uprising, although he acknowledges that these factors are to be found in many other Southern cities as well. He mentions the four-pronged approach that had been devised at the meeting on July 30, and closes by insisting that racial segregation is doomed, both because it is politically obsolete and because it is ethically corrupt: "Why Albany? Because Albany symbolizes the bastions of segregation set upon by the compounded forces of morality and justice."

16. King, "Why It's Albany," *New York Amsterdam News*, August 18, 1962, 1, 1.

The Birmingham Campaign[17]

Though Albany was hardly a success, King was determined that it should not be a total failure, and the lessons learned there paid off handsomely eight months later in the stunning victory at Birmingham. Two of these lessons deserve special attention. First, King learned that a nonviolent direct-action campaign required clear and attainable objectives and that the most promising targets were areas in the political and economic life of a community where even modest concrete achievements would have a major impact. Thus, in a district where the citizens were relatively evenly divided on certain key political issues, the registration of even a relatively small number of new voters, casting their ballots as a block, could determine the outcome of elections. Or a business operating on a thin profit margin would be bankrupted by a sustained boycott by even a modest number of its regular customers. Thus, the key to social change was to determine those areas of civic life in which the dominance of Whites depended on the resigned or terrified compliance of Blacks—and then to inspire the Blacks to stop complying. Second, King discovered that a successful campaign needed a simple, flexible method, and one in which the intended outcome was already foreshadowed and exemplified in the process used to attain it. King had to show that racial segregation contradicted cherished American values, and he saw two distinct but closely related and equally significant ways to do that: first by showing that the Bible, which the vast majority of Americans held sacred, defended the rights of the poor, the weak, the defenseless, and the oppressed; and second, by showing that freedom and equality for all citizens were explicitly guaranteed in the founding documents of the nation. But for a civil rights campaign to exert leverage on the laws and institutions of the land, the demonstrators had to display in their conduct and comportment precisely the kind of dignity, decency, courage, and compassion that reflected the best ideals of Christian discipleship and American citizenship. King did not teach that African Americans *deserved* freedom *because* they were exemplary Christians and exemplary citizens. That would have turned inalienable rights into earned privileges—and thereby conceded the very point at issue. Rather, he insisted that when demonstrators acted in ways that reflected the values upon which the

---

17. Sources for the following account include: Garrow, *Bearing the Cross*, 231–86; King, *Autobiography*, 170–217; King, *Why We Can't Wait*; King Research and Education Institute Encyclopedia, "Birmingham Campaign (1963)"; Oates, *Trumpet*, 209–43.

Christian faith and the American republic stood, the defenders of segregation could no longer pretend that Blacks were inherently inferior beings, to whom the franchise need not be extended.

King devised a four-step method by which demonstrators could display in the very act of demonstrating the virtues commensurate with the rights they were demanding: (1) careful inquiry into the social, political, and economic conditions of the local community; (2) good-faith negotiation with its elected officials and other leaders; (3) rigorous self-purification by the demonstrators prior to the demonstrations, to assure that if violence were done to them during the demonstrations, they would not retaliate in such a way that would only justify the use of coercive force by the authorities; and (4) nonviolent direct action itself, consisting of non-cooperation with unjust laws, public demonstrations, economic boycotts, voter registration drives, etc.[18] The Montgomery campaign, which had not been planned in advance but was an impromptu response to the arrest of Rosa Parks, lacked the preliminary research and careful self-purification called for by steps 1 and 3, but those deficiencies were rapidly overcome by the inspired leadership and brilliant tactical improvisation of King and other leaders. The Albany Movement self-destructed partly because the SCLC had entered late in the game and had no time to prepare the demonstrators in steps 1, 2, and 3, and partly because the authorities did not play into the demonstrators' hands by using unnecessary force or outright brutality. In contrast, the Birmingham campaign, for all its twists and turns, was executed "by the book," at least in the sense that all four steps were scrupulously followed. Accordingly, the demonstrators consistently held the moral high ground against the authorities, while the Birmingham authorities seemed strangely determined to hold the moral *low* ground, a fact that King adroitly exploited. It was in Birmingham that the prophetic words with which King had ended his earlier article, "Why It's Albany," were fulfilled: "the bastions of segregation [were] set upon by the compounded forces of morality and justice."

The great challenge of the Birmingham Campaign, at least in the early stages, was the *timing* of the thing, a point on which King dwells at length in his "Letter from Birmingham Jail," and which he acknowledged in the very title of his book about the campaign, *Why We Can't Wait*.[19] In

---

18. These steps represent the schematization of the methods of Mahatma Gandhi, whose writings King had studied in the spring of 1950. They are outlined in King's "Letter from Birmingham Jail" in *Why We Can't Wait*, 87–90.

19. King, *Why We Can't Wait*, 90–92.

September 1962, King was invited by the Rev. Fred Shuttlesworth, pastor of the Bethel Baptist Church of Birmingham and head of the Alabama Christian Movement for Human Rights (ACMHR), a local affiliate of the SCLC, to join in the civil rights efforts that had already been going on for several years. Segregation was firmly entrenched in the city, almost bizarrely so. For example, a children's book had recently been banned from the schools because it featured white and black rabbits, and a drive was afoot to prevent "Negro music" from being aired on White radio stations.[20] Assaults of Black citizens and bombings of their homes and churches were common, and the local police, under the leadership of Commissioner Eugene "Bull" Connor, not only turned a blind eye to outbreaks of racial violence, but used fiercely repressive tactics to squelch the ACMHR's efforts to integrate the city's public facilities. Knowing the dangers that awaited them in Birmingham, and still smarting from their failure in Albany, King and his associates laid careful plans.

But in November 1962 the city voted to change the structure of its local government and set mayoral elections for March 5, 1963. King rescheduled the opening of his campaign for two weeks after the election. But when the ballots were counted there was no clear winner, and a run-off election was needed. The two leading candidates, Connor and Albert Boutwell, were equally committed to racial segregation, but Boutwell was known to be less violent of temper, and when he won the run-off on April 2, the local newspapers declared that a "new day had dawned" for the city. Unfortunately, Connor and other city commissioners contended that the term of the offices to which they had been elected some years earlier did not expire until 1965 and refused to yield power. Thus, although Boutwell was now the mayor, Connor remained in control of the city's police and fire departments. Many leading citizens of Birmingham, including some Blacks, as well as the Kennedy administration and the national media, believed that the scheduled civil rights campaign should be suspended indefinitely to give the courts time to sort out who was actually going to govern the city, and, presuming that the results of the recent election were upheld, to give Boutwell time to establish his new administration and ease the city's racial tensions. King and Shuttlesworth, however, doubted that much was likely to change under Boutwell for the city's Black citizens, and refused to delay their campaign any longer. Thus, beginning on April 3,

---

20. Oates, *Trumpet*, 210.

marches and lunch counter sit-ins took place during the daytime, while evening pep rallies and songfests were staged in Black churches.

On Wednesday, April 10, a state circuit court issued an injunction against the demonstrations, giving the city government(s) power to arrest the protestors. Some three hundred were promptly jailed. Next day, King and Abernathy held a press conference and pledged to disobey the injunction and go to jail, too. Late that evening, however, word came that the SCLC bail bond fund had run out. Up to that point, King had been restricting the ranks of the protestors to those who had undergone the prescribed regimen of "self-purification," and as promptly as the members of his "nonviolent army" were arrested, they were bailed out and sent back to the lines. But now, with so many in lockup, the number of properly trained demonstrators was dwindling, and if King too were to go to jail, the chances of raising new bond money might dwindle, causing the Birmingham campaign to suffer the same ignominious end as that of Albany. Yet if King broke his vow to violate the injunction, he would lose the credibility and moral authority on which his leadership depended. Over the objections of his lieutenants, he decided to "make a faith act," that is, to lead a march and go to jail—uncertain of when he and his followers would be released.[21] On April 12—Good Friday—he and Abernathy were arrested, charged with civil and criminal contempt, and committed to the Birmingham city jail.

But if the injunction and the depletion of bail funds were ill-timed for King, the protests themselves seemed so to eight of Alabama's most prominent White religious leaders, who, on the same day that King was arrested, ran a "public statement" in the *Birmingham News*, "denouncing [his] efforts."[22] The statement acknowledges the "natural impatience of people who feel that their hopes are slow in being realized," but insists that "recent public events" have created an "opportunity for a new constructive and realistic approach to racial problems," rendering the ongoing demonstrations "unwise and untimely." It contends that the "facing of issues can best be accomplished by citizens of our own metropolitan area," and applauds the "local news media and law enforcement officials . . . on the calm manner in which these demonstrations have been handled."

King did not read the statement until four days later, for he was being held incommunicado in a narrow, ill-furnished cell, with only a

---

21. King, *Why We Can't Wait*, 81.
22. Carpenter et al., "Public Statement by Eight Alabama Clergymen."

barred window high overhead for light. Fortunately, on the second day of his confinement, his circumstances began to improve. He received visits from his attorneys on Saturday and again on Easter Sunday, and learned that his brother, the Rev. A. D. King, had led a huge march. On Easter Monday, still another attorney, Clarence Jones, brought word that singer Harry Belafonte had raised $50,000 in bail money, which was available immediately, and had pledged to raise as much more as would be needed. Additionally, King was permitted to call his wife, who informed him that President Kennedy had interceded on his behalf—which explained why he had just been given a mattress, a blanket, a pillow, and telephone privileges. King was deeply moved by these developments:

> I found it hard to say what I felt. Jones's message had brought me more than relief from the immediate concern about money; more than gratitude for the loyalty of friends far away; more than confirmation that the life of the movement could not be snuffed out. What silenced me was a profound sense of awe. I was aware of a feeling that had been present all along below the surface of consciousness, pressed down under the weight of concern for the movement: I had never been truly in solitary confinement; God's companionship does not stop at the door of a jail cell. I don't know whether the sun was shining at that moment. But I know that once again I could see the light.[23]

These words indicate his frame of mind when, on Tuesday, April 14, his lawyers brought him a copy of Friday's newspaper, in which the eight clergymen had published their open letter to him. His response, written with a pen surreptitiously left in his cell by his attorney, and scribbled on the margins of the newspaper, pieces of toilet paper, and sheets of contraband stationery, is the greatest apologia of the Civil Rights Movement, and one of the greatest pieces of Christian prison literature ever composed. Its form and contents are analyzed below.

King and Abernathy posted $300 bail on Friday, April 19, and were released. During the following week, King, Abernathy, Shuttlesworth, and SCLC staff member Wyatt Walker stood trial for criminal contempt—the charge of civil contempt had been dropped by the judge—and, upon being found guilty, were sentenced to five days in jail. They appealed, however, and it was not until late October 1967 that they served their time.

During the two weeks that King was in jail and in court, the movement faltered. But one of King's lieutenants, James Bevel, suggested a way

---

23. King, *Why We Can't Wait*, 84.

to jumpstart it, namely, by "manning" the demonstrations with youth and children. Predictably, the so-called "Children's Crusade" evoked a storm of controversy, although King parried the sanctimonious expressions of concern for the young people's welfare by asking why the critics had never said much about the deplorable conditions of the city's Black schools or the laws that closed parks and playgrounds to Black children. Yet the critics were right that these new recruits were in danger, and the carnivalesque atmosphere that their youthful enthusiasm soon gave to the marches utterly infuriated Bull Connor, who ordered that attack dogs and high-pressure fire hoses be used to "control" them. The ghastly spectacle that ensued was captured by television cameras and broadcast to the world—and was met with widespread revulsion. Using public opinion for leverage, Burke Marshall, assistant attorney general for civil rights, was able to broker a tentative settlement on May 10 between King and Birmingham's business leaders (not the city government).

But the segregationists were not through. On May 11, the Gaston Motel, where King had his command post, was bombed, and on May 20, the local board of education suspended or expelled over a thousand Black students who had participated in the demonstrations. An appellate court swiftly overturned the school board action, and the Alabama Supreme Court upheld the results of the citywide elections of April 2, thereby ending Bull Connor's reign of terror. The desegregation of public facilities proceeded, and the movement rightly claimed victory, although a tragic postscript occurred on the morning of Sunday, September 15, when the Sixteenth Street Baptist Church, one of the hubs of the movement's earlier activities, was dynamited and four children were killed.[24]

"Letter from Birmingham Jail," April 16, 1963[25]

We saw earlier that the great challenge faced by King during the Birmingham Campaign was timing, and his "Letter" repeatedly stresses the urgency of the civil rights cause and the moral impossibility of further delay. Yet he expresses this urgency in gentle tones of disappointed love for his critics. It is this paradoxical blend of unyielding fervor and patient

24. A transcript of King's "Eulogy for the Martyred Children" is printed in King, *Testament*, 221–23, and a sound recording, with the slightly altered title, "Eulogy for the Young Victims of the Sixteenth Street Baptist Church Bombing," is included in King and Shepard, *Call*, Disk 4.

25. King, *Why We Can't Wait*, 85–109. Page references will be given in the text.

reasonableness that accounts for the work's extraordinary rhetorical power. King is writing to people whom he admires and respects, and who are generally sympathetic to the cause of racial equality and civil rights, but who have failed to rise to the defense of that cause at a critical moment in national and world history. Indeed, it is precisely because he regards them as "men of genuine good will," whose criticisms have been "sincerely set forth," that he decides to reply to their letter (85). If they had been strident opponents of the cause, King might have responded with fiery defensiveness. But if they had been vocal supporters of the movement, a brief word of cordial thanks might have sufficed. These clergymen, however, had agreed that his cause was just, but had criticized his tactics as inflammatory and his timing as inauspicious. The aim of his response, therefore, was to use the moral leverage created by their admission that his cause was just to explain why his tactics were suitable and why his campaign could not be further delayed.

To accomplish this aim, his argument oscillates between detailed explanations of the theory and practice of nonviolent direct action and forceful vindications of his decision to press forward with the campaign, despite the recent vagaries of the city's electoral politics. This powerful thematic oscillation may be seen in the following series of quotations. Those passages pertaining to the theory and practice of nonviolence are shown in regular type, while those pertaining to the timing of the Birmingham campaign and its place in history are shown in italics. A glance at the successive page numbers reveals how the pattern works.

> In any nonviolent campaign there are four basic steps: collection of the facts to determine whether injustices exist; negotiation; self-purification; and direct action. (87)

> *For years now I have heard the word "Wait!" . . . This "Wait!" has almost always meant "Never." We must come to see, with one of our distinguished jurists, that "justice too long delayed is justice denied." (91)*

> There are two types of laws: just and unjust. . . . One has not only a legal but moral responsibility to obey just laws. Conversely, one has a moral responsibility to disobey unjust laws. (93)

> *The time is always ripe to do right. Now is the time to make real the promise of democracy and transform our pending national elegy into a creative psalm of brotherhood. Now is the time to lift*

our national policy from the quicksand of racial injustice to the solid rock of human dignity. (98)[26]

The Negro has many pent-up resentments and latent frustrations, and he must release them. So let him march; let him make prayer pilgrimages to the city hall; let him go on freedom rides—and try to understand why he must do so. (100)

We will reach the goal of freedom in Birmingham and all over the nation because the goal of America is freedom. Abused and scorned though we may be, our destiny is tied up with America's destiny. (106)

Over the past few years I have consistently preached that nonviolence demands that the means we use must be as pure as the ends we seek. (107)

One day the South will know that when these disinherited children of God sat down at lunch counters, they were in reality standing up for what is best in the American dream and for the most sacred values in our Judaeo-Christian heritage. (108)

Sprinkled throughout the "Letter" are numerous references to figures from the Western religious and philosophical tradition whose combined moral authority lend great weight to King's argument, and it is a testimony to King's erudition that he could cite so many of these so effortlessly, when he had no access to his library.[27] He deflects his critics' charge that he was an "outsider," who had no business meddling in Birmingham's problems, by mentioning the eighth-century-BCE prophets

---

26. Four months later, in his "I Have a Dream" speech at the close of the March on Washington, King again used the refrain, "Now is the time," with telling rhetorical effect. See King, *Testament*, 281. A sound recording is included in King and Shepard, *Call*, Disk 3.

27. In his article, "Black Theology—Black Church," James Cone stresses the extent to which King's theology was shaped by his heritage in the Black Church and laments the fact that this is often overlooked in studies of King's spiritual and intellectual development. He remarks: "The references to the intellectual tradition of western philosophy and theology are primarily for the benefit of the White public so that King could demonstrate to them that he could think as well or better than any other seminary or university graduate" (411). Although I cordially agree with Cone's overall argument, I am not sure that this remark applies to the "Letter from Birmingham Jail" (which, admittedly, Cone does not reference in his article). In the "Letter," King cites a wide variety of sources: not only the giants of western philosophy and theology, but also heroes from Christian Scripture and the Civil Rights Movement. And he does so, not to certify his academic credentials, but to embed the Civil Rights Movement in the long and honorable heritage of principled dissent to social injustice. The wide array of citations fortifies his argument and increases its rhetorical effectiveness for *all* readers.

and the apostle Paul, who left their homelands to preach where their message was needed (86). He buttresses his claim that disobedience to an unjust law is a moral duty by citing the writings of Augustine and Aquinas (93). He demonstrates the evils of racial segregation by mentioning Martin Buber's theory of I-Thou relationships and Paul Tillich's theory of sin as separation (93). He supports the practice of civil disobedience by mentioning the opposition of the Three Youths to Nebuchadnezzar in Daniel 3:1–30, the provocative philosophical inquiries of Socrates in Athens, and the protest mounted by American colonists against Britain's exorbitant tax policies at the Boston Tea Party (95). He invokes Hegel's philosophy of history to situate the American Civil Rights Movement within the ongoing efforts by persons of color around the world to free themselves from colonial domination (100). He proudly aligns himself with other "extremists" of history, such as Jesus, the prophet Amos, the apostle Paul, Martin Luther, John Bunyan, Abraham Lincoln, and Thomas Jefferson (100–101).[28] He quotes a line from a T. S. Eliot play, *Murder in the Cathedral*, to draw a parallel between the assassination of Thomas Becket by King Henry II and the persecution of protestors by Commissioner Connor and Chief Pritchett (107–8). And he crowns this list of luminaries by honoring two heroes of the movement: James Meredith, who had integrated the University of Mississippi in 1962, despite ferocious White opposition, and an "old, oppressed, battered Negro woman" (known in Movement lore as "Mother" Pollard), who had, during the Montgomery Bus Boycott of 1956, "responded with ungrammatical profundity to one who inquired about her weariness: 'My feets is tired, but my soul is at rest'" (108). This array of citations is intended to show that the urgent quest by African American citizens for their God-given and constitutionally guaranteed rights stood squarely within a tradition of moral discourse and political action that his critics themselves had to honor and showed that it was the subtext of his critics' appeal to "the principles of law and order and common sense," not the ongoing demonstrations, that was "unwise and untimely."

Also conspicuous in King's "Letter" is his forthright account of the deep disappointment he feels in the White liberal churches, whom his clergy critics represent. He chides them for being more devoted to domestic tranquility than social justice (95–99), and for their tendency to "stand on the sideline and mouth pious irrelevancies and sanctimonious

28. King offered a similar response to being called an "extremist" in an interview he gave for *Playboy Magazine*, January 1965, and reprinted in King, *Testament*, 356.

trivialities" (103), instead of boldly engaging the pressing moral and social issues of the day. Yet he expresses this double disappointment with grave courtesy, suggesting that he hopes his counter-rebuke will register with these well-intentioned ministers and their flocks. One suspects that the powerful experience of "God's companionship," which had occurred the night before reading their monitory statement in the local newspaper, was still fresh in his mind, and enabled him to rise above the rancor he might naturally have felt toward them, and to refrain from the ridicule to which he might justifiably have subjected them. He writes from his heart, but he does not take personal umbrage at their words.

Before we leave the "Letter from Birmingham Jail," let us analyze more deeply his four-step outline of a properly conducted nonviolent direct-action campaign. It is noteworthy that the outline focuses on the actions taken by the protestors. It says little about the anticipated reactions of the local authorities, or about the media attention that the confrontation between the protestors and the authorities might attract, or about the wider public response that the media attention was expected to arouse. Clearly, however, the actual success of any given campaign depended heavily on these factors, and a large part of King's genius as the leader of the Civil Rights Movement was his ability to foresee how his adversaries would react to his initiatives and his skill in exploiting his adversaries' blunders and atrocities in the court of public opinion. The moral force that King was able to exert against the Jim Crow laws hinged largely on the tendency of the local authorities to enforce those laws with brutally repressive tactics, and on the habit of local White supremacists to commit acts of wanton violence against their Black neighbors with almost complete impunity. The wider world had turned a blind eye to the structural evils of segregation for decades, but King realized that it could not ignore the televised evidence that disproportionate force was being used by the police to defend these evils, and that violent crimes were being committed by thugs under the aegis of local laws.[29] Thus, to understand King's four-step strategy properly—and to understand the true brilliance of his implementation of that strategy in the Birmingham Campaign of 1963 and the Selma Campaign of 1965—we must fill in some of the gaps

29. Conversely, when the authorities responded to King's nonviolent protestors with restraint and courtesy, as happened at Albany in 1962, the status quo which the authorities were upholding did not look so bad. Among the reasons that King selected Birmingham and Selma for his subsequent campaigns was that he could count on the lawmen of those cities to make exactly the kind of mistakes that would play into his hands.

left in the account given in the "Letter." We must take note of the way he anticipated and made allowance for those contingencies that might have derailed or discredited his campaigns before they began, and of the skillful "moral jiu-jitsu" he employed against the heavily armed law enforcement officers who were trying to derail his campaigns.[30] Here we shall restate King's four steps a bit more expansively than before and add some of the specific considerations that he and his lieutenants had to keep in mind when executing each step in turn.

Step 1: Fact-finding. Before a nonviolent direct-action campaign begins, and to ensure its moral legitimacy, careful fact-finding is necessary. A target city must be one in which the violation of the civil rights of Blacks is systemic, egregious, and easily documented, and in which the ecclesiastical and civic institutions of the local Black community are strong enough and unified enough to enable the efficient organization of massive public protest.[31] A nonviolent direct action campaign cannot be successfully executed in a city whose Black community is divided against itself or otherwise incapable of being mobilized, as internal dissension will discredit the campaign in the eyes of the public and gravely reduce the effectiveness of whatever tactics are used (as at Albany).

Step 2. Negotiation. Before nonviolent direct action is used, sincere and sustained efforts at good-faith negotiation must be made with local elected officials and/or business leaders regarding those laws and customs that the African American community finds particularly offensive and injurious. As a sign of their good faith, the campaign negotiators begin with the assumption that the representatives of the White establishment intend to follow through with any promises or concessions they make during the talks, and they, the campaign negotiators, agree not to begin public protest unless and until talks break down or it becomes clear that the establishment's promises were little more than disingenuous stalling tactics.

Step 3. Self-purification. Before prospective demonstrators are sent into action, they must receive careful training in the theory and practice of nonviolence, surrender any weapons they might be tempted to use,

---

30. The phrase "moral jiu-jitsu" was coined, to the best of my knowledge, by Gregg, *Power*, 43, who writes: "The non-violence and good will of the victim act like the lack of physical opposition by the user of physical jiu-jitsu, to cause the attacker to lose his balance." King had studied Gregg's book on Gandhian satyagraha, and corresponded with him personally, though I am not aware that he used this pithy phrase in any of his speeches or writings.

31. See King, *Why We Can't Wait*, 47–61.

even in self-defense, against law enforcement officers or counter-protestors, and pledge to endure verbal abuse and/or physical assault without retaliating in kind. A direct-action campaign cannot be justifiably conducted or successfully executed without a critical mass of persons willing to undergo this advance preparation and self-purification, to follow the prescribed nonviolent regimen, and to obey the instructions of the designated leaders during public demonstrations.[32] Nor can a campaign be successfully executed unless sufficient bail funds are available to assure that those demonstrators who do get arrested will be promptly sprung from jail, whether or not they intend to rejoin the protests.[33] And once under way, a campaign that leads to outbreaks of violence by members of the oppressed community against the establishment must be temporarily suspended until tempers cool. This holds true even if those members of the oppressed community who resort to violence are acting independently of the movement and have not received proper training in non-violence. Thus, the campaign assumes some responsibility for the behavior of all persons who stand to benefit from the attainment of its objectives, including those who have not pledged to abide by its discipline.[34]

Step 4. Non-violent direct action. The methods of the campaign may include the refusal to obey demonstrably unjust laws, the refusal to patronize places of business that adhere to these laws, and the staging of mass public demonstrations (sit-ins, marches, rallies, etc.) to dramatize the injustice of those laws and the grave need of reform. Once under way, the campaign depends for its success on the use by local officials of repressive police tactics, which glaringly illustrate the injustice of the very laws they are supposed to enforce, and/or criminal actions carried out by local White supremacists, which grimly exemplify the inequities and brutalities endemic to local society. It also depends on the presence of journalists willing to publicize any instances of police brutality or

32. See King, *Why We Can't Wait*, 66–70.

33. King's decision to go to jail on April 12, 1963, after word had come the night before that the bail bond fund had been depleted, is the exception that proves the rule. Many of King's SCLC lieutenants objected to his decision to violate the court injunction of April 10, believing that only he could raise the needed money, and believing that he could not do so from inside a jail cell. King saw the logic of this, but he decided to violate the injunction because he had already vowed to do so before learning that the bail money was gone and could not go back on his vow without compromising the very moral authority on which his ability to raise the needed funds depended.

34. This principle had been put into dramatic effect on the Day of Penance that King called on July 25, 1962, at the height of the Albany Campaign, after an outbreak of violence by Black citizens who were not trained in the theory and practice of nonviolence.

racist hate crimes.[35] And a campaign can only be deemed a success if it eventuates in the reforms called for in the earlier negotiations with local leaders, and preferably in the passage and enforcement of federal laws that mandate similar reforms throughout the land.[36]

The Selma Campaign[37]

King deployed his four-fold strategy with great skill during the Selma Campaign of 1965 and either presupposes or explicitly cites it in the two documents he penned during his five-day lockup in the Selma City Jail and in the public statement he issued upon his release.

Despite the considerable gains the Civil Rights Movement had made by 1963 in overturning Jim Crow laws throughout the South, many municipalities refused to extend the franchise to African Americans. Voter registration offices were seldom open, the lines of applicants were long, the registrars were lackadaisical, the qualifying tests that applicants had to pass were lengthy and difficult, and the commission of even a trivial error on a form could disqualify an applicant. The chief objective of the movement in 1964–65, therefore, was to reform voter registration procedures and to add large numbers of Blacks to the voter rolls.[38] But efforts to do so met with fierce opposition. During the Freedom Summer project of 1964 in Mississippi, three civil rights workers were murdered, dozens more were beaten and harassed, and the homes of many local Blacks were bombed. And the Credentials Committee at

---

35. The newsreels of the tactics used against the "Children's Crusade" during the Birmingham Campaign were instrumental in arousing national and international outrage against segregation. And news coverage of the "Bloody Sunday" debacle and the murders of Jimmie Lee Jackson, James Reeb, and Viola Liuzzo during the Selma Campaign would have an even greater impact on world opinion.

36. Thus, the 1957 and 1960 Civil Rights Acts were direct and indirect consequences, respectively, of the Montgomery Bus Boycott; the 1964 Civil Rights Act was the result of the Birmingham Campaign; and the 1965 Voting Rights Act was passed in response to the great Selma-to-Montgomery March (see below).

37. Sources for the following account include: Garrow, *Bearing the Cross*, 357–414; King, *Autobiography*, 270–89; "Selma to Montgomery March (1965)" on the King Research and Education Institute website; Oates, *Trumpet*, 325–64.

38. See, e.g., Martin Luther King Jr., "Hammer on Civil Rights," *Nation* 198, March 9, 1964, 230–34; "Negroes Are Not Moving Too Fast," *Saturday Evening Post* 237, November 7, 1964, 8–9; and especially "Civil Right No. 1: The Right to Vote," *New York Times Magazine*, March 14, 1965, 26–27. These articles are reprinted in King, *Testament*, 169–75, 176–81, and 182–88, respectively.

the 1964 Democratic National Convention seated only two members of the Mississippi Freedom Democratic Party, for fear that the delegations from the states of the Deep South would withdraw their support from the party ticket if Blacks were given their fair share of power.

But the Movement would not be thwarted. On January 2, 1965, the SCLC joined with the SNCC and several local organizations to launch a voter registration drive in Selma, Alabama. Selma was chosen for two reasons. First, the disenfranchisement of Blacks was especially egregious: despite repeated efforts by civil rights workers, only 2 percent of the city's Black population were on the voter rolls. Second, the local police authorities could be counted on to use the kinds of brutality that would arouse national outrage. Both the mayor of Selma, Joe Smitherman, and the city's new public safety director, Wilson Baker, proved to be reasonably temperate in their management of the protests. But the sheriff of Dallas County, Jim Clark, was a rabid and foul-mouthed segregationist, and once demonstrators passed into his jurisdiction, they were sure to be met with violent repression. Clark's jurisdiction included the Dallas County Courthouse, which was located within the Selma city limits, and the undeveloped land just across the Edmund Pettus Bridge, on the south side of the Alabama River.

King arrived in Selma on January 2, 1965, and put his lieutenants, James Bevel and Hosea Williams, in charge of local operations. He returned on January 18, the next date set for voter registration, and led a march to the courthouse. No violence broke out on that occasion, but a week later, on January 25, an elderly woman was savagely beaten at the courthouse by Clark himself, with King and Bevel feverishly managing to restrain the protestors from retaliating. With his city seething in anger, Mayor Smitherman called in state troopers, who were commanded by another notorious segregationist, Al Lingo, director of the Alabama Department of Public Safety. King, always sensitive to moments of "creative tension,"[39] led another march, with some two hundred and fifty participants, on February 1, and this time refused to comply with Baker's standing order to subdivide his followers into small groups spaced widely apart. They were all arrested, and, because the city jail was too small to accommodate them all, taken to the county jail—a predictably abysmal place. On February 5, he was visited by Coretta, who brought the stunning news that she had met that day with Malcolm X, who had come

---

39. Cf. his comments in the "Letter from Birmingham Jail," *Why We Can't Wait*, 89–90.

to Selma to support King's work. "If the White people realize what the alternative is," Malcolm remarked to her, "perhaps they will be more willing to hear Dr. King."[40] King was released later that day.

On February 18, during voter registration activities in nearby Marion, Alabama (Coretta Scott King's hometown), an upstanding young Black citizen, Jimmie Lee Jackson, was shot by Lingo's state troopers. Jackson died on February 26, and King presided at his funeral. After the funeral, James Bevel announced that King would lead a march from Selma to the state capitol in Montgomery, beginning on Sunday, March 7. King subsequently asked that the march be delayed a day to allow him to preside over Sunday services at Ebenezer, but a group of over five hundred marchers assembled that morning as planned, and from his church office in Atlanta King reluctantly gave them the go-ahead, intending to join them later. The march had been banned by Governor George Wallace, however, and when the throng crossed the Pettus Bridge they were met by a cohort of state troopers, who, almost immediately after ordering the marchers to disband, charged them with billy clubs flailing, fired tear gas into their midst, and then charged again. As the marchers retreated to a nearby church, Clark's deputies, mounted on horseback and armed with bullwhips, attacked them from the side. Over one hundred and forty marchers were injured.

When King got word of the events of "Bloody Sunday," he bewailed his decision not to be present for the march, flew immediately to Selma, and hurriedly summoned the nation's clergy—especially its White liberal clergy, whose failure to involve themselves in the struggle he had excoriated in his great "Letter from Birmingham Jail"—to join him in a follow-up march, scheduled for Tuesday, March 9. The plan was not for the marchers to try to breach the line of troopers, but to turn back peaceably when the troopers' intention to use violence against them was made obvious to the world. A federal judge issued an injunction against this second march, but King forged ahead, telling federal and state officials that he "would rather die on the highway in Alabama than make a butchery of [his] conscience by compromising with evil."[41] The march proceeded, and when the protestors crossed the Pettus Bridge and again found their way blocked, they simply knelt in prayer and

---

40. Oates, *Trumpet*, 341.

41. "Behind the Selma March," in King, *Testament*, 130. King had used the "butchery" remark, which he borrowed from John Bunyan, in his "Letter to Birmingham Jail," *Why We Can't Wait*, 101.

then dispersed as ordered. But King pledged that the twice-averted pilgrimage from Selma to Montgomery would eventually take place. That night, James Reeb, a Unitarian minister from Boston, Massachusetts, who had come to Selma in response to King's call, was beaten to death by a group of White thugs.

The deaths of Jackson and Reeb finally stirred the government to action. President Lyndon B. Johnson submitted a Voting Rights Bill to Congress on March 17, and the federal judge, who had earlier prohibited the second march, now proclaimed himself satisfied that the third march was prudently planned and would not lead to violence or mayhem. So, on March 21, King and three hundred pilgrims set out from Selma, arriving in the state capital four days letter, where they were met by a crowd of some twenty-five thousand supporters.[42] The flush of victory was spoiled later that evening, however, when Viola Liuzzo, a woman from Michigan who had come to Alabama for the march, was shot and killed in her car by members of the Ku Klux Klan as she was ferrying demonstrators back to their homes.

Three documents survive from King's brief incarceration in the Dallas County Jail in Selma: a public statement of the movement's objectives, an open letter to the world, soliciting support for the movement's work, and a sheet of instructions to his lieutenants, bidding them to keep up the pressure during his incarceration.

Statement on Voter Registration, February 1, 1965[43]

At a rally at Brown Chapel African Methodist Episcopal Church in Selma, just prior to his arrest, King issued a forceful, even pugnacious, statement to the press, outlining the movement's demands and summoning the nation's government and citizenry to support its efforts. The tone suggests that King is confident of his ultimate victory, but he is also aware, and wants the nation to be aware, that no concrete gains have yet been made, and that the stonewalling tactics used to prevent the registration of Black voters are still in use. Moreover, he understands the ferocity of the opposition arrayed against his campaign, and clearly enunciates the bitter paradox facing—and driving—the Civil Rights Movement: "If Negroes

---

42. A transcript of the speech King gave at the state capitol building, under the title, "Our God Is Marching On!" is printed in King, *Testament*, 227–30; a sound recording is included in King and Shepard, *Call*, Disk 5.

43. King, *Autobiography*, 275.

could vote," he promises, "there would be no Jim Clarks, there would be no oppressive poverty directed against Negroes." But it is precisely because of the Jim Clarks that Blacks are prevented from voting. The aim of the movement is that "the whole community might live together in harmony," but first it must expose the *dis*-harmony built into the system of racial segregation. The present demonstrations do not *cause* disharmony in a hitherto just, prosperous, and tranquil social order, as the guardians of the status quo contend. Rather, they reveal the injustices and humiliations under which an oppressed minority has long been suffering but against which it has hitherto been too terrified and disorganized to resist. But the time of silent despair and dull resignation is over. "This is our intention: to declare war on the evils of demagoguery. The entire [Negro] community will join in this protest, and we will not relent until there is a change in the voting process and the establishment of democracy." Persons who are not truly free when they are not in jail must be willing to go to jail to dramatize their oppression and to express their refusal to cooperate any longer with a system that deprives them of their God-given and inalienable constitutional rights.

Letter from a Selma, Alabama Jail, February 1, 1965[44]

On the day of King's arrest, King wrote another "letter from jail," which was published four days later in the *New York Times*. It is much shorter than the famous missive from Birmingham, occupying about half a sheet of newsprint and furnished with a large print headline and a coupon at the bottom for persons interested in making a financial contribution to the SCLC in support of the Selma campaign. The letter is partly an exposé of the conditions against which the movement is protesting and partly a solicitation for funds. King claims the moral high ground by reminding readers that he had recently been awarded the Nobel Peace Prize, adding wryly that the Norwegian monarch could scarcely have guessed at the time that the recipient of this high honor would soon be jailed for continuing the very fight for which he had earned it. But, King insists, there is "unfinished business in the South." It is one thing for the U.S. Congress to pass laws and for international committees to hand out prestigious awards to movement leaders, but quite another for

---

44. Martin Luther King Jr., "A Letter from a Selma, Alabama Jail," *New York Times*, February 5, 1965, 15; reprinted in Oates, *Trumpet*, 342–43.

American Blacks to exercise their right to vote. They are made to stand in line all day at registration offices, and when finally called to fill out the necessary forms, they are subjected to lengthy qualifying exams larded with obscure questions that most ordinary citizens could not answer. He underscores the absurdity of the situation by noting that there are more Negroes presently serving jail time for protesting this obstructionism than there are on the voting rolls. Yet the right to vote is not the only aim of their protest: human dignity and decency are at issue here. King notes that when "reporters asked Sheriff Clark if a woman defendant was married, he replied, 'She's a n----r woman and she hasn't got a Miss or a Mrs. in front of her name.'" King then pleads for donations to the cause, reminding readers that although Southern Blacks are willing to endure jail time in the pursuit of their rights, their incomes are meager in the best of times and utterly cut off during their incarceration. It is a bit unclear whether King means that donations will support the families of the jailed or will be used for bail bonds, so that protestors can return to work. King closes his letter by noting: "Your help can be a message of unity which the thickest jail walls cannot muffle."

"The Letter from a Selma Jail" contains no fresh exposition of its author's religious or political convictions and no testimony to his latest carceral experience. It certainly burns with moral passion, and it uses King's stature as an internationally recognized apostle of social justice and racial reconciliation to solicit much-needed financial support for those who are suffering nobly for a righteous cause.[45] But it lacks the loftiness of style, the display of erudition, the forcefulness of argument, and the dignity of tone that marked King's Birmingham masterpiece.

Instructions to Movement Associates, February 2 (?), 1965[46]

The third document from the Selma jailing is a page of instructions, written on Waldorf-Astoria Hotel stationery, which King wrote to Andrew Young and his other lieutenants, assuring them that the campaign would

45. It may be worth noting that whereas the Black press cites King's professional titles in his bylines—he is "Rev. M. L. King" in *Jet* and "Dr. Martin Luther King Jr." in *The Amsterdam News*—*The New York Times* simply gives his name. Perhaps this is due to differing editorial policies or subcultural practices. Still, the very fact that King's titles are *not* given in the *Times* suggests either that the paper took for granted his moral authority with its readers or assumed that mention of his titles either wasn't needed or wouldn't help to enhance his moral authority in their eyes.

46. King, *Autobiography*, 274. The stationery is mentioned by Oates, *Trumpet*, 341.

keep going strong during his confinement. King's tactical genius is fully displayed here. There are thirteen numbered items. The first four pertain to public officials whose support King hopes to solicit. He begins by suggesting that Leroy Collins, former two-term governor of Florida and then the director of the Community Relations Service under the 1964 Civil Rights Act, be invited to make a "personal visit to Selma, to talk with city and county authorities concerning speedier [voter] registration and more days for registering." He then suggests that Congress be asked to send a delegation, that the president dispatch a "personal emissary" from the Justice Department, and that Judge Thomas of the U.S. Court of Appeals for the Fifth Circuit (whose jurisdiction at that time included Alabama) be urged to enjoin further arrests of demonstrators and to speed up voter registration. The remaining items involve various aspects of the campaign itself, their overall aim being to assure that the protestors maintain the "offensive" and establish a "sense of drama" in the eyes of the public. Some attention-getting activity is to be organized for every day, including a night march to the jail to protest his own arrest, and another to the courthouse "to let [Sheriff] Clark show [his] true colors." Public school teachers, traditionally among the most widely respected (and politically conservative) members of the African American community, should be recruited for a march. Bond money must be carefully husbanded, so that "staff members essential for mobilization" who get arrested would be promptly released. Selma's mild-mannered director of public safety, Wilson Baker, must not be allowed to "control our movement." And entertainer Sammy Davis should be asked to stage a fund-raiser in Atlanta—a point to which King adds the rather amusing observation, "I find that all of these fellows respond better when I am in a jail or in a crisis." Withal, this document shows not only that King maintained firm control of the Selma campaign from his jail cell, but that he was taking full tactical advantage of his incarceration itself. The Dallas County Jail has become both his command post and his bully pulpit.

King's Theological Convictions

Let us now summarize and analyze the religious and political convictions that suffuse King's prison literature.

1. An unjust social order will tend to be enforced by violent or coercive means, but the injustice of the social order may be disguised by the apparent tranquility of day-to-day life, because the oppressed are afraid of the violence that the state may use lawfully (or that vigilantes may use unlawfully but with complete impunity) to maintain the status quo

Therefore, an effective means of reforming an unjust social order will be to provoke the police (and/or the vigilantes) to squelch protest or harass protestors. This will expose both the injustice of the social order and the violent or coercive means by which it is maintained. This is clearly a Type A conviction. Indeed, it might seem more like a political strategy statement than a theological or ethical tenet. Yet it presupposes that the injustices of a given social order—in this case, of the Deep South during the Jim Crow Era—represent standing contradictions to the professed principles of that social order, as articulated in Christian Scripture (e.g., that all human beings are made in the image of God and are offered redemption by Christ) and in the founding documents of the United States (e.g., that all human beings are "endowed by their Creator with certain unalienable rights, that among these are life, liberty, and the pursuit of happiness"). But King also recognized that the actual means that people use to protect their interests and privileges are a better index of their true character and values than the religious and political principles they may publicly profess. Or worse, the solemn profession of those principles by the privileged classes may serve to justify in their minds the cultural, legal, political, economic, and/or religious arrangements that benefit themselves, and therefore also to justify in their minds the use of coercive force against the oppressed classes. Yet it is precisely the willingness of the privileged classes to protect their privileges with means that contradict the very principles that ostensibly justify those privileges that provides the oppressed classes with the moral leverage needed to justify their campaign for reform. In short, when the injustices, contradictions, and hypocrisies of the status quo are defended by egregious displays of violence, when these displays of violence are publicized to the world, and when the oppressed demonstrate their willingness to endure these displays nonviolently, rather than retaliate in kind, then the *concrete realities* of society are delegitimized by the very *principles* upon which the society is supposedly based. The oppressed have thus gained the moral high ground by conducting themselves in accordance with the principles that everyone supposedly espouses, and they have demonstrated the justness of their demand to exercise the rights and enjoy the opportunities that the system theoretically accords to all.

2. Therefore, efforts to reform an unjust social order must themselves be scrupulously just, issuing in no death or injury to any person, and no destruction or damage to property

That is, the justness of the means of reforming an unjust social order must embody and illustrate the justness of the reforms that those means are intended to bring about. Again, a Type A conviction, and a corollary of Conviction 1. Efforts by the oppressed to bring about social reform depend not only on the exposure of the injustices and hypocrisies of the status quo, but also on the demonstration of the moral integrity of the agents of reform. This certainly does not mean that the oppressed can be said to "deserve" justice only if they demonstrate their moral integrity. No, the inalienable right to be treated justly is a function of people's citizenship, and indeed, of their humanity, not of their virtue.[47] But it does mean that those who set out to reform the existing social order must demonstrate their respect for the principles on which that order professes itself to be based and must demonstrate further that the reforms for which they are calling are actually more closely in line with those principles than the concrete arrangements of the status quo. King's campaigns for social, cultural, political, legal, and economic reform affirmed beliefs and values that were cherished by most Americans in the mid-1960s, including most Southern Whites, namely those of Christianity and of constitutional democracy. And the moral appeal of his work hinged largely on his ability to orchestrate public demonstrations in which those very beliefs and values were dramatically put into practice—and never more dramatically than when the police or White supremacist groups flagrantly contradicted them in the very process of "enforcing" them. King realized that responding to brutality with mob violence was suicidal, and he often pointed this out. The White majority

---

47. The notion that people must somehow prove their virtue before claiming their rights fails to acknowledge the fact that the systematic violation of people's human rights often has a profoundly demoralizing and dehumanizing effect upon their character. The defenders of the status quo can then point to the resulting "character flaws" of the oppressed as justification for "keeping them in their place," i.e., for denying them their constitutionally guaranteed rights. But without the human dignity and socioeconomic opportunities afforded by those rights, the oppressed find it difficult to emerge from their state of demoralization. This evil state of affairs thus perpetuates itself indefinitely.

had vast tactical advantages over the Black minority: superior numbers, greater financial resources, deadlier weapons, and complete control of the socioeconomic infrastructure.[48] But King taught his followers to "turn the other cheek," not just because fighting back was futile, but because doing so contradicted the teachings of Jesus (in whom most Whites of that time, as well as most Blacks, professed to believe), and because doing wrong in the service of the right would have brought the protestors down to the moral level of their oppressors, thereby nullifying the two great tactical and rhetorical advantages that Blacks enjoyed, namely, their warranted confidence in the justice of their cause and the slowly growing support of the wider American public.

3. *Now is the time!*

This is simultaneously a Type A and a Type B conviction. It fits Type A criteria because it is a call to immediate action. Although African Americans had to endure suffering patiently in their quest for justice, according to King the time to demand it—proudly, insistently, militantly, but nonviolently—had come. Whatever the federal, state, or local governments might do to advance or retard the cause, any further delay on the part of Blacks to demand their rights would have amounted to unjustifiable collusion with an oppressive system. King quoted the legal maxim, "justice too long delayed is justice denied," when rebutting the charge that he was moving too far, too fast,[49] and he routinely invoked the principle, if not the maxim itself, in his speeches and writings.[50] He fiercely de-

---

48. In this respect, the American Civil Rights Movement was significantly different from the nonviolent campaigns for self-rule led by Gandhi in India and Kwame Nkrumah in Ghana. In those situations, the oppressors were a small, foreign minority, wealthy and powerful, to be sure, but vastly outnumbered by those whose lands they had colonized, and therefore both geographically remote from their power base and completely without the moral and political legitimacy held by the native majority.

49. King, *Why We Can't Wait*, 91. King ascribes this maxim to "one of our distinguished jurists," but he does not cite the source.

50. See, e.g., "Equality Now: The President Has the Power," *Nation* 192, February 4, 1961, 91–95; "The Time for Freedom Has Come," *New York Times Magazine*, September 10, 1961, 25–27; "In a Word: Now," *New York Times Magazine*, September 29, 1963, 91–92; "I Have a Dream" (August 28, 1963); "Negroes Are Not Moving Too Fast," *Saturday Evening Post* 237, November 7, 1964, 8–9; and "Showdown for Nonviolence," *Look* 32, April 16, 1968, 23–25. These articles are reprinted in King, *Testament*, 152–59; 160–66; 167–68; 217–20; 176–81; and 64–72, respectively. Compare King's insistence that "Now is the time!" with the gradualism of Walter Rauschenbusch, who insisted

nounced the obstructionist methods of "nullification and interposition," which were used by segregationist authorities to block civil rights laws and court orders.[51] He chided those Black citizens who failed to join the cause, either because they feared reprisals or because they had found ways to profit from the existing system. And he blasted White liberals for professing their sympathy to the cause of freedom but failing to give concrete support for fear of social unrest. Speaking as a social prophet and Christian moralist, rather than a calculating politician, King insisted that "the time is always ripe to do right,"[52] and conversely, that history has repeatedly shown that "the oppressor never voluntarily gives freedom to the oppressed."[53] Therefore the oppressed must demand their birthright, fight for it, and if necessary sacrifice their time, resources, personal liberty, and physical safety for it. King comes very close to suggesting that the test of the sensitivity of one's conscience is the urgency with which, and the courage by which, one fights for freedom—one's own, and that of other people, including one's enemies.

But Conviction 3 also fits the criteria for Type B, because it assumes that the struggle against social injustice is in alignment with God's providential purposes for human history. As he said only a few days before his death, "We're going to win our freedom because both the sacred heritage of our nation and the eternal will of the almighty God are embodied in our echoing demands. And so, however dark it is, however deep the angry feelings are, and however violent the explosions are, I can still sing,

---

that "The kingdom of God is always but coming." See Rauschenbusch, *Christianity and the Social Crisis*, 309 and 421. King tells us in his intellectual autobiography, "Pilgrimage to Nonviolence," that this book left "an indelible imprint" on his thinking; but he also criticizes Rauschenbusch for falling victim "to the nineteenth century 'cult of inevitable progress,' which led him to an unwarranted optimism concerning human nature." King, *Testament*, 37.

51. See, e.g., "Give Us the Ballot—We Will Transform the South" (May 17, 1957) speech contained in *Congressional Record* 103, May 28, 1957, 7322–24; "The Rising Tide of Racial Consciousness," *YWCA Magazine*, December 1960, 4–6; "Facing the Challenge of a New Age," *Phylon* 28, April 1957, 24–34. These articles are reprinted in King, *Testament*, 197–200; 145–51; and 135–44, respectively. See also his sermon, "Antidotes for Fear" in King, *Strength to Love*, 108–17.

52. King, *Why We Can't Wait*, 98.

53. From "The Birth of a New Nation," a sermon preached at Dexter Avenue Baptist Church, Montgomery, AL, April 7, 1957, shortly after returning from the ceremonies that made the Gold Coast, formerly a British colony, the independent nation of Ghana. A transcript is available at the website of the King Research and Education Institute; a sound recording is included in King and Shepard, *Call*, Disk 1.

'We Shall Overcome.' We shall overcome because the arc of the moral universe is long, but it bends toward justice."[54]

4. Suffering (including imprisonment) is not per se redemptive and is certainly not to be sought for its own sake. Indeed, the purpose of reforming an unjust social order is to reduce the suffering of those who routinely endure injury, deprivation, and humiliation. But voluntary suffering endured for the sake of social justice is redemptive—not only to the persons who endure it, but also to the persons who inflict it or in whose name it is inflicted

This is clearly a conviction of Type B. King taught his people to overcome the injustices that the system of segregation inflicted upon them by voluntarily and nonviolently enduring the punishments meted out to them for refusing to cooperate any longer with that system. To win the right to ride on a bus, they might suffer the indignity of being hauled away in a paddy wagon. To win the right to eat a hamburger at a downtown lunch counter, they might spend a week choking down the swill served at the county jail. To win the right to vote, they might have to face down state troopers armed with nightsticks, bullwhips, and firehoses. And they would endure all this suffering willingly, without retaliating against their persecutors. There is an almost alchemical principle at work here: to escape suffering they must endure suffering without inflicting suffering. That is, the just way to defeat unjust laws is to peaceably endure the unjust punishments used to enforce them; the honorable way to protest social injustice is to put the establishment in the morally untenable position of having to use increasingly violent methods in order to "keep the peace." King did not valorize suffering, although one mark of his leadership was his way of paying eloquent and heartfelt tribute to the valor of his people, who had bravely endured the miseries of slavery and the indignities of segregation, and who now had a morally admirable and spiritually defensible way of gaining redress for their grievances without wreaking vengeance upon their oppressors.

The thing that gave the civil rights struggle its extraordinary moral leverage, however, is that King always insisted that Whites, no less than Blacks, were its intended beneficiaries. The marches, sit-ins, and freedom

---

54. From "Remaining Awake Through a Great Revolution," a sermon preached at the National Cathedral in Washington, DC on Passion Sunday, March 31, 1968, in King, *Testament*, 277. The full text is printed on pp. 268–78.

rides were intended not only to end the social and political inequalities from which Blacks suffered, but also to prevent Whites from continuing to sin against their Black neighbors, if only by unthinkingly supporting and profiting from a corrupt and oppressive system. The true measure of the Civil Rights Movement, therefore, was not just that Blacks, who had patiently but resignedly suffered injustice for so long, now intentionally put themselves in harm's way to reform degrading and injurious social arrangements. Warranted as such efforts surely were, at that level they were still essentially self-serving. But protestors were *not* merely serving their own temporal interests by advocating radical social change. They were also serving the spiritual interests of their oppressors, many of whom had never acknowledged that institutional racism contradicted the cherished principles of American democracy and the Christian faith.

Conclusion

Introduction

THE AIM OF THIS book has been to show how our four ambassadors articulated in their prison writings those religious convictions *for which* they were incarcerated (Type A convictions) and those *by means of which* they resisted pressure from the state to renounce their convictions and endured their punishment for resisting (Type B convictions). Broadly speaking, our ambassadors were imprisoned for affirming by word or deed their Type A religious convictions (and/or those "political" convictions that seemed to them logically entailed by them), and they bore their imprisonment by embracing their Type B religious convictions. But as we have seen, the distinction between the two types is fuzzy, and some of their convictions fit both types.

I have argued that convictions are a central feature of a person's identity, that moral and spiritual integrity consist in living in accordance with one's convictions, that relinquishing a conviction would entail the loss or radical alteration of one's identity, and therefore that such a relinquishment is honorable if and only if one has solid rational grounds for deeming that conviction erroneous. For a Christian, the relinquishment of one's convictions is apostasy. But when a Christian's convictions contradict the dominant ideology of her society, such that the state demands their relinquishment, her refusal to relinquish them—that is, her refusal to apostatize—would be regarded by the state either as outright treason (as in the cases of Perpetua, Maximus, and More) or as subversiveness (as in the case of King). The prison literature of our ambassadors was intended, first, to defend the validity of those religious convictions that their contemporaries deemed dangerous, and second, to steel those who held them—the authors themselves, but perhaps also their sympathetic readers—against persecution.

The stories we have told differ widely in many ways. Yet there are some remarkable commonalities as well. To conclude this work, I wish to explore these commonalities. The table below displays the salient convictions articulated in the prison writings of our four ambassadors and indicates their "types." The discussion that follows investigates five ways in which our ambassadors' religious convictions, though expressed differently due to the vast differences in their respective historical situations, often share deep underlying affinities.

Ambassador	Conviction	Type A	Type B
Vibia Perpetua: resistance to pagan idolatry	1. The Triune God is the supreme good and the sovereign power in the universe.	x	x
	2. God freely and continuously communicates his will and grace to his followers.	x	x
	3. The church is a community of witness in a world indifferent to God and hostile to God's church.	x	x
Maximus the Confessor: resistance to imperial heresy	1. The Christian conscience is bound by the testimony of the apostles and the orthodox fathers and by the doctrines and canons promulgated by the ecumenical councils.	x	
	2. Because Jesus Christ possesses both divine and human natures, and because the will is a function of the nature (not of the person), we must conclude that he possesses both divine and human wills.	x	
	3. Although a Christian state is responsible for supporting the orthodox church, it has no authority to promulgate new doctrines for the sake of political advantage or to force the state church to do so.	x	
	4. In a Christian state, principled resistance to state-sponsored heresy is the highest form of patriotism.		x
	5. The Christian who resists the state and/or the state church must display humility and courtesy toward those civil and ecclesiastical officials who are sent to bring pressure to bear on his conscience.		x

CONCLUSION 183

Ambassador	Conviction	Type A	Type B
Thomas More: resistance to national apostasy	1. The conscience of a Christian is bound by the non-negotiable doctrines of the universal church.	x	x
	2. In a state whose laws reflect the teachings of the Catholic Church, one's duties as a citizen are usually morally consistent with one's duties as a Christian, and the performance of one's civic duties is a tangible expression of one's Christian discipleship. But when and to the extent that the state apostatizes, one's duty as a Christian is to withdraw one's support from the state apparatus, while abstaining, if possible, from illegal conduct.	x	x
	3. The Christian life is a journey, in the company of fellow Christians, toward the eternal, merry fellowship of heaven.		x
	4. The communal merriment of heaven must be adumbrated in the way we treat others here and now.		x
Martin Luther King Jr.: resistance to racial injustice	1. An unjust social order will tend to be enforced by violent or coercive means, but the injustice of the social order may be disguised by the apparent tranquility of day-to-day life, because the oppressed are afraid of the violence that the state may use lawfully (or that vigilantes may use unlawfully but with complete impunity) to maintain the status quo.	x	
	2. Efforts to reform an unjust social order must themselves be scrupulously just, issuing in no death or injury to any person, and no destruction or damage to property.	x	
	3. Now is the time!	x	x
	4. Voluntary suffering (including imprisonment) is not *per se* redemptive and is not to be sought for its own sake. But voluntary suffering endured for the sake of social justice is redemptive—not only to the persons who endure it, but also to the persons who inflict it or in whose name it is inflicted.		x

Commonalities

1. Conscientious objection and the preservation of personal integrity

Conspicuous in the stories of all four ambassadors are the challenges they faced when the state demanded that they speak or act in ways contrary to their conscience. It is crucial to note once again that all four understood their conscience to have been formed by the doctrinal and moral teachings of the historic Christian church,[1] and all four remained committed to those teachings. None of them regarded the convictions to which their conscience was bound as "private opinions." One's conscience is, of course, one of the most fundamental features of one's "personhood." But for a Christian, one's personhood is always construed in terms of one's God-relatedness, and one's conscience is that feature of one's personhood whereby one voluntarily accepts the will of God as the rule of life, and the teachings of the church as the deposit of divine self-revelation. Thus, when the states in which our four ambassadors lived required them to disobey what they took to be God's will, or to affirm what they regarded as false doctrine, they felt obliged, "in good conscience," to dissent. (See Perpetua, Conviction 1; Maximus, Convictions 1 and 2; More, Conviction 1; and King, Convictions 2 and 3.)

The word "conscience" does not appear in *The Passion of Saints Perpetua and Felicitas*, but the following vignette from her diary indicates that she understood herself to be conscience-bound to her faith and believed that her new affiliation with the church defined her identity: "Now while . . . we were with the prosecutors my father desired to topple me with words and kept trying to hinder me, out of his affection. 'Father,' I said, 'do you see, for the sake of an example, this vase lying there, or pitcher or whatever it is?' He said, 'I see it.' I said to him: 'Can it be called by another name than what it is?' He said: 'No.' 'So also I cannot call myself anything but what I am, a Christian.'"[2]

---

1. I acknowledge the fuzziness of the term "historic Christian church." I use it to include the very different ecclesiastical judicatories to which Perpetua, Maximus, More, and King belonged, respectively, all of which in some sense affirmed the Triune nature of God, the "two natures" of Christ, and the inspiration and authority of the Christian Scriptures. (Perpetua, of course, lived over a century before the promulgation of the Creed of Nicaea or the formal canonization of the Bible, but her *Passion* indicates that the Carthaginian church to which she belonged, including its proto-Montanist faction, stood within the so-called "Great Tradition.")

2. *Passion of Perpetua and Felicitas* II.3.1–2 in Cobb, *Passion*, 22–25.

CONCLUSION

Two references to "conscience" (*syneidēsis*) appear in close succession in the transcript of Maximus' first trial. In answer to the suggestion that he was acting as if he thought that everyone who disagreed with his views was damned, Maximus first compares himself to the Three Young Men in the Book of Daniel, who adhered to their own faith without passing judgment on anyone else, and then to Daniel himself, who "chose to die and not to backslide from God, and to be flayed by his own conscience (*mastigōthēnai syneidēsēs*) in a matter of the transgression of natural law." He then adds: "To the best of my ability I'll choose to die rather than have on my conscience the worry that in some way or other I have suffered a lapse with regard to belief in God."[3] The phrase "flayed by [one's] own conscience" is fiercely graphic: the verb *mastigoō* is related to the noun *mastix* (horsewhip). Thus, for Maximus to comply with the government's latest decree would be to flog himself forever with guilt—a self-torture far worse in his estimation than any punitive measures the government might mete out. To preserve his integrity, he must refuse the state's demands.

As for Thomas More, we have already explained in some detail how the theme of obedience to his conscience pervades his prison writings. It will suffice to quote the remark he made to the royal commissioners shortly before his imprisonment, when pressed to comply with what by that point had become the consensus—albeit a *coerced* consensus—of the realm: "If there were no more but myself upon my side and the whole Parliament upon the other, I would be sore afraid to lean to mine own mind only against so many. But on the other side, if it be so that in some things for which I refuse the oath, I have (as I think I have) upon my part as great a council and a greater too, I am not then bounden to change my conscience, and conform it to the council of one realm against the general council of Christendom."[4] Like Maximus, More believed that coercion by the government would not exonerate him from the guilt of violating his conscience.

And as for King, his entire public career was driven by his profound moral sense, and he frequently accepted—indeed, sometimes

---

3. *Report of the Trial* §6, in Allen and Neil, *Maximus*, 60–63. The Scripture references are to Daniel 3:1–30 and 6:1–28 (and perhaps to the Prayer of Azariah and the Song of the Three Jews). But Maximus may also be obliquely comparing himself to Orestes, the protagonist in Aeschylus' play, *The Furies*.

4. Letter to Margaret Roper, c. April 17, 1534, in More, *Last Letters*, 60. I have slightly modernized More's diction in a couple places in accordance with de Silva's editorial notes.

invited—imprisonment to dramatize his conscientious objection to unjust laws, customs, and socioeconomic conditions. Oddly, the word "conscience" does not appear in his writings as frequently as one might suppose. But it does occur. In an early sermon titled, "A Knock at Midnight," he remarks: "The church must be reminded that it is not the master or the servant of the state, but rather the conscience of the state. It must be the guide and the critic of the state, and never its tool."[5] The term appears again in the "Letter from Birmingham Jail," when he quotes a remark by John Bunyan: "I will stay in jail to the end of my days before I make a butchery of my conscience."[6] (The eerie similarity between Bunyan's "butchery" remark and Maximus' statement that he will not "flay his own conscience" is noteworthy, but probably coincidental.)

2. Serving as the "loyal opposition"

Three of our four prisoners of conscience opposed the policies of the state for what they regarded as the ultimate benefit of the state, or at least for the spiritual and moral health of their fellow citizens. They resisted what they perceived to be the evils of their society out of loyalty and love, not out of spite or scorn. (See Maximus, Conviction 4; More, Conviction 2; and King, Conviction 1).

Maximus believed that monenergism and monotheletism implicitly contradicted the Christology of the Council of Chalcedon. But orthodox Christianity was the official religion of the Byzantine state, and the state believed that its security depended on the blessing of God, which in turn hinged on its fidelity to the orthodox Christian faith as defined by the ecumenical councils. Thus, when a sizable number of citizens in the Eastern provinces rejected Chalcedon, the government sought to conciliate them by an "arrangement" that seemed to Maximus to negate the doctrinal foundation on which the government's legitimacy rested. No doubt his opposition to that arrangement was driven by explicitly theological considerations. But in his social world, theology and power politics were inextricably intertwined, and a state church

---

5. King, *Strength to Love*, 47. The Chronology on the King Research and Education Institute website indicates that this sermon was preached to Baptist gatherings on July 31, 1958 in Selma, Alabama, on August 31, 1958 in Pittsburgh, Pennsylvania, and on September 14, 1958 in Chicago. King included it in his collection of sermons, *Strength to Love*, which was published ten years later.

6. King, *Why We Can't Wait*, 101.

that periodically adjusted its doctrines for flagrantly pragmatic reasons could easily lose its legitimacy in the eyes of the faithful. As it turned out, the two heresies failed to appease the dissident Christian populations of Syria, Palestine, and Egypt anyway, and they proved to be political non-starters as well as theological blunders. And although Maximus was not mentioned by name at the Sixth Ecumenical Council, his contributions to Christology and theological anthropology were embraced and became part of the Byzantine theopolitical legacy.

Thomas More, who had spent his entire adult life as a successful and popular servant of the Tudor government, regarded the early phases of the Henrician Reformation as a catastrophe for England. When he could no longer support government policy, he resigned his office and returned to private life, refusing to profess what he did not believe, but also refusing to embarrass the government by openly asserting his opposition. When further laws were passed that decreed his silence to be treasonous, he knew he was doomed. But his conscience not only forbade him to swear oaths whose content he disagreed with; it also forbade him to renounce his loyalty to king and country. According to one account, his last words on the scaffold were that he "died the king's good servant, and God's first." His choice of the word "and" in this testimony, rather than the word "but," is suggestive. He was affirming that his obedience to God superseded his obedience to the king but was not antithetical to it—until the king himself made it so. More opposed the Henrician Reformation because he regarded England's schism from the papacy as spiritually suicidal, but his opposition did not imply that his loyalty to England ever wavered.

Martin Luther King Jr.'s early campaigns in Montgomery, Albany, Birmingham, and Selma were intended to secure the civil rights and to improve the living conditions of the oppressed Black populations of those cities. And by obtaining Supreme Court support and promoting the passage of new federal laws, he sought to advance the interests of all Black citizens in the South. But in a larger sense, King's work served the common good of the American people as a whole—even those, and indeed especially those, who feared that his proposed reforms would eradicate their social, economic, and political privileges. In King's view, these folks were unaware that the systemic racism on which their privileges depended was spiritually and morally damaging to them and gave the lie to the religious values that they piously professed. The use of lawful means to change unjust laws would therefore benefit not just those who suffered most directly and egregiously from those laws, but also those who fought so fiercely to preserve them. In his "Letter from Birmingham Jail" he wrote: "I am cognizant of the interrelatedness of all communities and states.... Injustice anywhere is a threat to justice everywhere. We are caught in an inescapable network of mutuality, tied in a single garment of destiny. Whatever affects one directly, affects all indirectly."[7]

Vibia Perpetua is the exception here. There is nothing in the *Passion* to suggest that she or her companions understood themselves to be the "loyal opposition" or to be acting for the "common good." Nor, on the other hand, were they trying to overthrow the empire (though perhaps they expected God to do so). The Carthaginian martyrs simply refused to participate in the ceremonies that constituted Roman civil religion, and it was for that refusal that they were condemned to the arena. As Christians, they undoubtedly rejoiced when their public witness succeeded in converting people to their faith. But their aim simply *was* to convert people to their faith, not to transform the imperial status quo.

3. The transformation of carceral space

Three of our four ambassadors report that during their time in lockup their attitude toward imprisonment underwent a radical transformation. Prisons are designed as places where no one wants to be. But Perpetua, More, and King all found divine consolation there, even "inward" freedom. (See Perpetua, Conviction 2; More, Convictions 3 and 4; and King, Conviction 4.)

Perpetua offers this extraordinary testimony of her experience of imprisonment:

> Then Tertius and Pomponius, blessed deacons who were ministering to us, settled on a bribe, so that we might be sent for a few hours into a better part of the prison and refresh ourselves. When we went out of the prison everyone took time for themselves. I was nursing my baby, who was already weakened from fasting. Concerned for him, I spoke to my mother and comforted my brother, and I entrusted my son to them. I was

---

7. King, *Why We Can't Wait*, 86–87. In *Why We Can't Wait*, chapter 5 is the full text of the "Letter from Birmingham Jail," and chapter 6 is titled "Black and White Together." The word "together" here is carefully chosen. Whereas the "Letter" upbraids those white liberal clergy who advised that the Birmingham protests be delayed, the very next chapter gratefully acknowledges those whites who actively supported the movement, knowing that racial reconciliation would ultimately bless everyone.

languishing because I saw them languishing because of me. Such concerns I suffered for many days; and then I was granted that my baby might stay with me in prison, and right away I recovered; I was relieved from the struggle and concern for my baby, and suddenly the prison became my palace, and there was nowhere else I wanted to be.[8]

More, too, found divine consolation in his cell, although he does not tell us of any sudden or dramatic experience. But as many of his biographers have noticed, his youthful yearnings to become a monk were strangely fulfilled in the last months of his life, as he transformed his room in the Tower into a place of contemplation and prayer.

> [God] hath ... put in the King toward me that good and gracious mind, that as yet he hath taken from me nothing but my liberty (wherewith, as help me God, his Grace hath done me so great good by the spiritual profit that I trust I take thereby, that among all his great benefits heaped upon me so thick, I reckon upon my faith my prisonment even the very chief).[9]

And King writes from his Birmingham jail cell, upon hearing several pieces of unexpectedly good news in the wake of a previously desperate situation:

> What silenced me was a profound sense of awe. I was aware of a feeling that had been present all along below the surface of consciousness, pressed down under the weight of concern for the movement: I had never been truly in solitary confinement; God's companionship does not stop at the door of a jail cell. I don't know whether the sun was shining at that moment. But I know that once again I could see the light.[10]

As for Maximus, the transcripts of the *Report of the Trial* and *The Dispute at Bizya* do not indicate much about his prison experience as such, or any radical changes in his attitude toward imprisonment. But he had been a monk for forty years at the time of his arrest in 553, so perhaps he was already quite used to finding God's presence in the confinement of a cell.[11]

8. *Passion of Perpetua and Felicitas* II.2.7–9, in Cobb, *Passion*, 24–25.
9. Letter of Margaret Roper to Alice Alington, August 1534, in More, *Last Letters*, 88.
10. King, *Why We Can't Wait*, 84.
11. I cannot resist sharing an experience of my own that seems germane here. Many

4. The sanctification of carceral time

The existential question that incarceration puts to a Christian prisoner of conscience is how the time spent behind bars can be redeemed, either for the purpose of bearing witness to others through one's writings or for the purpose of deepening one's own spiritual resources. (See Perpetua, Conviction 3; Maximus, Conviction 5; More, Conviction 4; and King, Conviction 4.)

We know from Perpetua's diary that she and her friends did both: they engaged in various devotional practices (prayers, psalmody, a baptism, a love feast, the kiss of peace), and they managed to make converts by their display of spiritual power. We do not know much about Maximus' life in prison, except what we learn from the records of his interrogations. But these records suggest that he somehow managed to maintain his regimen of prayer and theological reflection during his time of lockup, and he met such visitors as were sent to secure his capitulation with courtesy and modesty, suggesting that his long confinement had not dampened his spirits or dulled his wits, as his captors must have hoped. More, as we have seen, spent many of his hours in the Tower of London engaged in literary pursuits: drafting letters, annotating his prayer book, and composing theological treatises. In all these works, both public witness and spiritual self-cultivation play a part. As for King, toward the end of his "Letter from Birmingham Jail," he asks the ironical question, "What else can one do when he is alone in a narrow jail cell other than write long letters, think long thoughts and pray long prayers?"[12] But in Birmingham he had been placed in solitary confinement (though he did have limited guest privileges). During some of his other jailings, however, he conducted worship services and led his fellow prisoners in singing hymns

---

years ago, when I was the pastor of a rural church in southern Wisconsin, one of my parishioners, whom I shall call "Ned," was arrested on a minor drug charge and was jailed for several months. During one of my visits, at his request, I took him holy communion. When I arrived, however, the cubicles used by visiting clergy and attorneys were all occupied, so the officer put us in the chamber where prisoners met with friends and family members—face-to-face, but separated by a thick, steel-reinforced window, and speaking by telephone. On this occasion, however, Ned and I were both on the inside chamber, seated on stools bolted to the floor, with a stool between us serving as the Lord's Table. After reading a passage from Scripture, saying a few impromptu prayers, and celebrating the sacrament, we fell into companionable silence. At last, Ned spoke up: "From now on, this room will be holy ground for me." If I hadn't been there, that probably wouldn't have happened; but it certainly didn't happen simply because "I" was there.

12. King, *Why We Can't Wait*, 109.

and protest songs. By various means, therefore, our four ambassadors redeemed their time behind bars.

5. Counting the cost

All four of our ambassadors anticipated their own deaths. I am not suggesting that their premonitions were the *direct* consequence of their religious convictions. But they knew the deadly danger they were in for holding their Type A convictions, and they drew upon their Type B convictions to help them prepare to make the supreme sacrifice, should that ever prove necessary. (See Perpetua, Convictions 2 and 3; Maximus, Conviction 5; More, Convictions 3 and 4; and King, Conviction 4.)

Perpetua and Maximus had actual visions of their impending deaths. In the first of her four visions, Perpetua "saw" a golden ladder by which she was to ascend to heaven. But a dragon lay at its base, and its sides were studded with deadly blades. So, the ascent would be perilous. When she awoke, she related her vision of this dangerous climb to her brother (a fellow Christian, but apparently a visitor to the prison and not himself incarcerated). "And," she writes, "we understood that suffering was coming, and we began to no longer have hope in this world."[13] A few days later, in her fourth vision, she saw herself doing combat in the arena. She proved victorious, but upon awakening she writes: "I understood that I wasn't going to animals but that I was going to be fighting against the Devil."[14] Maximus' vision is known to us through the letter of Anastasius the Apocrisiarius to another member of the beleaguered dyothelite party. Though imprisoned in different imperial fortresses in Lazica in 662, Anastasius had somehow learned that Maximus had "seen a divine vision" in which the date on which God "would take him up" was revealed. Maximus did, in fact, die of his wounds and general maltreatment later that year.[15]

Neither More nor King saw visions of their deaths, but both anticipated their fate. In More's case, the longer his imprisonment in the Tower lasted, the more certain he was that the outcome of his eventual

---

13. *Passion of Perpetua and Felicitas* II.4.10 in Cobb, *Passion*, 26–27.

14. *Passion of Perpetua and Felicitas* II.10.14, in Cobb, *Passion*, 30–31. Of course, she and her companions *did* soon face the beasts in the arena. But she is reading her vision allegorically, looking beyond its literal sense to its spiritual meaning.

15. Letter of Anastasius the Apocrisiarius to Theodosius of Gangra §5, in Allen and Neil, *Maximus*, 137.

trial would be execution. As we saw, in his last letter, dated July 5, 1535, he says his goodbyes to his family and makes some final arrangements for the disposition of his personal effects.[16] He was beheaded the following day—but apparently with a twinkle in his eye and a joke upon his lips. King anticipated that he would die as a result of his labors. In a sermon delivered from his home pulpit at Ebenezer Baptist Church on February 4, 1968, he described how he hoped to be remembered, namely "as a drum major for justice . . . and for peace . . . and for righteousness."[17] And in a sermon delivered at Mason Temple in Memphis, Tennessee, on April 3, 1968, at the height of the Sanitation Workers Strike, he told his audience that although he had "seen the promised land," he might not get there with them, though he wasn't worried if he didn't.[18] On April 4, his heartbreakingly prophetic words came true, and he was assassinated while getting ready to attend a dinner party.

Epilogue: Prison Literature and the Examination of Conscience

This book has been an exercise in historical theology. Yet I believe that the commonalities among our four ambassadors' stories and the deep affinities between the religious convictions expressed in their prison literature have great theological relevance for our own time. As I write these words in the summer of 2024, I foresee that nonviolent resistance against an increasingly oppressive state has become a moral and missiological imperative for orthodox Christians in America. This is especially so because the demagoguery and authoritarianism now gripping American politics are supported by what has come to be called "Christian nationalism," a virulent heresy reminiscent of the worst features of Byzantine toadyism, Henrician megalomania, and Jim Crow bigotry. Indeed, something akin to the pagan Roman practice of venerating the image of the emperor has recently come back into fashion.

Perpetua, Maximus, More, and King can help us respond to this ominous situation, both by challenging us to examine our consciences and by encouraging us to respond faithfully and creatively. They illustrate how, under the direst of circumstances, the followers of Jesus can deploy

---

16. Letter to Margaret Roper, in More, *Last Letters*, 127–28.
17. From "The Drum Major Instinct," in King, *Testament*, 267.
18. From "I Have Seen the Promised Land," in King, *Testament*, 286.

their Christian convictions to diagnose the evils and injustices of their culture. And they exemplify how, when doing this difficult and dangerous work, the followers of Jesus can put their Christian convictions to good use when facing ostracism and backlash. Their prison writings certainly cannot tell us exactly how to combat the political and religious pathologies of our time. But the list of commonalities among their writings may help us to formulate some of the questions we should be asking ourselves as we begin forging concrete strategies of principled protest and conscientious objection. Such questions might look something like these:

1. Conscientious objection and the preservation of personal integrity

Do we distinguish carefully enough between those nonnegotiable religious convictions that define our identity as followers of Christ and those personal opinions and private preferences that we can relinquish or modify without sacrificing our integrity?

2. Serving as the "loyal opposition"

Do we conduct ourselves in a way that demonstrates Christian love for neighbors—and "enemies"? Do we show that our disagreement with certain policies is not driven by, or confused with, antipathy to those enforcing them? Do we display respect and courtesy toward our opponents without appearing obsequious or cowardly?

3. Transforming conflictual spaces

Do we enter public spaces with the intention of striking up an earnest conversation or only with the desire to grab the microphone? Do we expect any manifestation of divine power and presence when we speak words of prophetic outrage and Christian grace in God's name?

4. Redeeming our times

Do we pass our days with the unruffled confidence of those who see God's hand at work in human history, or do we act as if we felt the panicky need to control affairs? Do we have the urgency to say, "Now is the time!" but also the patience to say, "The arc of the moral universe is long, but it bends toward justice"?

5. Counting the cost

Have we considered the potential consequences of public dissent? Are we prepared to make sacrifices for the cause? Sacrifices of what kind? Sacrifices of what severity?

If the study of the prison literature of Vibia Perpetua, Maximus the Confessor, Thomas More, and Martin Luther King Jr. leads us to ask such questions of ourselves, then they were not merely ambassadors of the gospel to their contemporaries, but to us as well.

Bibliography

Ackroyd, Peter. *The Life of Thomas More*. New York: Doubleday, 1998.
Aelius Spartianus. *Severus*. In *Scriptores Historiae Augustae*, translated by David Magie, 1:370–429. Loeb Classical Library 139. 1921. Reprint, Cambridge: Harvard University Press, 2000.
Ahnert, Ruth. "Writing in the Tower of London During the Reformation, ca. 1530–1558." *Huntington Library Quarterly* 72 (2009) 168-92.
Allen, Pauline, ed. *Sophronius of Jerusalem and Seventh-Century Heresy: The "Synodical Letter" and Other Documents*. Oxford Early Christian Texts. Oxford: Oxford University Press, 2009.
Allen, Pauline, and Robert Hayward, eds. *Severus of Antioch*. Early Church Fathers. London: Routledge, 2004.
Allen, Pauline, and Bronwen Neil, eds. *Maximus the Confessor and His Companions: Documents from Exile*. Oxford Early Christian Texts. Oxford: Oxford University Press, 2002.
Amat, Jacqueline. *Passion de Perpétue et de Félicité suive des Actes*. Paris: Editions du Cerf, 1996.
Ameling, Walter. "*Femina Liberaliter Instituta*—Some Thoughts on a Martyr's Liberal Education." In *Perpetua's Passions*, edited by Jan Bremmer and Marco Formisano, 78–102. Oxford: Oxford University Press, 2012.
Ansbro, John. *Martin Luther King, Jr.: The Making of a Mind*. Maryknoll, NY: Orbis, 1982.
Athanasius. *The Life of Antony and the Letter to Marcellinus*. Translated by Robert C. Gregg. Mahwah, NJ: Paulist, 1980.
Auerbach, Erich. *Mimesis: The Representation of Reality in Western Literature*. Translated by Willard R. Trask. Princeton: Princeton University Press, 1968.
Augustine. *Nicene and Post-Nicene Fathers*. First Series. Vol. 5, *Saint Augustin: Anti-Pelagian Writings*. Translated by Peter Holmes et al. Peabody, MA: Hendrickson, 1994.
———. *The Works of Saint Augustine*. Part III, Vol. 8, *Sermons, 273–305A*. Translated by Edmund Hill. Edited by John E. Rotelle. Hyde Park, NY: New City, 1994.
Barnes, T. D. "Legislation Against the Christians." *Journal of Roman Studies* 58 (1968) 32–50.

Bennett, Lerone, Jr., *What Manner of Man: A Biography of Martin Luther King, Jr.* 4th rev. ed. Chicago: Johnson, 1976.

Blowers, Paul M. "The Dialectics and Therapeutics of Desire in Maximus the Confessor." *Vigiliae Christianae* 65 (2011) 425–51.

———. "Gentiles of the Soul: Maximus the Confessor on the Substructure and Transformation of the Human Passions." *Journal of Early Christian Studies* 4 (1996) 57–85.

Boeft, Jan den. "The Editor's Prime Objective: *Haec in Aedificationem Ecclesiae Legere.*" In *Perpetua's Passions*, edited by Jan Bremmer and Marco Formisano, 169–79. Oxford: Oxford University Press, 2012.

Bolt, Robert. *A Man for All Seasons: A Drama in Two Acts.* New York: Random House, 1962.

Boswell, James. *Life of Samuel Johnson, LL.D.* Great Books of the Western World 44. Chicago: Encyclopædia Britannica, 1952.

Branch, Taylor. *At Canaan's Edge: America in the King Years, 1965–68.* New York: Simon & Schuster, 2007.

———. *Parting the Waters: America in the King Years, 1954–63.* New York: Simon & Schuster, 1988.

———. *Pillar of Fire: America in the King Years, 1963–65.* New York: Simon & Schuster, 1998.

Bremmer, Jan. "Felicitas: The Martyrdom of a Young African Woman." In *Perpetua's Passions*, edited by Jan Bremmer and Marco Formisano, 35–53. Oxford: Oxford University Press, 2012.

Bremmer, Jan N., and Marco Formisano, eds. *Perpetua's Passions: Multidisciplinary Approaches to the Passio Perpetuae et Felicitatis.* Oxford: Oxford University Press, 2012.

Brock, Sebastian. "An Early Syriac Life of Maximus the Confessor." *Analecta Bollandiana* 91 (1973) 299–346; photo-reprinted (with original pagination) in *Syriac Perspectives on Late Antiquity*, chapter 12. London: Variorum Reprints, 1984.

Butler, Rex D. *The New Prophecy and "New Visions": Evidence of Montanism in The Passion of Perpetua and Felicitas.* Washington, DC: Catholic University of America Press, 2006.

Carpenter, C. C. J., et al. "Public Statement by Eight Alabama Clergymen Denouncing Martin Luther King's Efforts, April 12, 1963." https://www.massresistance.org/docs/gen/09a/mlk_day/statement.html.

Cassell's Latin Dictionary: Latin-English, English-Latin. New York: Wiley, 1968.

Chadwick, Henry. "John Moschus and His Friend Sophronius the Sophist." *Journal of Theological Studies* 25 (1974) 41–74.

Cobb, L. Stephanie. *Dying to Be Men: Gender and Language in Early Christian Martyr Texts.* New York: Columbia University Press, 2008.

———, ed. *The Passion of Perpetua and Felicitas in Late Antiquity.* Translations by Andrew S. Jacobs and L. Stephanie Cobb. Oakland, CA: University of California Press, 2021.

Cone, James. "Martin Luther King, Jr.: Black Theology—Black Church." *Theology Today* 40 (1984) 409–20.

Crisp, Oliver D. "Problems with Perichoresis." *Tyndale Bulletin* 56 (2005) 119–40.

Cummings, Brian. "Conscience and the Law in Thomas More." *Renaissance Studies* 23 (2009) 463–85.
Curtwright, Travis. "Thomas More as Author of Margaret Roper's Letter to Alice Alington." *Moreana* 56 (2019) 1–27.
Davies, Ioan. *Writers in Prison*. Oxford: Blackwell, 1990.
Davies, J. G. "Was the Devotion of Septimius Severus to Serapis the Cause of the Persecution of 202–203?" *Journal of Theological Studies* 6 (1954) 73–76.
Derrett, J. Duncan M. "The Trial of Sir Thomas More." *The English Historical Review* 79.312 (1964) 449–77.
De Ste Croix, G. E. M. "Why Were the Early Christians Persecuted?" *Past & Present* 26 (1963) 6–38.
de Voragine, Jacobus. *The Golden Legend*. Vol. 2. Translated by William Granger Ryan. Princeton: Princeton University Press, 1993.
Dio Cassius. *Roman History*. Books LXXI–LXXX. Translated by Earnest Cary. Loeb Classical Library 177. 1927. Reprint, Cambridge: Harvard University Press, 2001.
Dionysius the Areopagite. "Letter 4 to Gaius Therapeutes." *The Works of Dionysius the Areopagite*. Translated by John Parker. https://en.wikisource.org/wiki/The_Works_of_Dionysius_the_Areopagite/Letters/Letter_IV.
Dodds, E. R. *Pagan and Christian in an Age of Anxiety*. London: Norton, 1970.
Dronke, Peter. *Women Writers of the Middle Ages: A Critical Study of Text from Perpetua (†203) to Marguerite Porete (†1310)*. Cambridge: Cambridge University Press, 1984.
Duffy, Eamon. *Marking the Hours: English People and Their Prayers, 1240–1570*. New Haven: Yale University Press, 2006.
Ekonomou, Andrew J. *Byzantine Rome and the Greek Popes: Eastern Influences on Rome and the Papacy from Gregory the Great to Zacharias, A.D. 590–752*. Lanham, MD: Lexington, 2007.
Erasmus, Desiderius. *Praise of Folly and Letter to Maarten Van Dorp, 1515*. Translated by Betty Radice. Introduction and Notes by A. H. T. Levi. London: Penguin, 1993.
———. *Ten Colloquies*. Translated by Craig R. Thompson. Indianapolis: Bobbs-Merrill, 1957.
Eusebius, *History of the Church*. Translated by G. A. Williamson. Revised and edited by Andrew Louth. Harmondsworth: Penguin, 1989.
Farrell, Joseph P. *Free Choice in St. Maximus the Confessor*. South Canaan, PA: St. Tikhon's Seminary Press, 1989.
Fenlon, Dermot. "Thomas More and Tyranny." *Journal of Ecclesiastical History* 32 (1981) 453–76.
Frei, Hans. *The Eclipse of Biblical Narrative*. New Haven: Yale University Press, 1974.
Frend, W. H. C. *Martyrdom and Persecution in the Early Church*. New York: New York University Press, 1967.
Garrow, David. *Bearing the Cross: Martin Luther King, Jr. and the Southern Christian Leadership Conference*. New York: HarperCollins, 2004.
Gregg, Richard B. *The Power of Non-Violence*. Philadelphia: Lippincott, 1934.
Guy, J. A. *The Public Career of Sir Thomas More*. Brighton: Harvester, 1980.
Haldon, John F. *Byzantium in the Seventh Century: The Transformation of a Culture*. Cambridge: Cambridge University Press, 1990.
———. "Ideology and the Byzantine State in the Seventh Century. The 'Trial' of Maximus Confessor." In *From Late Antiquity to Early Byzantium: Proceedings of*

the *Byzantinological Symposium in the 16th International Eirene Conference*, edited by Vladimir Vavřínek, 87–91. Prague: Academia, 1985.

Halporn, James W. "Literary History and Generic Expectations in the *Passio* and *Acta Perpetuae*." *Vigiliae Christianae* 45 (1991) 223–41.

Harpsfield, Nicholas. *The Life and Death of Sir Thomas More, Knight*. Dallas: CTMS, 2020. https://essentialmore.org/wp-content/uploads/Harpsfield_s-Life-5-18-2020.pdf.

Harris, J. Rendel, and Seth K. Giffort. *The Acts of the Martyrdom of Perpetua and Felicitas: The Original Greek Text Now First Edited from a MS in the Library of the Convent of the Holy Sepulchre at Jerusalem*. London: C. J. Clay & Sons, 1890.

Harrison, Verna. "Perichoresis in the Greek Fathers." *St. Vladimir's Theological Quarterly* 35 (1991) 53–65.

Hauerwas, Stanley, and Thomas L. Shaffer. "Hope Faces Power: Thomas More and the King of England." *Soundings* 61 (1978) 456–79.

Hippolytus. *Apostolic Tradition*. Translated by Alistair Stewart-Sykes. Crestwood, NY: St. Vladimir's Seminary Press, 2001.

Hopkins, Keith. "Murderous Games." In *Death and Renewal*, 1–30. New York: Cambridge University Press, 1983.

Hovorun, Cyril. *Will, Action, and Freedom: Christological Controversies in the Seventh Century*. The Medieval Mediterranean 77. Leiden: Brill, 2008.

Howard-Johnston, James. *Witnesses to a World Crisis: Historians and Histories of the Middle East in the Seventh Century*. Oxford: Oxford University Press, 2011.

Huizinga, Johan. *Homo Ludens: A Study of the Play Element in Culture*. Boston: Beacon, 1955.

Hussey, J. M. *The Orthodox Church in the Byzantine Empire*. Oxford: Clarendon, 1986.

Kelly, J. N. D. *Early Christian Doctrines*. 2nd ed. New York: Harper & Row, 1960.

Kenny, Anthony. *Thomas More*. Oxford: Oxford University Press, 1983.

King, Martin Luther, Jr. *The Autobiography of Martin Luther King, Jr.* Edited by Clayborne Carson. New York: Intellectual Properties Management, 2001.

———. *The Papers of Martin Luther King, Jr.* Vol. 5, *Threshold of a New Decade, January 1959–December 1960*. Edited by Clayborne Carson et al. Berkeley: University of California Press, 2005.

———. *The Papers of Martin Luther King, Jr.* Vol. 6, *Advocate of the Social Gospel: September 1948–March 1963*. Edited by Clayborne Carson et al. Berkeley: University of California Press, 2007.

———. *The Papers of Martin Luther King, Jr.* Vol. 7, *To Save the Soul of America, January 1961–August 1962*. Edited by Clayborne Carson et al. Berkeley: University of California Press, 2014.

———. *Strength to Love*. New York: Harper & Row, 1963.

———. *A Testament of Hope: The Essential Writings and Speeches of Martin Luther King, Jr.* Edited by James M. Washington. San Francisco: HarperCollins, 1986.

———. *Why We Can't Wait*. Boston: Beacon, 2010.

King, Martin Luther, Jr., and Kris Shepard. "*A Call to Conscience: The Landmark Speeches of Dr. Martin Luther King, Jr.*" 7 audio discs. New York: Intellectual Properties Management, Inc. in association with Warner Books, 2001.

Lewis, C. S. *Studies in Words*. Cambridge: Cambridge University Press, 1967.

Lewis, David L. *King: A Biography*. 2nd ed. Champaign, IL: University of Illinois Press, 1978.

Lightfoot, J. B., and J. R. Harmer, eds. *The Apostolic Fathers: Revised Greek Texts with Introductions and English Translations*. Grand Rapids: Baker, 1984.

Linder, Douglas O. "The Trial of Sir Thomas More Knight, Lord Chancellor of England, for High Treason in Denying; the King's Supremacy, May 7, 1535. the 26th of Henry VIII." https://famous-trials.com/thomasmore/997-moretrialreport.

Marc'hadour. "Thomas More's Spirituality." In *St. Thomas More: Action and Contemplation*, edited by Richard S. Sylvester, 125–59. New Haven: Yale University Press, 1972.

Marius, Richard. *Thomas More: A Biography*. New York: Vintage, 1985.

Markshies, Christoph. "The *Passio Sanctarum Perpetuae et Felicitas* and Montanism." In *Perpetua's Passions*, edited by Jan Bremmer and Marco Formisano, 277–90. Oxford: Oxford University Press, 2012.

Martz, Louis L. *Thomas More: Search for the Inner Man*. New Haven: Yale University Press, 1990.

Martz, Louis L., and Richard S. Sylvester, eds. *Thomas More's Prayer Book: A Facsimile Reproduction of the Annotated Pages*. New Haven: Yale University Press, 1976.

Maximus the Confessor. *The Disputation with Pyrrhus of Our Father Among the Saints Maximus the Confessor*. Translated by Joseph P. Farrell. Waymart, PA: St. Tikhon's Monastery, 1990.

———. *Maximus the Confessor*. Edited by Andrew Louth. Early Church Fathers. London: Routledge, 1996.

———. *Maximus the Confessor: Selected Writings*. Introduction by Jaroslav Pelikan. Translated by George C. Berthold. New York: Paulist, 1985.

McClendon, James Wm., Jr., and James M. Smith. *Convictions: Defusing Religious Relativism*. Rev. ed. Valley Forge, PA: Trinity, 1994.

Metzger, Bruce M. *A Textual Commentary on the Greek New Testament*. Swindon: United Bible Societies, 1971.

Miller, William Robert. *Martin Luther King, Jr.: His Life, Martyrdom, and Meaning for the World*. New York: Weybright and Talley, 1968.

More, Thomas. *The Complete Works of St. Thomas More*. Vol. 12, *A Dialogue of Comfort Against Tribulation*. Edited by Louis L. Martz and Frank Manley. New Haven: Yale University Press, 1976.

———. *The Complete Works of St. Thomas More*. Vol. 13, *Treatise on the Passion, Treatise on the Blessed Body, Instructions, and Prayers*. Edited by Garry E. Haupt. New Haven: Yale University Press, 1976.

———. *The Complete Works of St. Thomas More*. Vol. 14, Parts I and II. *De Tristitia Christi*. Edited and translated by Clarence H. Miller. New Haven: Yale University Press, 1976.

———. *The Correspondence of Sir Thomas More*. Edited by Elizabeth Frances Rogers. Princeton: Princeton University Press, 1947.

———. *A Dialogue of Comfort Against Tribulation*. Translated by Mary Gottshalk. Introduction by Gerard B. Wegemer. Princeton: Scepter, 1998.

———. *The Last Letters of Thomas More*. Edited by Alvaro de Silva. Grand Rapids: Eerdmans, 2000.

———. *The Sadness of Christ and Final Prayers and Instructions*. Edited by Gerard Wegemer. Translated by Clarence Miller. Princeton: Scepter, 1993.

———. *Selected Letters*. Edited by Elizabeth Frances Rogers. New Haven: Yale University Press, 1961.

———. *Thomae Mori Omnia Latina Opera*. Louvain: Peter Zangrius, 1565. https://thomasmorestudies.org/library/#works.

———. *The Works of Sir Thomas More Knyght, sometime Lorde Chauncellour of England, written by him in the English tonge*. London: William Rastell, 1557. https://thomasmorestudies.org/library/#works.

Musurillo, Herbert, ed. and trans. *The Acts of the Christian Martyrs*. Oxford: Clarendon, 1972.

Neil, Bronwen, and Pauline Allen, eds. *The Life of Maximus the Confessor: Recension 3*. Early Christian Studies. Strathfield: St. Paul's, 2003.

Niebuhr, H. Richard. *Christ and Culture*. Expanded ed. San Francisco: HarperCollins, 2001.

Nikodimos of the Holy Mountain and Makarios of Corinth. *The Philokalia*. Vol. 2. Translated by G. E. H. Palmer et al. London: Faber and Faber, 1984.

Norwich, John Julius. *Byzantium: The Early Centuries*. New York: Knopf, 1992.

Oates, Stephen B. *Let the Trumpet Sound: A Life of Martin Luther King, Jr.* New York: HarperCollins, 1994.

Oxford English Dictionary. Oxford: Oxford University Press, 2023.

"The Paris Newsletter Account of More's Trial and Execution, August 4, 1535." In *Letters and Papers of Henry VIII*, Vol. 8, No. 996, edited by J. S. Brewer and James Gairdner. London: Longmans, 1882. https://thomasmorestudies.org/wp-content/uploads/2020/09/The-Paris-Newsletter-Account-of-More.pdf.

Parsons, Nicholas T. "The Reformation in Hungary." *Hungarian Review* 9 (2018). https://hungarianreview.com/article/20180119_the_reformation_in_hungary/.

Pelikan, Jaroslav. *The Christian Tradition: A History of the Development of Doctrine*. Vol. 2, *The Spirit of Eastern Christendom (600–1700)*. Chicago: University of Chicago Press, 1974.

Pettersen, Alvyn. "Perpetua—Prisoner of Conscience." *Vigiliae Christianae* 41 (1987) 139–53.

Pieper, Josef. *Leisure the Basis of Culture: The Philosophical Act*. Translated by Alexander Dru. 1963. Reprint, San Francisco: Ignatius, 2009.

Platnauer, Maurice. *The Life and Reign of the Emperor Lucius Septimius Severus*. 1918. Reprint, Westport, CT: Greenwood, 1970.

Powicke, Maurice. *The Reformation in England*. London: Oxford University Press, 1961.

Prestige, G. L. *God in Patristic Thought*. 2nd ed. London: SPCK, 1981.

———. "Περιχωρέω and περιχώρησις in the Fathers." *Journal of Theological Studies* 29 (1928) 242–52.

Price, S. R. F. "The Future of Dreams: From Freud to Artemidorus." *Past & Present* 113 (1986) 3–37.

Quasten, Johannes. *Patrology*. 3 vols. Westminster, MD: Newman, 1960–62.

Rader, Rosemary. "The *Martyrdom of Perpetua*: A Protest Account of Third-Century Christianity." In *A Lost Tradition: Women Writers of the Early Church*, by Patricia Wilson-Kastner et al., 1–32. Lanham, MD: University Press of America, 1981.

Rauschenbusch, Walter. *Christianity and the Social Crisis*. 1907. Reprint, Louisville: Westminster John Knox, 1992.

Rives, James. "The Piety of a Persecutor." *Journal of Early Christian Studies* 4 (1996) 1–25.

Robeck, Cecil M., Jr. *Prophecy in Carthage: Perpetua, Tertullian, and Cyprian*. Cleveland, OH: Pilgrim, 1992.

Ronsse, Erin Ann. "Rhetoric of Martyrs: Transmission and Reception History of the 'Passion of Saints Perpetua and Felicitas.'" Ph.D. diss., University of Victoria, 2008.

Roper, William. *The Life of Sir Thomas More*. In *Two Early Tudor Lives*, edited by Richard S. Sylvester and Davis P. Harding, 195–254. New Haven: Yale University Press, 1962.

Rossi, Mary Ann. "The Passion of Perpetua, Everywoman of Late Antiquity." In *Pagan and Christian Anxiety: A Response to E. R. Dodds*, edited by Robert C. Smith and John Lounibos, 53–86. Lanham, MD: University Press of America, 1984.

Rouselle, Robert. "The Dreams of Vibia Perpetua: Analysis of a Female Christian Martyr." *Journal of Psychohistory* 14 (1987) 193–206.

Salisbury, Joyce E. *The Blood of Martyrs: Unintended Consequences of Ancient Violence*. London: Routledge, 2004.

———. *Perpetua's Passion: The Death and Memory of a Young Roman Woman*. London: Routledge, 1997.

Scalise, Brian T. "Perichoresis in Gregory Nazianzen and Maximus the Confessor." *Eleutheria* 2 (2012) 58–76.

Sherwin-White, A. N. "The Early Persecutions and Roman Law Again." *Journal of Theological Studies* 3 (1952) 199–213.

Sherwood, Polycarp. *An Annotated Date-List of the Works of Maximus the Confessor*. Studia Anselmia Fascicle 30. Rome: Herder, 1952.

Stapleton, Thomas. *The Life and Illustrious Martyrdom of Sir Thomas More*. Translated by Philip E. Hallett. Dallas: CTMS, 2024. https://essentialmore.org/wp-content/uploads/Stapleton-Biography-04-24-2024.pdf.

Stark, Rodney. *The Rise of Christianity*. San Francisco: HarperCollins, 1997.

Suetonius. *The Twelve Caesars*. Translated by Robert Graves. Harmondsworth: Penguin, 1969.

Tabbernee, William. "To Pardon or Not to Pardon? North African Montanism and the Forgiveness of Son." In *Studia Patristica*, edited by M. F. Wiles and E. J. Yarnold, 36:375–86. Leuven: Peeters, 2001.

Taylor, Charles. *Sources of the Self: The Making of Modern Identity*. Cambridge: Harvard University Press, 1989.

Thunberg, Lars. *Man and the Cosmos: The Vision of St. Maximus the Confessor*. Crestwood, NY: St. Vladimir's Seminary Press, 1985.

———. *Microcosm and Mediator: The Theological Anthropology of Maximus the Confessor*. 2nd ed. La Salle, IL: Open Court, 1995.

Van Henten, Jan Willem. "The *Passio Perpetuae* and Jewish Martyrdom: The Motif of Motherly Love." In *Perpetual's Passions*, edited by Jan Bremmer and Marco Formisano, 118–33. Oxford: Oxford University Press, 2012.

Verghese, Paul. "The Monothelite Controversy—A Historical Survey." *Greek Orthodox Theological Review* 13 (1968) 196–211.

Von Franz, Marie-Luise. *The Passion of Perpetua: A Psychological Interpretation of Her Visions*. Irving, TX: Spring, 1980.

Weitbrecht, Julia. "Maternity and Sainthood in the Medieval Perpetua Legend." In *Perpetua's Passions*, edited by Jan Bremmer and Marco Formisano, 150–66. Oxford: Oxford University Press, 2012.

Wilken, Robert Louis. *The Christians as the Romans Saw Them*. 2nd ed. New Haven: Yale University Press, 2003.

Wolfson, Harry Austryn. *The Philosophy of the Church Fathers*. Vol. I, *Faith, Trinity, Incarnation*. 3rd ed. Cambridge: Harvard University Press, 1970.

Zim, Rivkah. "Writing Behind Bars: Literary Contexts and the Authority of Carceral Experience." *Huntington Library Quarterly* 72 (2009) 291–311.

Websites

The Essential Works of Thomas More. Center for Thomas More Studies. https://essentialmore.org.

Dr. Martin Luther King, Jr. Archive at the Howard Gottlieb Archival Research Center, Boston University. https://www.bu.edu/library/gotlieb-center/collections/dr-martin-luther-king-jr.archive/.

Martin Luther King, Jr. Research and Education Institute of Stanford University. https://kinginstitute.stanford.edu.

Thomas More Studies. Center for Thomas More Studies. https://thomasmorestudies.org.

Subject Index

activity. *See* energy.
Africa (Roman Province), 1, 10, 13, 18, 19, 49
Africa (Exarchate), 49, 51n3, 53, 59, 62–63, 69, 69n33
Albany, GA, 147, 149–55, 155n16, 156, 157, 158, 159, 165n29, 166, 167n34, 187
ambassadors in chains, 1–9, 142, 144, 181–94. *See also* prisoners of conscience.
Antioch (city), 18, 50, 56
Antioch (Patriarchate), 3, 11, 25, 30n34, 87

Birmingham, AL, 142n2, 148, 149, 156–68, 168n36, 187, 188n7, 190. *See also Letter from Birmingham Jail.*
Bizya (city in Byzantine Thrace), 65, 78, 79, 84, 85, 86n49, 87. *See also Dispute at Bizya.*
Byzantium (Byzantine Empire), 2, 4, 49–54, 51n3, 58, 63–64, 66, 69, 69n33, 72, 73, 88n54, 89, 90, 91, 186–87, 192
Byzantine Church (Byzantine Orthodoxy), 1, 57, 58, 73, 73n37
Byzantium (city). *See* Constantinople.

Caesar (Roman imperial official), 4, 23, 30, 35

Caesaropapism, 72, 90
Carthage, 1, 10, 15, 17–19, 18n14, 20, 20n18, 21n19, 25, 49, 55, 58, 59, 69
Chalcedon (Fourth Ecumenical Council), Chalcedonianism, 50–53, 55n11, 58, 61, 61n22, 75, 80, 81, 89, 186
communal merriment, eschatology of (Thomas More) 108, 111, 112, 118, 128, 138, 139, 141, 183
Constantinople (capital city of Byzantine Empire), 49n1, 50, 53n, 54, 56, 63, 64, 64n5, 65, 65n27, 66, 68, 79, 86, 88
Constantinople (Patriarchate), 50, 51, 52, 53, 58, 59, 62, 63, 74, 77, 80, 81, 83, 85, 87
Constantinople II (Fifth Ecumenical Council), 52, 74
Constantinople III (Sixth Ecumenical Council), 66
Conscience (*syneidēsis*), 39n46, 74–75, 75n40, 85, 88–89, 91–92, 95, 103, 104, 107, 110n32, 111–20, 115n35, 116n36, 117n40, 127–28, 135, 139–40, 144, 148, 151, 170, 178, 182–94. *See also* prisoner of conscience.
convictions, 5–8, 42–47, 49, 88–92, 116, 117, 139–41, 174–80, 181–94

deities (Roman). *See* gods (pagan).
Definition of Chalcedon. *See* Chalcedon (Fourth Ecumenical Council), Chalcedonianism
dreams, 24n23, 40–41n49, 44, 44n53, 69–71, 69–70n34. *See also* Visions.
Dyophysitism, Dyophysites, 51, 53, 75
Dyotheletism, Dyothelites, 51n4, 60, 75, 82, 83, 88, 191

Eastern Roman Empire. *See* Byzantine Empire.
Ekthesis (*Exposition*), 56n16, 57–60, 63, 76, 81
energy (*energeia*), energies (*energiai*), 53, 56, 57, 59, 63, 72, 80, 82, 84, 89, 90
Ephesus (Third Ecumenical Council), 50
essence (*ousia*), 84
Eucratas (monastery), 55, 55n11, 59
Eucratas (surname), 74, 75

Georgia State Prison, Reidsville, 148, 148n6
gods (pagan), 1, 4, 19, 23, 24, 30, 36, 46, 48

hypostatic union, 56, 57n17, 59, 60, 62, 82, 83

Jerusalem (city), 58
Jerusalem (Patriarchate), 55, 57, 87. *See also* Sophronius.

Lazica (Province of Byzantine Empire), 55, 65, 88, 191

Magnolia Tea Room, 148, 148n6
martyr, martyrdom, 2, 3, 10–47, 11n1, 13n5, 14n6, 15n8, 15n10, 19n17, 24n28, 25n29, 35n41, 38n45, 41n51, 47n56, 93n1, 110n32, 121, 127, 130, 132, 141, 188
martyrology, 2, 7, 10, 13, 14, 16n11
miaphysitism, miaphysites, 51n3

Monastery of St. Theodore, Rhegium (western suburb of Constantinople), 84
monenergism, monenergites, 53, 55, 56–59, 66, 82, 89, 186
monophysitism, monophysites, 50–59, 51n3, 53n5, 74, 82, 89. *See* miaphysitism, miaphytes.
monotheletism, monothelites, 53, 56–66, 55n12, 72, 73, 73n37, 75, 80, 81, 82, 89, 186
Montanism, Montanists, 13, 13n4, 14, 22, 43, 45, 184n1
Montgomery, AL, 146, 149, 157, 164, 168n36, 170–71, 178n53, 187
Mutual interchange (*epallagē*), 83
Mutual interpenetration (*perichōresis*), 83, 83n47

National Association for the Advancement of Colored People (NAACP), 146, 149
nature (*physis*), human and/or divine of Christ, 50–62, 51n3, 51n4, 61n21, 73n37, 75n40, 80, 82, 83, 84, 89–90, 132, 133, 182, 184n1. *See also* hypostatic union.
Nestorianism, Nestorians 50, 51n4, 59, 83. *See also* Nestorius

operation. *See* energy.
Origenism, 74

paganism. *See* gods (pagan)
papacy. *See* Rome (papacy).
person (*prosōpon*) of Christ, 50–61, 51n3, 51n4, 73n37, 82, 83, 89–90, 182. *See also* Nature.
play, playfulness, 33, 34, 40–41, 41n50, 141
premonitions 143n3, 191. *See also* Visions.
prison literature, 1–8, 8n2, 10–17, 27, 37n44, 64, 67–88, 109–39, 148–74
prisoner of conscience, 1–9, 31, 47n56, 186, 190. *See also* ambassadors in chains

Psēphos (Resolution), 56, 56n16, 59

Ravenna (Exarchate), 49, 58, 62, 63, 64, 71
realistic historical narrative, 16–17, 16n11
Reformation Parliament, 96, 101–3, 105, 106, 107, 116, 123, 185
Rome (city), 25, 49, 58, 62, 63, 66, 69, 75, 95
Rome (empire), 4, 11, 17, 18, 30, 38, 42, 43, 44. *See also* Byzantine Empire.
Rome (papacy), 49n1, 51, 52, 64, 82–83, 84, 87, 87n53, 95, 96, 102, 106, 116, 140

Schemaris (town in Byzantine Georgia), 65
scruple, 112, 114, 115, 115n34, 115n35, 117
Southern Christian Leadership Conference (SCLC), 147, 149, 152–53, 157, 158, 159, 160, 167n33, 169, 172
Student Nonviolent Coordinating Committee (SNCC), 149, 169

Theopaschitism, 52
Tower of London (English prison), 93, 102, 103–4, 104n17, 108, 109, 109n29, 110, 110n32, 111, 114, 123n44, 124n46, 126n47, 136, 138, 141, 142, 189, 190, 191
Type A Convictions. *See* Convictions.
Type B Convictions. *See* Convictions.
Typos (Edict), 63, 65n27, 72, 73n37, 76–77, 80, 81, 85

visions, 12, 12n2, 13n4, 20, 21, 22, 24, 24n23, 27, 28–29, 30, 31, 32, 32n37, 33, 34, 36, 38, 40, 40–41n49, 41, 42, 43–44, 47, 47n56, 69–70n34, 88, 141, 143, 191, 191n14. *See also* dreams *and* premonitions.

will (*thelēma*; *proairesis*), human and/or divine of Christ, 43, 51n4, 53, 55n12, 56–63, 62n23, 66, 70–72, 73n37, 75, 80, 82, 83, 89–90, 133, 134, 182

Name Index

Abernathy, Ralph (Pastor of First Baptist Church, Montgomery, AL and aide to Martin Luther King Jr.), 150, 150n11, 151, 152, 152n14, 153, 155, 159, 160

Acacius (Patriarch of Constantinople), 52

Aeschylus (Greek tragedian), 185n3

Agatho (Pope of Rome), 66

Alington, Alice (Stepdaughter of Thomas More), 111, 113–14, 115n35, 117, 118, 189n9

Anastasius the Apocrisiarius (Roman papal diplomat and disciple of Maximus the Confessor), 55n10, 64, 65, 65n27, 68, 68n31, 83, 86–87, 87–88, 191, 191n15

Anastasius the Monk (Disciple of Maximus the Confessor), 54, 55, 55n10, 63, 64, 65, 67, 68, 68n31, 71, 72, 73–74, 76, 77, 78, 86–87, 87n53

Anthony (Egyptian Desert Father), 122–23, 123n44

Aquinas, Thomas (Medieval Latin Theologian), 164.

Audley, Thomas (Lord Chancellor of England), 103, 111, 113–18, 120

Augustine of Canterbury (Papal missionary to Britain), 107

Augustine of Hippo (Latin Church Father), 13n5, 14–15n7, 16n12, 32n36, 35n41, 164

Bevel, James (Aide to Martin Luther King Jr.), 160–61, 169–70

Boleyn, Anne (Queen of England), 72n36, 95, 96, 101, 102

Bolt, Robert (English playwright), 97, 97n7, 98, 98n9, 139

Boutwell, Albert (Mayor of Birmingham, AL), 158

Bowne, Borden Parker (American theologian), 146

Brightman, Edgar Sheffield (American theologian), 146

Buber, Martin (Jewish philosopher), 164

Catherine of Aragon (Queen of England), 93–96, 100, 102

Charles V (King of Spain and Emperor of the Holy Roman Empire), 95

Chosroes II (King of Persia), 52

Christ. *See* Jesus Christ.

Clark, Jim (Sheriff of Dallas County, AL), 169, 173, 174

Connor, Eugene "Bull" (Commissioner of Public Safety, Birmingham, AL), 158, 161, 164

Constans I (Roman Emperor), 73n38

NAME INDEX

Constans II Pogonatus (Byzantine Emperor), 49, 53, 54, 58, 59, 62–66, 67, 68, 69, 70, 71–72, 73, 75, 76, 76n44, 78, 80, 81, 84, 85, 86, 87, 87n53
Constantine I "the Great" (Roman Emperor), 73
Constantine III (Byzantine Emperor), 58
Constantine IV (Byzantine Emperor), 66
Cranmer, Thomas (Archbishop of Canterbury), 96, 101, 102, 103, 120
Cromwell, Thomas (Chief Minister to King Henry VIII), 96, 100, 103, 104, 106, 107, 107n23, 110, 111, 120, 137n63
Cyril (Patriarch of Alexandria), 50, 52, 55, 82,
Cyril (Patriarch of Constantinople), 63
Cyrus (Monenergist Patriarch of Alexandria), 55–56

DeWolf, L. Harold (American theologian), 146
Dinocrates (brother of Vibia Perpetua), 14n7, 27, 32, 32n36, 33, 34, 39–41

Epiphanius (Byzantine senator), 71, 74, 85
Erasmus, Desiderius (Dutch humanist), 96, 97–98, 97n5, 99, 129n50
Eugenius I (Pope of Rome), 64, 75, 86
Evagrius Ponticus (Origenist theologian), 74

Felicitas (Carthaginian Christian slave woman), 10, 27, 28, 31, 32, 33, 34, 35n41, 36, 37, 37n43, 38
Fitzjames, John (English jurist), 107, 116
Freud, Sigmund (German psychoanalyst), 38

Gandhi, Mohandas K. ("Mahatma") (Indian statesman), 145, 157n18, 177n48
Geta Caesar (son of Septimius Severus), 35
God (Christian), 4–5, 6, 14n7, 15, 15n10, 26, 28, 34, 38, 39n46, 43–47, 47n56
Gregory (Byzantine Exarch of North Africa), 59, 63, 69–71
Gregory, son of Photinus (Byzantine official), 71–73
Gregory I (Pope of Rome), 107

Henry VIII (King of England), 72n, 93–96, 100, 101, 102, 103, 104, 105, 106, 107, 108, 108n27, 110, 111, 113, 116, 119, 120, 122n43, 139
Heraclius (Byzantine Emperor), 53, 53n5, 54, 55, 58, 69, 76
Heraclius the Elder (Byzantine Exarch of Africa), 51n3
Hilarianus (Roman procurator), 23, 24, 25–26, 27, 28, 31, 33n38, 35, 45
Holy Spirit, 11, 27, 28, 29, 40–41n49, 43, 44, 45, 75
Honorius (Pope of Rome), 56–59, 57n17, 66

Jacob Baradaeus (Monophysite theologian), 50–51, 51n3
Jesus Christ, 1, 4, 5, 8, 23, 26, 26n32, 32n36, 37, 38–39, 39n46, 43, 45, 48–49, 50–63, 51n4, 62n23, 73n37, 75, 78, 80–81, 82–84, 89–90, 106, 112, 123, 130–34, 138, 164, 175, 177, 182, 184n1, 192–93.
John IV (Pope of Rome), 58
Johnson, Samuel (English essayist), 140, 140n65
Julius Caesar (Roman commander and statesman), 18
Justin I (Byzantine Emperor), 52
Justin II (Byzantine Emperor), 52
Justinian I (Byzantine Emperor), 49, 52

NAME INDEX

Kennedy, John F. (President of the United States), 148
King, A. D. (Pastor of First Baptist Church of Ensley, Birmingham, AL and brother of Martin Luther King Jr.), 160
King, Alberta Williams (Mother of Martin Luther King Jr.), 145
King, Coretta Scott (Spouse of Martin Luther King Jr.), 146, 151, 152, 169, 170
King, Martin Luther Sr. (Pastor of Ebenezer Baptist Church, Atlanta, GA), 145
King, Martin Luther Jr, 1–7
  comparison of his imprisonments to those of Perpetua, Maximus, and More, 142–44; 143n3
  sketch of his life, 145–48
  Magnolia Tea Room incident, 148, 148n6
  Albany Movement, 149–55; 149n7, 150n10, 151n13, 152n14, 153n15, 155n16
  Albany *Jail Diaries*, 151–52, 153–55
  Why It's Albany, 155
  Birmingham Movement, 156–68; 156n17, 157n18, 157n19, 159n21, 160n23, 161n24, 163n26, 163n27, 164n28, 165n29, 166n30, 166n31, 167n32, 167n33, 167n34
  Letter from Birmingham Jail, 8n2, 143, 153, 157, 157n18, 157n19, 161–68, 163n27, 169n39, 170, 172, 173, 186, 188, 188n7, 189, 190
  Selma Campaign, 148, 149, 165, 165n29, 168–74, 168n36, 168n37, 170n41, 171n42
  Statement on Voter Registration, 171–72; 171n43
  Letter from a Selma, Alabama Jail, 172–73, 172n44
  Instructions to Movement Associates, 173–74, 173n46
  I Have a Dream, 147, 163n26, 177–178n50
  King's theological convictions, 174–80, 177n48, 178–179n54, 183
  King's commonalities with Perpetua, Maximus, and More, 184–92, 184n1, 186n5, 186n6, 188n7, 189n10, 190n12
  his relevance for today, 192–94, 192n17, 192n18

Leo I (Pope of Rome), 51, 52
Leo II (Pope of Rome), 66
Leo X (Pope of Rome), 95
Lewis, C[live] S[taples] (English author and literary critic), 115–16, 116n36, 116n37, 116n38
Lingo, Al (Director of Alabama Department of Public Safety) 169, 170
Louis II (King of Hungary), 122

Martin I (Pope of Rome), 58, 59, 63, 64, 65, 77
Marx, Karl (German philosopher), 38, 145
Maurice (Byzantine Emperor), 52
Maximus the Confessor, 1–9; 48–92
  comparison of his imprisonment with Perpetua's, 48–49
  historical and religious background of his life, 49–54
  sketch of his life, 54–67, 54n6, 54n7, 54n8, 54n9, 64n26
  Disputation with Pyrrhus, 59–62, 59n20, 61n21, 62n23
  prison literature, 67–88
  Record of the Trial (also known as the *Relatio Motionis*, the *Report of the Trial*, and "The Trial of Maximus"), 67–78, 67n30, 68n31, 69n33, 78, 79, 86n49
  Dispute at Bizya, 78–86, 78n45, 86n49, 87n52, 185n3, 189
  Letter of Maximus to Anastasius the Monk, 86–87, 87n58
  Maximus' theological convictions, 88–92, 88n54, 182
  his view of conscience compared to More's, 103

Maximus the Confessor *(continued)*
   his view of the dual natures of Christ compared to More's, 133
   comparison of King's imprisonments to those of Perpetua, Maximus, and More, 142–44
   Maximus' commonalities with Perpetua, More, and King, 184–92, 184n1, 185n3, 191n15
   his relevance for today, 192–94
McClendon, James Wm., Jr. (American theologian), 5, 5n1
Mongo, Peter (Patriarch of Alexandria), 52
More, Agnes Graunger (mother of Thomas More), 98
More, Alice Middleton (second wife of Thomas More), 99, 111, 129n50
More, Jane Colt (first wife of Thomas More), 99, 129n50
More, John (father of Thomas More), 98
More, Thomas, 1–9, 93–141
   "silence implies consent," 72n
   historical and religious background of his life, 93–96, 93n1, 95n2
   sketch of his life, 96–109, 97n8, 99n10, 100n11, 103n12, 104n15, 104n15, 105n20, 106n21, 106n22, 107n24, 108n27, 108n28
   his prison literature, 109–139, 109n29; *Last Letters* (or *Prison Correspondence*), 110–21, 110n30, 114n33, 115n35, 116n38, 117n40
   Dialogue of Comfort Against Tribulation, 112, 121–30, 121n42, 122n43, 123n44, 124n45, 124n46, 126n47, 128n48, 129n49, 129n50, 130n51
   Sadness of Christ, 8n2, 130–34, 130n52; 131n53, 131n54,131n55, 131n56, 133n57, 135n59
   Instructions and Prayers, 135–39, 135n60, 136n61, 136n62, 137n63, 138n64
   More's theological convictions, 139–41
   comparison of King's imprisonments to those of Perpetua, Maximus, and More, 142–44
   More's commonalities with Perpetua, Maximus, and King, 184–92, 184n1, 185n4, 189n9
   his relevance for today, 192–94, 192n16
Morton, John (Archbishop of Canterbury), 98

Nestorius (Patriarch of Constantinople), 50, 50n2, 52. *See also* Nestorianism.
Niebuhr, H. Richard (American theologian), 26, 26n32, 26n33, 45n54
Niebuhr, Reinhold (American theologian), 145
Nietzsche, Friedrich (German philosopher), 38

Olympius (Byzantine Exarch of Ravenna), 63–64
Origen of Alexandria (early Christian theologian), 74. *See also* Origenism.

Paul (Byzantine consul), 79, 84
Paul the Apostle, 4, 11, 99, 108, 164,
Paul II (Monothelite Patriarch of Constantinople), 58, 62, 63, 64, 64n24, 66, 81
Perpetua, 1–9
   the *Passion of Saints Perpetua and Felicitas*, 10–47
   the *Passion* as prison literature, 10–15, 11n1, 12n2, 13n3, 14n7, 15n8, 16n11
   historical and religious background of Perpetua's life, 15–26, 16n12, 17n13, 18n14, 19n16, 20n18,

21n19, 22n20, 22n21, 23n22, 24n28, 25n29
  structure, rhetorical design, and literature devices in the *Passion*, 26–42, 30–31n34, 31n35, 32n36, 32n37, 33n38, 34n39, 35n41, 37n43, 38n45, 39n46, 40–41n49, 41n51, 42n52
  theological convictions, 42–47, 44n53, 47n56, 49, 141
  comparison of King's imprisonments to those of Perpetua, Maximus, and More, 142–44
  Perpetua's commonalities with Maximus, More, and King, 184–92, 184n2, 189n8, 191n13, 191n14
  her relevance for today, 192–94
Philippikos Bardanes (Byzantine Emperor), 66
Pritchett, Laurie (Chief of Police, Albany, GA), 149–55, 164
Pseudo-Dionysius the Areopagite (Christian theologian), 56, 56n15
Pudens (Roman military adjutant), 20, 27, 28, 35, 36, 39, 41–42
Pyrrhus I (Monothelite Patriarch of Constantinople), 58, 59–63, 59n20, 61n, 64n21, 66, 73–74, 81

Rauschenbusch, Walter (American theologian), 145, 177–78n50
Rich, Richard (Solicitor General for England and Wales), 105–6, 110n31, 120
Roper, Margaret More (Daughter of Thomas More), 103, 103n13, 103n14, 104n16, 105n18, 105n19, 110, 111, 112–15, 123, 185n4, 189n9, 192n16
Roper, William (Son-in-law and first biographer of Thomas More), 93n1, 95n2, 96n3, 97n8, 105n20, 106n22, 107n25, 107n26, 108n27, 108–9n28, 116n38, 123n44

Saturus (Carthaginian Christian catechist), 8n2, 10, 11, 11n1, 12, 12n2, 13–14, 15, 19, 20, 22, 27, 28, 29, 30, 32–33, 34, 35, 36, 38, 39, 40–41n49, 41, 42, 45, 141
Selma, AL, 148, 149, 165, 165n29, 168–74, 168n37, 170n41, 171n42, 172n44, 186n5, 187
Septimius Severus (Emperor of Rome), 19, 23–24, 24n27, 25
Sergius I (Monothelite Patriarch of Constantinople), 53, 56–58, 56n16, 57n17, 63, 66, 81
Sergius Eucratas (Byzantine official), 74–76
Sergius Magoudas (Byzantine official), 69–71
Severinus (Pope of Rome), 58
Severus of Antioch (Monophysite theologian), 50, 56, 56n15
Shuttlesworth, Fred (Pastor of Bethel Baptist Church, Birmingham, AL), 158, 160
Smith, James M. (American philosopher), 5, 5n1
Sophronius (Patriarch of Jerusalem), 55–59, 55n11, 57n17, 58n18, 65, 66, 75n40

Tertullian, 19, 22, 26, 30–31n34, 32n37, 42n52
Thuburbo Minus (city in Roman North Africa), 18n14
Theodore I (Pope of Rome), 58, 62, 63, 65n27, 70, 77
Theodore I Calliopas (Byzantine Exarch of Ravenna), 64, 64n26
Theodore Chila (Byzantine official), 71
Theodore Spoudaeus (Supporter of Maximus), 88
Theodosius (Byzantine consul), 79, 82
Theodosius (Byzantine bishop of Bithynian Caesarea), 79–85

Theodosius of Gangra (Supporter of Maximus), 65, 88, 191n15
Theophilus (Bishop of Antioch), 30–31n34
Tiberius (Roman Emperor), 96–97
Tiberius II Constantine (Byzantine Emperor), 52
Tillich, Paul (American theologian), 164
Troilas (Byzantine patrician and state official), 74–76, 77, 84–85

Vibia Perpetua. *See* Perpetua of Carthage.
Vitalian (Pope of Rome), 64, 66

Williams, Adam Daniel (Pastor of Ebenezer Baptist Church, Atlanta, GA), 145
Williams, Hosea (Aide of Martin Luther King Jr.), 169

Zeno (Byzantine Emperor), 52

Scripture Index

Exodus
19:6	46

Leviticus
20:21	94

Deuteronomy
25:5	94

Psalms
3:1–6	137
38:13	137

Daniel
3:1–30	74, 164, 185, 185n
6:1–28	74, 185, 185n

Joel
2:28	21

Prayer of Azariah and the Song of the Three Young Men
1–68	185n

Matthew
7:2	69
18:7	70
26	130
26:15	133n
26:39	57
26:50	134

Mark
8:3	76
14	130
14:10	133n
14:51–52	134
15:16–24	84

Luke
16:26	32n
22	130

John
16:25	76
18	130

Acts

2:17–18	21, 28–29, 40n, 43
7:54–8:1a	108
21:39	4
22:25–29	4

1 Corinthians

12	37
13:3	70, 70n

2 Corinthians

1:5	39
3:12	76
5:20	4
7:4	76

Ephesians

2:19	4
5:1	84
6:18–20a	4

Philippians

1:20	76
2:7–8	84
3:20	4

Titus

4	89

1 Peter

3–4	39n
3:21	39n

Jude

3	84

www.ingramcontent.com/pod-product-compliance
Lightning Source LLC
Chambersburg PA
CBHW031356230426
43670CB00006B/564